Law Against the People

LAW

AGAINST

THE

PEOPLE

*Essays to Demystify
Law, Order and
the Courts*

Edited by Robert Lefcourt

 Random House   New York

To Jenny,

       our new-born future

Preface

The idea for this anthology grew out of the "liberation school" that was organized after the April 1968 uprising at Columbia University. Before April I had worked with community groups protesting Columbia's plan to build a gymnasium on the edge of Harlem, and I had done some of the research exposing the backgrounds of Columbia's board of trustees, so as part of this work, I attended the liberation school's Legal RAP (Research-Action Project) meetings. In the Legal RAP, students, community residents, law students, lawyers, and other Movement sympathizers worked to analyze the American legal system and plan actions against the criminal courts.

About six of us in the RAP formed a writers' collective to support the actions. We did research, wrote leaflets, and published articles. One group exposed the operation and ideology of the Legal Aid Society; another studied the grand jury system; another wrote a pamphlet called "The Bust Book: What To Do Till the Lawyer Comes" (subsequently published as a book) to inform white youth about the procedures in arrest situations stemming from protest activities.

In the fall of 1968, a number of lawyers, along with three of us in the writers' collective, began to discuss a new kind of law firm, a "law commune" which would bring together Movement activists, writers and young lawyers to develop a radical approach to law and law practice. One of the purposes of the Law Commune, like the Legal RAP, was to attempt to break through the "professionalism" of the legal apparatus, its mystique, its removal from us as people, to understand it like it is—demystified.

Demystification of the law is a central purpose of many groups around the country, in high schools and colleges, political collectives, and community action groups. One such group was organized among Black, Puerto Rican and white residents in the neighborhood surrounding Columbia University soon after the 1968 strike. These people demanded and received funds from the school for courses related to their own struggles around housing, health, education and the law. Other groups, dealing with other specific areas of the law, such as welfare, students' and women's rights, have been organized in numerous cities. The desire to know and to demystify the law has become contagious.

This book also is an action about law in America. It is not written by specialists for other specialists; rather, the writers try to escape the esoteric jargon which usually prevents the lay person from comprehending legal concepts. Their purposes are political and social, not legal and professional.

For their influence on this book I am indebted to the 1968 Columbia University students, the Legal RAP people, and Columbia's neighborhood residents; to Flo Kennedy, for the encouragement to do, as she does for so many others; to Stanley Aronowitz, for much of my political re-education; to Kathy Boudin and Brian Glick, for early discussions on and early drafts of the "Law Against the People" essay; to Arthur Kinoy, for useful dialogues; to the Workers Collective at the Law Commune, most especially Ruth Silber, Eunice Burnett and Carol Birnbaum, for much of the typing, editing and criticism; to my editors at Random House, Hilary Maddux and John J. Simon; and to those who read and commented upon portions of the manuscript, members of the Law Commune, Saul Shapiro, J. Judson Jenkins, John Cohen and others.

Finally, for their total influence on this book, I thank my wife, Carol, and my brother, Gerald, for becoming people's lawyers.

Robert Lefcourt
May 1971

Contents

PART TWO:
CHALLENGING THE LAW

Law Against the People

Introduction

Some critics have suggested that the title of this book is unnecessarily provocative, that it sounds like a slogan which instead of describing actual human relationships only serves to polarize. The title is not meant to suggest that law has been used by government *only* as a repressive instrument, but it is meant to question the legitimacy of law-making and law-enforcing institutions. In this questioning we are not alone. According to a report to the National Commission on the Causes and Prevention of Violence,

> While it may be argued that much . . . disaffection is due to naïve and unreal demands made of courts by the disaffected, it must be emphasized that the courts—and other branches of government—have themselves contributed to the decline of legal authority . . .[1]

The report also recognizes that ". . . Blacks, whether in the North or the South, have always been skeptical of the courts' capacity to administer fair and equal justice."[2] Whether the institutions are failing to respond to legitimate grievances or different groups have always questioned the likelihood of institutions to uphold their rights, there is a crisis of legitimacy within rule-making bodies.

Within the legal apparatus only a few judges, prosecutors, and prison officials are willing to criticize the system they have been taught to protect. A Supreme Court justice calls for radical change in society (and is threatened with impeachment), an occasional judge frees those unjustly arrested during a ghetto rebellion or hands down decisions favorable to people rather than property rights, or a prison guard sympathizes with prisoners' protests (and is indicted). For the time, it is mainly lawyers who are attacking the basic inequities in the legal system—in the courts, in their writings, and even in the streets. Many of these lawyers began to realize only after they became attorneys that law and legal institutions do not serve the majority of people. In allying themselves with movements for social change—even in writing articles—they risk disbarment; several contributors to this book have already been imprisoned for their protests.

What seems to threaten Establishment officials most is the relationship between Movement lawyers and their radical clients, a relationship in which political convictions and the exposition of a political program and beliefs are not outside the lawyer's province and not reserved for comment by the client alone. The legal profession is quite clear in its condemnation of such a relationship:

> The thesis (that) depicts defense counsel as an agent permitted, and perhaps even obliged, to do for the accused everything he would do for himself if only he possessed the necessary skills and training in the law . . . had been totally and unequivocally rejected for over one hundred years under canons governing English barristers and is similarly rejected by canons of the American Bar Association and other reputable professional organizations.[3]

Tradition and respectability define in clear gobbledygook the "proper role of a defense lawyer":

> As in other contexts of human endeavor, the intermediary brings to the controversy an emotional detachment which permits him to make a more dispassionate appraisal. He translates the desired course of action into those steps which the form and procedure of the system permit and professional judgment dictates.[4]

But more and more lawyers now denounce such "detachment" as a hoax and as the graveyard of any hope of social transformation. All lawyers choose their clients, and this choice reflects the lawyer's views of society: "Corporate" lawyers reveal their political commitments in their choice of corporate clients. People's lawyers have exposed the myth of the lawyer's neutrality and have turned to clients of all colors and classes who oppose established authority within decadent institutions.

Much has been written about "individual" lawyers who defend unpopular clients in their fight against injustice.* Much has been written about famous trials of radicals who have been attacked by the state, and defended by a dedicated (though not necessarily sympathetic) lawyer.† But historically, the lawyer class has not aligned itself with the forces of change. In fact, the role of the legal profession in relation to social movements reflects the class and racist orientation of the legal system itself.

The American legal profession has always boasted of the decisive role of lawyers during the first revolutionary period—25 of 56 signers of the Declaration of Independence and 31 of 55 members of the Constitutional Convention were lawyers. But the primary job of the lawyer class at that time was business, the collection of debts and foreclosures, for example—and during the revolution most attorneys either remained loyal to England, or withdrew from practice altogether.⁵ Those who did sign the new Constitution ignored Blacks' petitions for freedom, and ignored demands for a Bill of Rights which an angry public finally forced upon the new government fifteen years later. In fact, Shays' Rebellion in 1786 in Massachusetts was directed largely against lawyers and judges who imprisoned people and confiscated land because of an inability to pay high taxes. Debtors in Vermont set fire to their courthouse; in New Jersey the people nailed up the courthouse doors.

---

* William M. Kunstler, whose article in this book is a dramatic departure from the individualist role of the lawyer, wrote such a book about ten famous lawyers, *The Case for Courage*. New York: William Morrow and Co., 1962.
† Richard B. Morris' *Fair Trial: Fourteen Who Stood Accused From Anne Hutchinson to Alger Hiss*. New York: Harper & Row, 1952, is typical.

The evidence drawn particularly from the period 1776 to 1791 indicates that the generation that framed the first state declarations of rights and the First Amendment was hardly as libertarian as we have traditionally assumed. They did not intend to give free rein to criticism of the government that might be deemed seditious libel, although the concept of seditious libel was—and still is—the principal basis of muzzling political dissent.[6]

While the myth of the lawyer who champions the cause of equal rights has its roots in the American revolutionary period, the myth of the "family lawyer" derives from the nineteenth century.

There are few more reassuring images in American folklore than the family-serving practitioner. The family doctor and the family lawyer—constant, competent . . . —are stock characters in the idealized picture of the American family.[7]

The actual family lawyer personified the deprofessionalization of the law and law practice prior to the Civil War.

With the advent of Jacksonian democracy, which held to the popular belief that every man should find open the gates to self-advancement, (this) trend toward deprofessionalization set in.[8]

The influx of the lower classes into law practice even saw some nonlawyers become judges. But as a group

the lawyer class has been anathema to our agrarian and debtor classes, to the Jacksonian, Populist, muckraking and other movements seeking large reforms.[9]

Near the end of the last century, as a result of the enormous economic development, the nature and practice of law took a decisive shift: American lawyers began to dominate political and economic affairs. It has been estimated that since the end of the Civil War well over fifty percent of all elected or government officials have been lawyers. Very few historians have been willing to explain the reasons for this. Alexis de Tocqueville, however, recalling that lawyers led the overthrow of the French monarchy in

1789 mainly because they were denied access to power, and believing that lawyers constituted "the most cultivated circle" and "enlightened class" of society, accepted their role: "They are naturally called upon to occupy most of the public stations." [10] Alexis de Tocqueville described lawyers as "eminently conservative and anti-democratic," and explained this by reasoning that because they "are attached to public order beyond every other consideration," they find that "the best security of order is (their) authority." [11] In the second half of the nineteenth century, beginning with the expansion of banks and other finance institutions and the growth of railroads, the large corporation became the *raison d'être* of the business world, and then became the core of the national economy. "Today the success of the corporation depends to a considerable extent upon minimizing its tax burden, maximizing its speculative projects through mergers, controlling government regulatory bodies, influencing state and national legislatures. Accordingly, the lawyer is becoming a pivotal figure in the giant corporation." [12]

With increased political and business power, general practitioners gave way to specialists in law—tax law, labor law, domestic relations, antitrust law, criminal law, and of course, administrative and corporation law. The legal profession has become entrenched in the business community. One prominent judge observes rather despairingly that:

All the signs and portents indicate that the organization lawyer will fuse into the organization man . . . He will never sing solo, but only raise his voice in the institutional chorus. But in the grand and glorious annals of the bar, it has been through singing solo that its men of mark have gained their strength and courage . . ." [13]

If there is nostalgia among some lawyers about the decline in the role of the lawyer as "advocate," that "many lawyers today are on a professional assembly line," [14] there is little reflection about the relationship between the organized bar and the government's legal repression of those who seek major reforms in society. During World War I, for example, the government enacted a selective service bill and censorship bills, and prosecuted the IWW conspiracy trials, academic and religious freedom cases, and trials aimed at the suppression of radicals, most notably the sedition trial of Eugene V. Debs, the Socialist Party leader. While the American Civil Liberties Union was formed to counter this repression of the progressive movement, the organized bar refused even to condemn assaults on union organizers (as in the 1930 convictions of seven Communist strike leaders who had allegedly killed a police chief in North Carolina) or the suppression of Blacks (as in the 1930s convictions of nine men accused of raping two white women hobos in the first of three trials in Scottsboro, Jackson County, Alabama). The American Bar Association, representative of corporate and business Establishment lawyers, had nothing better to attack than the "socialist" policies of Franklin Delano Roosevelt.

The National Lawyers Guild was founded in 1937 as an alternative to the big-business lawyers of the ABA and the civil liberties attorneys of the ACLU. During the 1940s the Guild was instrumental in proposing much of the more progressive New Deal legislation, and fought for the rights of labor and the disenfranchised. It also sought to counter the activities of the newly formed House Un-American Activities Committee and the propaganda of large business interests seeking to inoculate American public opinion with the notion that "Americanism" consists in the defense of the status quo. But the anti-Communist campaign of the late 1940s and the more virulent one of the McCarthy period all but destroyed the Guild's attempts to alter the lawyer's traditional role as handmaiden to the business class. The ACLU itself expelled suspected Communists from its own ranks, and by the 1960s the "safe grayness of the businessman-lawyer" seemed secure.

During the initial stages of the civil rights movement, lawyers' participation was limited—but later, when Southern Black leaders requested legal help, the response of the organized bar was the customary refusal. Howard Moore, one of sixty Black lawyers in Georgia—which has over 4,000 white lawyers—observed as recently as 1967 that he thought "it truthful to say that they (white lawyers) will not represent people in civil rights matters." [15] In 1960 in Mississippi a population of more than two million, over forty percent Black, had 2,100 white lawyers and three Black, plus one white sympathizer. The few Southern white attorneys who did defend Blacks in civil rights cases were ostracized by their communities.[16]

The "legal arm of the civil rights movement" in those early years was the NAACP Legal Defense and Educational Fund, Inc.; staff lawyers in New York and the few Black lawyers in Southern states fought many of the cases. When the political movement intensified from 1960 to 1964, the call for Northern and Western lawyers was answered by attorneys from the National Lawyers Guild, volunteers from civil-liberty-type organizations and numerous law students.[17]

Most of the time these lawyers and law students were on hand to give advice, get people out of jail, arrange bail, or to try to have a case removed from the local judge to a federal court to head off a trial in a Southern town. But when activists who refused to quit the struggle and still recognized the authority of the law were prosecuted, lawyers tried the cases. According to a 1964 report, "Project Mississippi":

> If no other achievements are credited to the project, this new respect, this new appreciation of the inviolability of the rights of even the lowest and the poorest has changed for all times the legal climate pervading the courts of Mississippi.[18]

Arthur Kinoy wrote in 1967:

> I think it has become increasingly understood throughout the profession that a new path in constitutional litigation has emerged, a path arising out of the struggle of the southern Negro freedom movement, a path that has opened up avenues and perspectives for a qualitatively different type

of role for the lawyer in every area of the struggle for the defense of American democratic rights.[19]

The lawyers attempted to translate the terms of the civil rights struggle into political and legal victories, and to a certain extent this was achieved. But whatever the legal accomplishments of the Southern movement (and some doubt that the passage of civil rights legislation and legal victories in the federal courts effected much change in the people's living conditions), those lawyers and law students who went South were members of the first generation since the Civil War to participate collectively in a struggle against white supremacy and its racist laws and institutions.

At the same time, without lawyers and in defiance of the law, a Black liberation struggle was taking its own course in the rebellions that erupted in Harlem, Chicago, Philadelphia, and Rochester in 1964, Watts in 1965, and dozens of other cities in the few years that followed. To this, the response of the legal system was severe. Overwhelming number of arrests, high bail used as preventive detention, and the denial of voluntary counsel defined legal relationships within dozens of predominantly Black communities. The bias of the courts was noted by a Presidential commission:

> By condoning and following such policies (as high bail) the courts contribute to the "breakdown of law" and to the establishment of an "order" based on force without justice.[20]

"During the riots," the report continues, "courts in various cities often became armed camps, and some lawyers were intimidated by police and troops in and around the courtrooms. . . . In Chicago, lawyers were initially turned away from the courts by police guards. Those that demanded and received entry were ignored and, in some cases, met with hostility from bailiffs and court officials."[21] It was not only that most volunteer lawyers, especially Black lawyers, could not perform their jobs in many cities, but:

The Bar Association refrained from criticizing the courts' actions during the riots, preferring instead to act as a broker between the courts and various legal defense organizations. This was seen by representatives of these organizations as quiescent support of the courts' policies.[22]

If during the early stages of the civil rights movement, when laws were broken in the name of higher federal laws, the legitimacy of the legal system was assumed, that legitimacy soon eroded, not only in Watts and other Black communities, but in the Free Speech Movement at Berkeley in 1964, in the anti-war march on the Pentagon and the emergence of Black revolutionary organizations such as the Black Panther Party in 1967, and in student takeovers of school buildings such as at Columbia and the protest demonstrations at the Chicago National Democratic Convention in 1968. As the commission report concludes:

> . . . Protestors do not accept the court's authority to decide the disputes. This situation is one in which even further disenchantment and erosion of the concept of legality are likely; as such it presents a crisis for the courts and the legal system.[23]

What characterizes this period in legal relationships, as contrasted with earlier periods, is precisely an "erosion of the concept of legality." The erosion is characterized by (1) a belief that the law and legal institutions are not only unresponsive but illegitimate; (2) a condemnation of the bureaucratic delays, judicial indifference, and overt racism of most courts; (3) a rejection, and in many instances a contempt for Establishment officials—police, judges and lawyers; and (4) an affirmation of individual rights and an identification with group, class, racial and sexual liberation.

Herbert Marcuse remarked in his *Essay on Liberation* that

> . . . there is no (enforceable) law other than that which serves the status quo, and that those who refuse such service are *eo ipso* outside the realm of law even before they come into actual conflict with the law.[24]

If the role of the lawyer is defined in these terms, it becomes severely restricted, if not irrelevant. Lawyers, it is argued, cannot transform the legal system; in addition, their class position and firm ties to the legal apparatus pose irreconcilable contradictions. For lawyers and law students who do not see in the law possibilities for advancing radical change, the alternatives have become cynicism, a sense of powerlessness, or "dropping out." Some have moved completely into political activism.

However, the legal system has not collapsed yet. As government repression increases and respect for legality decreases, the lawyer's role takes on a new importance. Of course, litigation "cannot be permitted to take precedence over the task of organizing for direct action. . . . (since that) concedes the legitimacy of procedures and institutions whose claim to legitimacy is now increasingly attenuated . . ."

> The task of the litigator, therefore, is a combination of offense and defense to protect the Movement against attack and to use the rules of the courtroom game to keep its leaders out of jail and to prevail in particular confrontations which circumstances dictate must take place in the courtroom.[25]

In addition, the legal system in its old forms, as a servant to corporate interests and as the bodyguard of the myth of "equality under law," has gone bankrupt, but a new content has taken hold.

> The traditional modes for public service by lawyers . . . have lost most of their effectiveness and allure. . . . A source of intense interest for the present generation of law students is the small number of practitioners outside government or corporate law practice whose prime goal is the promotion of significant social change.[26]

The new content of lawyers' involvement has been described as essentially three different pursuits:

> Aiding the poor; representing political and cultural dissidents and new radical movements; furthering substantive

but neglected interests common to all classes and races, such as environmental quality and consumer protection.[27]

These pursuits, however, are far from mutually exclusive. In fact, when lawyers and clients from any of these groups carry their struggle to a confrontation with the political and financial interests which control the institutions and exploit the people, the distinctions melt away. Even liberal theorists foresee this:

> The apparent successes of the (environment and consumer protection) movement . . . may pose an obstacle to the goals of those who see shoddy products and abuses of the environment as symbols of a deeper and more pressing need for public control over the institutions which have such enormous power over individual lives. It is not unrealistic to expect that as the battle becomes focused on issues affecting more significantly the distribution of power in American society, the most militant lawyers for consumer and environmental values will take on more of the forms and strategies of lawyers for political and cultural dissidents.[28]

When during the 1969 Chicago Eight Conspiracy trial, the lawyers for these "political and cultural dissidents" joined with their clients to protest the use of an unconstitutional riot statute to suppress dissent, the racism of the court in denying Bobby Seale the right to his own lawyer, and the politically repressive role of the court in denying all the defendants their right to fully present their defense, they were charged with contempt and sentenced to prison. William Kunstler's statement to the court just before he was sentenced to four years and thirteen days is an affirmation that the lawyer is a citizen whose grievances must be heard:

> I am not ashamed of my conduct in this court, for which I am about to be punished . . . I have the utmost faith that my beloved brethren at the bar, young and old alike, will not allow themselves to be frightened out of defending the poor, the persecuted, the radicals and militants, the Black people, the pacifists, and the political pariahs of this, our common land.[29]

But since the Chicago trial lawyers who defend protesters
and identify with the issues raised by their clients have
become an affront to the courts. Even if they play by the
rules, even if they speak the anachronistic phrase "Your
Honor," even if they use the full resources and protections
of the law, they are no longer allies of the court itself. In
political trials the courts are openly partial to the prosecution, as in Washington's Seattle Eight trial or New York's
Panther 21 Conspiracy trial. Even in nonpolitical cases
judges do not look with approval upon lawyers who reflect
new life styles in the way they dress or act in court.

The President of Harvard University, formerly dean of
the law school, believes that the law students of today:

> will not deviate very far from their predecessors when the
> time comes to choose a permanent job . . . Recent gradu-
> ates are likely to go into established (business or corporate
> law) firms.[30]

He correctly observes that the alternatives to Establishment law, such as poverty law programs or public interest
law firms, pay too little, are "often dull and frustrating,"
and cannot get sufficient funding to accommodate more
than a handful of lawyers.

> Under these circumstances, a cautious prediction is that the
> changing attitudes among law students will eventually re-
> sult, not in a wholesale defection from established firms
> and traditional forms of legal practice, but in a dialogue
> that will allow many firms to reappraise and renew them-
> selves in a way that is healthy for all institutions.[31]

But it is not so clear that young lawyers who join the established business and corporate law firms will be able to
operate so smoothly while the society around them disintegrates. Corporate control of the legal profession is not as
secure as Harvard's president indicates. It has taken a
sizeable increase in salaries to attract graduating law students, but the returns may not be long-lasting. The young
lawyers are still seeking alternatives to corporate and
business law practice.

Other lawyers continue the struggle against the economic, class, racial, religious, and sexual inequities that permeate a corrupt judicial system. To be sure, the lawyers have no pat answer as to how to change the legal system. For some, racism represents the central issue through which the legal system can be exposed. Arthur Kinoy argues that existing institutional forms, such as the legal system, must be protected in order to wage a long-range challenge from within, while Michael Kennedy, Kenneth Cloke, and Michael Tigar assume that the legal system itself is an enemy that must be challenged whenever possible. But the distinctions among these writers are not as sharp as these lines imply. All the lawyers contributing to this book are members of the revived National Lawyers Guild. All agree, as does a growing proportion of the population, that the legal system, like the system of education, the health and military establishments, and the political process itself, is collapsing and can no longer be saved in its present form. The process of radical change is not, as some would argue, devoid of direction. Continual challenge, such as periodic prison revolts, lawyer protests, and bail abolition demonstrations, cause confusion and disorder which can lead to a new order. The idea of People's Courts, as practiced in socialist countries, is one way of altering existing power relationships within the legal apparatus. Overall, the institutions which only pay lip service to democracy, to people's needs, and to the survival of the planet will have to be taken over and transformed by those who have been excluded from and oppressed by their operation, that is, the majority of the people.

R. L.

Notes

1. Jerome H. Skolnick, *The Politics of Protest*. Report of the Task Force on Violent Aspects of Protest and Confrontation of the National Commission on the Causes and Prevention of Violence. New York: Ballantine Books, 1969, p. 318.

2. Ibid., p. 139.
3. Proposed ABA Standards for Criminal Justice Relating to the Defense Function, as quoted in *American College of Trial Lawyers, Report and Recommendations on Disruption of the Judicial Process* (July 1970), p. 8.
4. Ibid.
5. Daniel J. Boorstein, *The Americans: The Colonial Experience.* New York: Vintage Books, 1958, p. 205.
6. Leonard W. Levy, *Legacy of Suppression: Freedom of Speech and Press in Early American History.* Cambridge, Mass.: Belknap Press of Harvard University Press, 1960, pp. vii–viii.
7. Bernard Botein and Murray A. Gorden, *The Trial of the Future.* New York: Cornerstone Library, Inc., 1965, p. 125.
8. Anton-Hermann Chroust, *The Rise of the Legal Profession in America.* Vol. 2, Norman, Oklahoma: University of Oklahoma Press, 1965, p. 286.
9. Botein and Gorden, pp. 128–129.
10. Alexis de Tocqueville, *Democracy in America,* Vol. I. New York: Schocken Books, 1961 (1835), pp. 323, 324.
11. Ibid., pp. 328, 329.
12. C. Wright Mills, *The Power Elite.* New York: Oxford University Press, 1957, p. 131.
13. Botein and Gorden, p. 140.
14. Ibid.
15. Howard Moore, Jr., "Black Barrister at Southern Bar," Vol. 26, no. 1, *the National Lawyers Guild Practitioner* (NLGP) (Winter 1967), p. 28.
16. *Southern Justice: An Indictment* (pamphlet). Atlanta, Georgia: Southern Regional Council and the Southern Regional Office of the American Civil Liberties Union, 1965, p. 11.
17. Len Holt, *The Summer That Didn't End.* New York: William Morrow and Co., 1965, p. 87.
18. Committee for Legal Assistance in the South, "Project Mississippi: Summer of 1964," Vol. 24, no. 2, *NLGP* (Spring 1965), p. 42.
19. Arthur Kinoy, "Brief Remarks on *Dombrowski v Pfister*—A New Path in Constitutional Litigation," Vol. 26, no. 1, *NLGP* (Winter 1967), p. 7.
20. *The Politics of Protest,* p. 316.
21. Ibid., pp. 298–299.
22. Ibid., p. 298.
23. Ibid., pp. 323–324.
24. Herbert Marcuse, *Essay on Liberation.* Boston: Beacon Press, 1969, p. 67.
25. Michael E. Tigar, "Lawyer's Role in Resistance," Vol. 27, no. 4, *NLGP* (Fall 1968), p. 147.

26. Robert Borosage, Barbara Brown, Paul Friedman, Paul Ger-
    wirtz, William Jeffress, Jr. and William Kelly, Jr., "The New
    Public Interest Lawyers," Vol. 79, no. 6, *The Yale Law Journal*
    (May 1970), pp. 1069–1070.
27. Ibid., p. 1072.
28. Ibid., p. 1105.
29. Mark L. Levine, George C. McNamee and Daniel Greenberg,
    eds., *The Tales of Hoffman.* New York: Bantam Books, 1969,
    p. 270.
30. Derek Curtis Box, "New Lawyers in Old Firms," *The New York
    Times,* February 3, 1971, p. 37.
31. Ibid.

1

Demystifying the Law: How It Really Is

Law Against
the People

by Robert Lefcourt

To the person who waits all day to pay a traffic fine, the young man who spends a few months in jail for possessing marijuana, the woman who finds no remedy in court for an exorbitant rent hike, the Black who still cries for implementation of "civil rights" legislation, and the student who resists serving in an illegal war, the judicial process appears to worsen pressing problems rather than solve them.

It is not only that the legal apparatus is time-consuming and expensive; that unjust laws remain unchanged; that the Supreme Court has long refused to consider such "political" questions as the continuing wars in Southeast Asia and the exclusion of nonwhites, young and poor people from most juries; and that the legal system has failed to meet the expectations of certain segments of society. The legal system is bankrupt, and cannot resolve the contradictions which, like air pollution, have grown visibly more threatening to society but whose resolution still is not given high priority.[1]

This bankruptcy is clearest in the priorities of law enforcement and in the criminal courts. Criminal courts protect existing economic, political, and social relations. Historically this role has created a pattern of selective law enforcement practices of which the white upper and middle classes are the beneficiaries. Bail requirements and plea bargaining victimize propertyless defendants who are, in effect, prejudged. The roles of the judge, the prosecuting attorney, and even the defense lawyer for the poor and near-poor reinforce the bias, because they are geared only to the efficient administration of overcrowded, understaffed, and dehumanized court bureaucracies. The proposed solutions of many court officials concentrate on material rather than human problems—automating court procedures, expanding facilities, allocating more funds. But the crisis in the legal system is more fundamental and cannot be cured by technical reform: it lies in the class-based and racist character of social relationships and in the court structures which maintain these relationships.

Who Does the Law Protect?

"Jail the Real Criminals"
—A poster seen at various demonstrations in the
1960s

The myth of "equality under law" would have us believe that everyone is subject to society's laws and those who violate the laws are subject to prosecution. Yet in criminal courts across the country it can be easily observed that law enforcement affects almost exclusively the working-man and the poor, and, in recent years, the political activist. In the big cities nonwhites predominate in regular court appearances. The other criminals, the extremely wealthy, the corporations, the landlords, and the middle class white-collar workers are rarely prosecuted and almost never suffer the criminal court process as defendants.

It is impossible to enforce all laws against all lawbreakers. One survey by the President's Crime Commission reports that ninety-one percent of all Americans have violated laws that could subject them to a term in prison.[2] Choices are made as to which laws will be enforced against which people, and law enforcement officials necessarily use guidelines to make these choices.

One of the most important guiding principles behind law enforcement decisions can be inferred from the Crime Commission report. On the one hand it is stated that

Each single crime is a response to a specific situation by a person with an infinitely complicated psychological makeup who is subject to infinitely complicated external pressures. Crime as a whole is millions of such responses.[3]

Accordingly, a corporate executive who arranges to fix prices for the sale of his company's milk product is just as much a "criminal" as a man who steals food from a vegetable market. On the other hand, it is argued that the individual perpetrator of a crime must be seen in the context of his or her environment.

. . . crime flourishes, and has always flourished, in city slums; those neighborhoods where overcrowding, economic deprivation, social disruption, and racial discrimination are endemic.[4]

. . . so long as the social conditions that produce poverty remain, no reforms in the criminal process will eliminate the imbalance. . . . The poor are arrested more often, convicted more frequently, sentenced more harshly, rehabilitated less successfully than the rest of society.[5]

Despite the fact that "individual responsibility" is the stated basis of our criminal law enforcement, just as "social conditions" explain the why of selected law enforcement, it is still the individual's economic and social class and the color of his skin that determine his relationship to the legal system.

Just as power in a capitalist society is not concentrated in the capitalist as an individual, the law's protection of the middle and upper classes is not exercised directly by individuals. The enforcement of criminal sanctions is dictated by the necessities of the economic and political system in which the profit motive is central. For example, it is not surprising that no law prevents industrial managers from laying off thousands of workers, or from moving plants to new locations in order to maximize profits. The people whose lives and communities may be shattered have no recourse in the legal system. No law requires institutions which control and profit from the materials and means of production to share their wealth equally among the people who produce it and need it. Despite the lip service, it is not a priority of any elected official to urge a district attorney's office to arrest the property owners and corporate managers who violate air and water pollution laws, antitrust laws, housing codes, and the health and safety laws of the drug and auto industries. The pollution, sickness, and death resulting from such illegalities have had little effect on law enforcement agencies; in fact, the corporate class exercises such control over Congress and law enforcement agencies that there are few statistics documenting abuses. The public continues to drink polluted water, breathe poisoned air, and ride unsafe automobiles.

The protection of lesser economic interests, such as those of the middle class, serves to camouflage the abuses of those higher up the ladder. The broker who sells phony stocks, the builder who deliberately uses defective materials, the dairy company executive who fixes prices, the embezzler and the tax evader are the white collar criminals. As the Crime Commission report states, "These criminals are only rarely dealt with through the full force of criminal sanctions." [6] Through a multitude of regulatory statutes, the law regulates the food and drug and other industries; but the law is not enforced. "The crucial fact is that these laws are violated on a vast scale, sometimes in deliberate disregard of the law, sometimes because businessmen, in their effort to come as close to the line between legality and illegality as possible, overstep it." [7]

Avoiding taxes is the common practice for many middle class business people. Of the more than forty billion dollars collected on personal income each year, eighty-six percent comes from people in the lower brackets. These figures reflect not only the vast scale of tax evasion, but the fact that the tax law rewards a capitalist's skillful shuffling of paper. Inheritance stipends and stock dividends are subject in practice to fewer taxes than the $10,000 or less in salary earned by carpenters or secretaries.[8]

Middle class "interest groups" also are favored in law enforcement practice. White New York City high school teachers are employed in a school system that is mostly nonwhite. Teachers who closed down schools in January 1969 were not arrested, although they clearly broke the law against strikes by public employees; but a headline the next month announced a legal crackdown on students who protested the conditions in those same schools. While the antistrike law is aimed at crushing worker demands, it will not be used against white, or for Black, interests. In the teachers' strike, the law defended a white middle class constituency against Blacks who were making inroads in the white-controlled school system.

White racism is rarely prosecuted, especially when property interests are involved. For example, real estate interests continue to profit from the age-old practice of "blockbusting" (although the courts may soon be forced to face the problem). This is a tactic used by speculators involving the sale of one or two homes in a white neighborhood to Blacks to persuade the remaining white home owners to leave the neighborhood, selling at low prices. The realtors then resell the homes to middle class Blacks at high prices. In spite of Supreme Court rulings upholding the civil rights of Blacks, the law has not been enforced against Southern politicians and landowners who discriminate in schools, public facilities, housing, and jobs. In 1970 a public park in one Southern town was returned by the Supreme Court to its original white owners. A will had turned the park over to the city with the restriction that only whites could enjoy the facilities, and the Court, rather than ordering the integration of the public park, chose to respect the interest of the dead property owner by returning the land to his estate.

Legal Oppression of the Innocent

> *"Much better hang wrong feller than hang no feller."*
> CHARLES DICKENS, Bleak House

No matter how willingly or unwillingly a criminal defendant cooperates with the rules of the legal game, he is forced to submit to his own undesirability, and in effect, his prejudged guilt under the law. The prejudgment is finalized by two traditional court practices: the requirements of monetary bail and the pressure to "cop a plea," whereby a defendant pleads guilty instead of going to trial. Less blatant than these techniques is the cooperation among officials—the judge, the prosecuting attorney, and the poor person's defense lawyer—who use the legal techniques to isolate the prejudged defendants. Common class and racial bonds unite court officials and set apart the defendant, more or less according to the particular crime he or she is alleged to have committed. In one study of arrests in Washington, D.C., ninety percent of the people taken into custody had incomes of less than $5,000; Blacks have a significantly higher rate of arrests nationally than whites in almost every offense category; nearly forty-five percent of all arrests are for crimes without victims, such as drunkenness, gambling, vagrancy, and prostitution.[9]

The poor and nonwhite, arrested at a proportionally higher rate than the rest of the population, are more likely to be jailed after arrest because of the court practice of imposing monetary bail. If the defendant cannot post the amount set by a judge or give a bail bondsman security to post it for him, he remains in jail. One study of New York bail practices indicates the extent to which the courts tend to incarcerate the innocent prior to trial: twenty-five percent of all defendants in this study failed to make bail at $500, forty-five per cent failed at $1,500, and sixty-three percent at $2,500.[10]

The Eighth Amendment guarantees against excessive bail and the Supreme Court has ruled that the only function of bail is to help guarantee the appearance of the defendant in court. But bail is most often used against a defendant to "teach him a lesson" or to "protect the community." [11] A poor or nonwhite defendant languishes in jail weeks, months, and even years before trial. Nor does this preventive detention count toward whatever sentence may be imposed if the defendant is convicted; thus more pressure is placed on the accused to plead guilty quickly.

It may surprise most people that there are almost no criminal trials in the United States; but since seventy percent (over ninety percent in many states) of all defendants plead guilty, the need for most trials is eliminated.[12] In 1966, there were 9,895 felonies recorded in New York City; 9,501 of these ended in convictions by a plea of guilty. The pressures on lower class, poor, or nonwhite defendants to plead guilty has received little attention, perhaps because those who are arrested and detained illegally are generally thought to be guilty anyway.

This huge number of guilty pleas is produced by the practice known as plea copping, in which the accused pleads guilty to an offense lesser than the one originally charged, or in exchange for a promise of leniency from the judge. Frequently, the accused will be charged with more crimes than actually took place in order to persuade him to plead guilty to lesser charges. A man may be charged with armed robbery on five counts: robbery first degree, assault second degree, assault third degree, carrying a dangerous weapon, and petit larceny. If the defendant goes to trial and is convicted on every count he faces many years in prison. Instead, if he has no previous record, he is offered a lesser charge—simple assault or petit larceny—to which he can plead guilty on the spot. Regardless of whether he committed the crimes, he will plead guilty to the misdemeanor because the risk of conviction at trial, especially for a Black man or woman, is great. Meanwhile the court saves the time and expense of a trial. In many states defendants in capital cases can avoid convictions carrying a mandatory death sentence only by pleading guilty. In such cases defendants who wish to exercise their right to trial by jury risk death.

In the practice of plea copping more than in any other court ritual the common class interest of all the participants in the "adversary system" of law is apparent. It is generally thought that the defense lawyer and prosecuting attorney are opponents whose struggle will bring out the true guilt or innocence of the accused. In reality, it is through the cooperation of the judge and the prosecuting and defense attorneys that bail requirements are established or a guilty plea obtained. Because there is no conflict in the class interest of judge, defense, and prosecuting attorneys, there is no reality to their apparent opposition in court. Their task is the disposition of cases, not the trial of people. Their function is to keep the guilty guilty.

The aim of the prosecutor is to "get" people. Obtaining the guilty plea is as necessary to his personal image as it is to the smooth functioning of the system. Election campaigns play up his conviction rate like a batting average. Whether a district attorney is elected or appointed, he must have the support—financial and otherwise—of the Democratic or Republican Party, and many prosecutors use their offices as political stepping stones or to build future careers in the business world. The prosecutor must therefore avoid disrupting the traditional court practices. His stake in the status quo leads him to view defendants as criminals who should be punished if they are even slightly implicated. The prosecutor's influence is great, as he determines whom the police arrest, the volume of cases in the courts, and whether convicted offenders are imprisoned.

The judge exerts a powerful influence on all stages of the criminal process. His enforcement of class distinctions in rulings, sentencing practices, and in the speed with which he disposes of cases determines many decisions by police, prosecutors, and defense counsel. Like the prosecutors, the judges have a stake in the status quo.

They are chosen by professional politicians, after nomination by the Democratic and/or Republican Parties, or appointed according to the patronage of local, state, or federal executives. It is therefore not unusual for judges to work hand in hand with prosecutors. A rebel Black judge from Michigan, George W. Crockett, Jr., states the relationship clearly: "I personally think that it's unfortunate that, for the most part, our judges are made up of members of the former ranks of the prosecutors' offices, or the U. S. District Attorney's office. I think they come to the bench conditioned to believe everything the policeman says and everything the prosecutor says." [13] Because a defendant can expect little from a court controlled by an Establishment judge, he is the more influenced to plead guilty.

Although the judge only acts as a rubber stamp in this process, his powers of setting bail and of sentencing, and the psychological effect of the aura of power that surrounds him, all serve to force the guilty plea. The great symbol of justice in the criminal courts, he in fact uses the prestige of traditional courtroom respect to cloak the procedure that takes place behind closed doors or before the bench itself. All must rise when the judge enters. U. S. District Court Judge Marvin E. Frankel writes, "Sitting on raised platforms, all draped in black, judges (even of lower courts) sometimes have ludicrously inflated images of themselves and of the supposed Olympian qualities of their decisions." [14] Because his role is the least questioned and the most respected of all the participants, the judge's decisions seem to confirm the guilt of the undesirables who plead guilty.

In a recent experiment in one Western county the prosecutor exchanged places in the courtroom with the defense attorney, supposedly so that each could learn the difficulties of the other's position. That the experiment could take place at all demonstrates the overt cooperation between supposedly opposing forces. The defense lawyer's role is that of a friend who leads the unsuspecting to the slaughterhouse. Of course the defense attorney is supposed to try to prove the innocence or defend the interests of his client; this is what he does when hired by a wealthy influential client. It is also true when a Movement attorney volunteers to defend a political activist. But a defense attorney for the poor or workingman, whether the state or a private agency reimburses him or whether the client pays directly, does not identify above all with the interests of the client. He is more interested in seeing the court process function smoothly—which means that his client should plead guilty.

Each year about sixty percent of all defendants in federal and state courts are financially unable to afford counsel. Most states provide lawyers by one or both of two methods. In the assigned counsel system, which covers about two-thirds of all indigent defendants, the county clerk uses a list of available lawyers to appoint an attorney for the indigent on a case-by-case basis. In large cities the "defender" system is in greater use. Here lawyers are mostly full-time salaried government employees. Since the 1963 *Gideon* decision, in which the U. S. Supreme Court decided that any person alleged to have committed a felony must have access to an attorney, the defender system has grown enormously.

Recent studies comparing both the defender and assigned counsel to the traditional private lawyer have shown that lawyers for the poor advise their clients to plead guilty somewhat more often than privately retained attorneys.[15] However, the experts do not begin to explain the relationship between the guilty plea and its class and race basis. The private "lawyer regulars," as one criminal lawyer calls them, use their professional role as attorneys to exploit moderate income and working class clients. These lawyers are

highly visible in the major urban centers of the nation; their offices—at times shared with bondsmen—line the back streets near courthouses. They are also visible politically, with clubhouse ties reaching into judicial chambers and the prosecutor's office. The regulars make no effort to conceal their dependence upon police, bondsmen, jail personnel, as well as bailiffs, stenographers, prosecutors, and judges.[16]

The private "lawyer regular" is not concerned with guilt or innocence—nine out of ten times he will lose in court—so he collects his fee in advance, then convinces his client that pleading guilty will be best because the charges or the sentence will be lessened. The trusting client agrees, forgetting that in so doing he is forfeiting his right to a trial by jury and, as in many states, getting a presentence hearing before a judge over facts that might mitigate the offense.

"As members of a bureaucratic system, defense attorneys become committed to rational, impersonal goals based on saving time, labor, and expense and on attaining maximum output for the system." [17] The assigned counsel or public defender has a close working relationship with the "impartial" judge and the "enemy" prosecutor. They appear again and again in the same courtroom, whereas clients come and go. One who has observed the casual offstage and onstage relations among the defense and prosecuting lawyers and the judge understands that the ties among these individuals override the interests of a particular defendant. This is not corruption in the traditional sense, although that also exists; this is the normal way that guilt is determined for the undesirables in our society. As a judge who sits on a higher court described the reality of the lower courts,

> Despite the presumption of innocence, the defendant in these police and magistrate courts is, prima facie, guilty. He is almost always uncounseled and sometimes he is not even informed of the charges against him until after the so-called trial. Often no records are kept of the proceedings, and in the overwhelming majority of cases, these courts are, in practice, courts of last resort.[18]

Law and Power in a "Pluralistic" Society

Karl Marx noted that "judicial relations, like state forms, can be explained neither as things in themselves,

nor by the progress of the human mind; they are rooted in
the material conditions of life." As the economic organization of our society is grounded in property relations, so
the law serves the most powerful property interests. The
masses of people who have little or no connection to the
centers of economic power are governed by rules intended
to maintain existing power relationships. Criminal law
enforcement controls the activities of those who are powerless because of their material conditions. While the
lower classes and nonwhites dominate the court calen-
dars, the court officers represent the interests of the power
structure. The class and racist practices inherent in the
bail system and plea bargaining contradict democratic
principles at the same time as they uphold the economic
relationships of a capitalist society. The legal superstructure is not designed to dispense justice to a whole community nor to allow changes in property relations. It legiti-
mizes the power of the few and punishes those who have
been defeated by or who challenge this power.

American social scientists use the term "pluralism" to
describe American "representative democracy." They de-
pict a society in which widely varied groups compete with
each other, in which decision-making rests on give-and-
take among various groups. Groups compromise, make
deals, and pressure each other; public officials and lawmakers respond to these various group pressures so that
no one political, economic, social, religious, regional, or
racial group will dominate. This creates the "natural" system of checks and balances which maintains a democracy. People become part of the decision-making process
as soon as they organize: as big labor checks big business,
Catholics check Protestants, farmers check urbanites, students check school administrators.

The plausibility of this description is such that today
many people are claiming that the answer to poverty is
community control and that racism can be ended by supporting Black power as a check on white power. Yet the
poor cannot check the rich and Blacks will never balance
whites; pluralism masks the fact that some groups and

individuals hold power in capitalist society while certain classes and races are excluded. It cannot be denied that important changes occur when pressures are exerted. High-level interest groups struggle for control in the top brackets of industry; the passage of civil rights legislation in 1964 and after came as a result of the nonviolent demands of the early 1960s. What can be denied is that property relations can be changed by the pluralist process. Economic guidelines and laws give the major corporations in this free enterprise system ownership of the means of production, while the populations underlying the upper class are divided (into income, religious, ethnic, and racial groups) so that they are prevented from determining the material conditions of their lives or the policies of their government. It is now a well-established (though not so well-known) fact that economic inequality within the United States has remained generally constant throughout this century,[19] showing that the "potential for unity" [20] of the upper class is much greater than that of the middle and lower classes. Sociologists have shown that a cohesive white upper class, consisting of approximately one-half of one percent of the people in this country, controls every major bank and corporation and personally owns over one-quarter of the country's wealth, while eighty percent of all stock value is owned by less than two percent of all families.[21]

The wealthy exercise their power through corporations.

> . . . great corporations are the important units of wealth, to which individuals of property are variously attached. The corporation is the source of the basis of continued power and privilege. All the men and the families of great wealth are identified with large corporations in which their property is seated.[22]

John Kenneth Galbraith and other apologists for monopoly capitalism argue that the increased need for technical knowledge and management expertise has come between large industrial enterprises and their owners and has democratized the corporations. Yet the profits of the top fifty

corporations represent about forty percent of all industrial earnings, and the corporations are now struggling for
still greater control of the economy by means of a new
phenomenon, the conglomerate. It is estimated that by
1975 three hundred corporations will own two-thirds of
the industrial assets of the world.[23]

Occasionally laws are passed which challenge ruling
class interests, e.g., New Deal legislation resulting from
workers' struggles strengthened unions and, to some extent, redistributed income. These changes, however, did
not substantially diminish corporate wealth and control.
The workers were diverted from the struggle to gain control over economic forces by the creation of a legal administrative bargaining structure in which the perpetuation of
the power structure was assumed. Other examples of laws
which challenge corporate control are consumer safety
regulations concerning food and drugs and, recently, air
and water pollution. The laws restrict those capitalists
whose activities are so obviously harmful that public
anger at them is a potential threat to corporate power.
They have clearly been forced to respond in some measure
to popular outcries; but the corporate elite, through its influence over law enforcement, insures that these new laws
are not used to impair basic operations.

"Legality" depends not only on who is powerful but also
on the intensity of the struggle by the people, which can
transform legal relationships. A labor union in the early
nineteenth century was defined as an illegal conspiracy to
interfere with employees' freedom of contact. Courts enjoined organizing activity and jailed organizers. Company
thugs were praised as protectors of law and order—that
is, company property—while workers out on strike were
criminals. By the late 1930s union organizing and the
right to strike were protected (except among weak groups
like agricultural workers and public employees) and
bosses were required to bargain. Union contracts became
enforceable in court. What had been criminal became
legal and previously legal activity was now illegal. The
changing law reflected the new power of the movement,

but it also coopted it. Property relations had been slightly modified by the struggles of the people; nevertheless, the right of ownership was safe.

Because the legal superstructure is largely powerless against the pervasive abuses of the corporate world and its oppression of the large segment of the population, it opens the way for popular attacks directed at its most valued assumption, its impartiality. Resistance to the legal oppression of the lower classes and nonwhite peoples has in recent years resulted in the arrests, jailing, and even murders of many who are aware that the system will not change itself. This resistance, especially among the Black population—supported by a growing number of white youth—has focused attention on the role the courts play in maintaining an illegitimate order. Those who are captured in the criminal court process experience its oppressiveness concretely and are radicalized by their experience; this process leads radicals to argue that all "criminals," as defined by the Establishment, are political prisoners.

For the majority, however, the legal superstructure does not seem to impose on daily life. The separation of the law from the people obscures the true class and racist nature of the entire economic and political system. People are now focusing their resistance on the institutions which directly affect them—at their schools, on their jobs, in their neighborhoods. But as the Establishment uses its law to cut off resistance, people will begin to see legal relationships as they actually are, coexisting with the economic and political system. Law will be demystified. People will no longer tolerate a system in which large corporations, wealthy individuals, and property owners receive the greatest benefits. They will no longer accept the pluralist mask behind which the law pretends to be an impartial voice among conflicting groups or individuals. The people themselves will then assume authority and become their own lawmakers.

Notes

1. See *The New York Times*, April 3, 1970, p. 48. "The Ford Foundation has appropriated $1,000,000-plus for grants to study what it feels is a growing lack of faith in this country's judicial process."
2. *The Challenge of Crime in a Free Society*, A Report by the President's Commission on Law Enforcement and the Administration of Justice. New York: Avon Books, 1968. Hereafter, the *Crime Commission Report*.
3. Ibid., p. 87.
4. Ibid., p. 88.
5. Patricia Wald, "Poverty and Criminal Justice," in the *Crime Commission Report*, p. 151.
6. The *Crime Commission Report*, p. 156.
7. Ibid., p. 157.
8. Gabriel Kolko, *Wealth and Power in America*. New York: Frederick A. Praeger, 1962, pp. 30–45.
9. The *Crime Commission Report*, pp. 149–50, 195.
10. Caleb Foote, "A Study of the Administration of Bail in New York City," *University of Pennsylvania Law Review*, Vol. 106 (1958), p. 633.
11. Ibid.
12. The percentage of trials in all states varies from none (South Dakota) to forty-five percent (Texas). The median is twelve percent. Lee Silverstein, *Defense of the Poor: The National Report*. Chicago: American Bar Foundation, 1965, Vol. 1.
13. George W. Crockett, "Racism in American Law," *The National Lawyers Guild Practitioner*, Fall 1968, p. 178.
14. Marvin E. Frankel, "Remarks on Law and Revolution," *Bar Bulletin*: New York County Lawyers' Association, Vol. 26, No. 2, 1968–1969, p. 51.
15. See Silverstein, *Defense of the Poor*, for a comparison of legal aid systems.
16. Abraham S. Blumberg, "Lawyers With Convictions," *Transaction*, July 1967, p. 18.
17. Ibid.
18. J. Skelly Wright, "The Courts Have Failed the Poor," *New York Times Magazine*, March 9, 1969, p. 26.
19. Kolko, pp. 13–14.
20. William Domhoff, *Who Rules America?*. Englewood Cliffs, New Jersey: Prentice-Hall, 1967, pp. 151–52.
21. Ibid., p. 11.

22. C. Wright Mills, *The Power Elite*. New York: Oxford University Press, 1957, Chapter 7.
23. See *Fortune*, May 15, 1969, for the Establishment's listing of the top corporations in the U.S., and some crude justifications for the growth of conglomerates.

Racism and American Law

by Haywood Burns*

The Kerner Commission told the nation something that most Black folk have known for a long time—America is a racist country.

> Race prejudice has shaped our history decisively; it now threatens to affect our future. White racism is essentially responsible for the explosive mixture which has been accumulating in our cities since the end of World War II.

Many white Americans recoiled from the charge of racism as it applied to them, and summarily dismissed the conclusions of the report. This all-too-easy evasion of some difficult and ugly truths was made more possible by the nature of the Kerner Commission Report. Despite its many valuable contributions, the report did not delve deeply into just how decisively racial animus has shaped our past and the extent to which it puts any future in doubt. The "explosive mixture" has been accumulating not just in our cities and not just since the end of World War II. The presence of white racism has been a constant in the American past. It has defined the American past.

We must move beyond the Kerner Commission Report to understand the exact way in which our institutions, group, and personal relationships were and are determined by the fact that this has been and continues to be a country permeated by racism. A look at the interaction of American attitudes toward race with the legal system provides one of the best avenues for this inquiry; for though it is often proclaimed that ours is a "government of laws, not men," the law does not exist as a "brooding omnipresence" somewhere off in the ether. It is made by men and, in America's case, by men in a racist society. In this country law has been the handmaiden of racism. It has been the way in which the generalized racism in the society is made specific and converted into particular policies and standards of social control which mirror the racism of the dominant society.

Inquiry into the racism-law interaction can perhaps best be made by first examining from an historical perspective the Indian, the Oriental, and the Black experiences with American law, and then by analyzing the manner in which racism continues to play a role in the structural apparatus of the American judicial system.

The social pathology of American white racism is not limited in its manifestations to negative attitudes towards and hostile treatment of Blacks. The Red brother has felt the brunt of the superiority complex of the white European and his descendants here in the new world. In the beginning, at least, some of the white newcomers felt the need to deal with the indigenous Indian population in an equitable manner. William Penn and Lord Baltimore both advocated and followed a policy attempting to acquire title to Indian land through mutual agreement and fair compensation. However, their approach proved to be the exception rather than the rule. As early as the seventeenth century, English settlers were setting up reservations for Indians in the environs. As early as the eighteenth century, legislative bodies were offering bounties for Indian scalps. On the question of Indian lands, the U. S. Supreme Court in *Johnson v M'intosh* (1823) took the position that "discovery gave exclusive title to those who made it"—upholding the land claim of whites who "discovered" certain lands occupied by Indians, and denying the Indians right and power to dispose of the land.

A treaty, once ratified by the Senate, is entered in the U. S. Statutes at Large and becomes part of the law of the land. Some of the greatest instances of official lawlessness chronicled in our nation's past are found in the pattern of treaty making followed by treaty breaking in dealing with Indians. It is the story of one continuous forked tongue. In 1830 Congress passed the Indian Removal Act, which was designed to effect the transfer of the so-called "civilized tribes" from their homeland in the East to lands west of the Mississippi. In exchange for their homeland the Indians were to receive perpetual title to the Western lands. "Perpetuity" lasted only until white Americans decided that the vast territory west of the Mississippi was too valuable to remain in Indian hands and to wrench it from them. It was illegal white encroachments which generated most of the Indian wars of the nineteenth century. Western lands taken away from the Indians and made available to white settlers under federal land grant law formed the basis for many white Americans' growth to economic independence and well-being. Many of today's middle Americans who are the staunchest advocates of law and order and free enterprise are where they are because of a land base that was provided for their forebears through theft of Indian land and the largesse of a big government benefit program.

One of the more striking examples of the perversion of the legal process in dealing with Indian land is the ruse used against the California Indians. The Indians gave up more than half the state of California in exchange for perpetual ownership of 7,500,000 acres. Because of pressure from white politicians, the Senate never ratified the treaties under which the Indians gave up their land in exchange for the 7,500,000 acres. The Indian Bureau, which had negotiated the treaties in 1851 with 119 California tribes, never told the Indians about the failure to ratify. The treaties stayed in the files of the Senate until 1905 when the 7,500,000 acres the Indians thought were theirs were sold to white settlers and land speculators.

As with Blacks, the law was used against Indians to make sure that these inferior beings stayed in their place —whatever that might be at the moment. In some parts of the country, Indians were not allowed to testify in court or become members of the bar. A special set of laws governed their social conduct in such matters as drinking and intermarriage. Custom and usage barred them from many public facilities. Governmental suggestions for dealing with "the Indian problem" ranged from penning them up on reservations to genocide. Ample efforts were made at both.

The record of the interaction of American racism and the legal system is far from unblemished in the area of this country's dealings with persons of Oriental descent. In the mid-nineteenth century Chinese were imported in droves to do the hard, dirty, and dangerous work of building the West. In particular, they were employed in the perilous tasks of cutting the first national railroad through the Western mountains. It was due to the number of Oriental workers who were injured or killed in this hazardous work that the expression "he doesn't have a Chinaman's chance" originated. As the need for Chinese labor decreased, and racial antagonism and fear of the Asiatic hordes grew, the Congress took under consideration and eventually passed a series of laws which barred the Chinese from immigrating to this country altogether. Such a legal move was unprecedented and was clearly based on race. The concern of domestic workers over foreign cheap labor is insufficient to explain this legislative action. Native American workers were worried about competition from the new immigrants of Southern and Central Europe as well, but Congress passed no comparable legislation to keep them out. The tired, the poor, the huddled masses yearning to breathe free, apparently did not include the Chinese.

In some areas, Chinese were not allowed to testify in

court. A California court upheld this rule even though there was no statutory exclusion of Chinese testimony. The reasoning of the court was that California law barred Indians from testifying, and since it was a well-known fact that Indians originally came to this continent from Asia and are racially related to Orientals, the intent of the statute was to bar Chinese testimony as well.

In the late nineteenth and into the twentieth century some Western states passed laws putting restrictions upon Orientals owning or leasing land or engaging in certain occupations. These statutes did not necessarily speak in terms of a bar to Orientals, but rather were phrased so that the exclusion from the "privilege" was based upon the person's status as an alien ineligible for citizenship. By this device the states were able to use the racist federal naturalization laws as a "neutral" cover—however transparent—for their discriminatory ends.

The Naturalization Act of 1790 limited naturalization to any alien who was a "free white person." It was not until after the Civil War that the "white only" naturalization law was altered. In 1870 it was amended to permit persons of African descent to become citizens, a change necessary to make citizenship for many former slaves possible. A racial bar to naturalization in one form or another existed throughout almost the entire history of the nation. In the 1920s, when faced with the question "who is white," the U. S. Supreme Court held (after looking to the intent of the framers) that "white" was not synonymous with Caucasian, and barred a Hindu from citizenship. It was not until 1943 that Chinese were allowed to be naturalized. This only came about because of the role of the Chinese as America's ally in World War II and because of pressure from groups and individuals on the home front —not the least of which was the resignation of the Director of the U. S. Immigration Service on this issue, who, in resigning, pointed out that the only other nation in the world at that time which had a legal barrier to naturalization based on race was Nazi Germany. When the last racial restrictions were removed by the Immigration and

Nationality Act of 1952, Burmese, Japanese, Koreans, Maoris, Polynesians, and Samoans were still excluded.

The experience of the Japanese in America during World War II is another recent example of the workings of racism and American law. One hundred and ten thousand persons of Japanese ancestry, 70,000 of them citizens—men, women, and children—were involuntarily removed from their homes, jobs and communities and placed in detention camps for periods ranging up to several years—all without benefit of a trial or any fair opportunity to be heard. This policy was initiated by General John L. DeWitt, the military officer in charge of Western states, an officer who made no secret of his racist sentiments. When questioned on his wholesale abridgement of the rights of tens of thousands of persons without any efforts to distinguish among them, General DeWitt is said to have replied simply, "A Jap is a Jap." The policy of internment of Japanese was followed nowhere in the Americas except General DeWitt's Western states region—not even in Hawaii where there was a much higher percentage of Japanese and Japanese-Americans in the population. It certainly was not applied to other enemy aliens as a group or persons with those nationality backgrounds. No one even suggested locking up persons of Italian and German descent for no other reason than their descent. Such a policy would have required the internment of Joe DiMaggio and Dwight David Eisenhower during World War II.

This unprecedented move by the government was in direct response to the virulent West Coast anti-Japanese feeling. The barbed-wire policy was authorized by the President, implemented by Congress, and ultimately approved by the Supreme Court, on the ground of national security. It was this last action that called forth special criticism from Professor E. V. Rostow of the Yale Law School. In a leading law journal article, written shortly after the Supreme Court's action, Professor Rostow saw reason for special concern over the action of the Court in sanctioning the Japanese Relocation scheme in that it "converts a piece of wartime folly into a permanent part of the law." The legal sanction for such a gross invasion of the personal liberties of a group of persons on the grounds of "national security" remains even now a potent threat to all those whom some administration may some day deem dangerous.

A close look at the work of the "founding fathers" in adopting the U. S. Constitution provides an excellent index of how they regarded the question of Black freedom. Though many professed an abhorrence of slavery, and moves were made toward its abolition, attempts to do away with it floundered and failed. Even among delegates of a liberal persuasion who opposed slavery there was great reluctance to tamper with so much property. Further, even in the most enlightened quarters there was a decided inability to view Blacks as men and as equals. This racism severely limited the boundaries of action of the slavery opponents, who were themselves racists. Black freedom was not a fundamental item as was white freedom, but rather a negotiable item, part of the barter and exchange system of trade-offs and accommodations by which white men conducted their affairs. Out of the welter of compromise of the Constitutional Convention came the document which constitutes our fundamental law. There enshrined, along with the guaranteed continuation of the slave trade and the obligation for the return of fugitive slaves, is the Black slave as three-fifths of a man.

It was through the law that the lives of slaves were governed in oppressive detail. The slave codes passed throughout the states of the South denied the legal personality of Blacks. Blacks could not bring lawsuits, no matter how grievously they had been wronged or how substantial their interest. They could not testify in a court of law when a white man's interests were involved. Apart from closely regulating the mobility of Blacks and their opportunities for social contact and interaction, the slave codes often made it a crime to teach slaves to read and write, and ruled out certain kinds of occupations for slave and free Blacks alike—especially occupations which involved work with drugs and explosives. Legal recognition of and protection for the family relationship was withheld by the slave codes and rejected by judicial decision. The criminal sanctions for slaves were governed by different rules or by no rules. This is partly a result of a system where men are held in bondage for life—for them the threat of jail has little or no meaning.

A special statutory penalty reserved for Blacks, and in some cases Indians, was sexual mutilation for sex crimes. Laws providing for emasculation of Black or Red offenders were passed in several jurisdictions. As late as 1857 white men sat in the Kansas Territory legislature and passed a bill which provided that a Black man convicted of having been involved in any of several different types of interracial liaisons should be castrated "by a person of suitable skill" and that the offender should be taxed with the costs of such a procedure.

As white racism was not an exclusively Southern phenomenon, neither were the laws reflecting it. While Northern politicians often attacked slavery in the South, many states above the Mason-Dixon line developed their own sets of laws for the so-called "free" Blacks. In many Northern states Blacks were banned by law from the ballot box and forced to attend segregated schools. Some areas even forbade Blacks to come within their geographical boundaries. The federal government barred Blacks from employment in the post office and vacillated greatly on the issue of granting passports to Blacks because of federal uncertainty as to the citizenship status of a Black man in America. Chief Justice Taney and the U. S. Supreme Court resolved the dilemma in *Dred Scott v Sanford*, making it quite clear that the slave Scott was not a citizen and, further (in effect, summing up the corpus of law on Blacks as it had developed to this time), Blacks "had no rights which the white man was bound to respect."

After emancipation and after Appomattox, the white South, relying on its tried and tested tool, the law, tried, insofar as was possible, to reestablish the previously existing superior position of whites. The notorious Black Codes were designed to assure a working relationship between whites and Blacks that would not offend the racist sentiments of the white South, one that would as closely as possible approximate the freedman's position to slavery. State legislatures passed bills which made it virtually impossible for freedmen to go into commercial fields or to work as artisans. Detailed, expensive licensing requirements and the necessity of serving an apprenticeship with someone already in the trade made it virtually impossible for Blacks to establish themselves in various areas of skilled labor and commercial enterprise. Service on the land was guaranteed, however. Black Codes set out in detail the obligations in the master-servant relationship, giving the master enormous control over the comings and goings of their workers, down to the most intimate details of their lives. Black Codes prohibited intermarriage, and permitted corporal punishment and convict labor. The latter was an especially useful legal device. Blacks could be arrested in numbers under exceedingly vague vagrancy and idleness statutes, and then farmed out to local landowners to work off their sentences of hard labor. Without the benefit of a date it is often difficult to tell a post-Civil War Black Code from a pre-Civil War Slave Code.

Reconstruction provided only a brief interlude in which the primary thrust of the law was turned away from suppression and denial of Blacks to progressive efforts in their favor; but even during this period the bold promises of sweeping legal changes to create an economically viable Black community went unfulfilled. Forty acres and a mule remained in the realm of dream stuff—a dream that began to fade the more rapidly as the white South snatched back power from the hands of a North grown tired of "the Negro question" and all too willing to let the former slave masters work their will with the former slaves in the interest of "national unity"—white national unity.

In the period following Reconstruction, the law was called into play to give definition and formal structure to the Southern practices, customs, and usages of apartheid. Jim Crow hospitals, schools, transportation, public accommodations, prisons, and cemeteries, one by one were required on a statewide basis as a matter of law. Whereas previously custom and usage allowed for some variance and local deviation, state legislatures in this period dictated a uniform standard of conduct with the full force of criminal sanctions behind it. Courtrooms were segregated as a matter of law, as were even the Bibles upon which witnesses took their oaths.

On a national level the Supreme Court in the post-Reconstruction era beat a retreat from the liberal directions of the postwar Congress. From the Civil Rights cases in 1883 invalidating post-Civil War public accommodations law to and beyond *Plessy v Ferguson* in 1896, upholding the doctrine of "separate but equal," the Supreme Court engaged in a systematic evisceration of the Civil War amendments and federal civil rights legislation that had been passed pursuant to those amendments. The Court imposed an increasingly restrictive view upon the scope of the Fourteenth Amendment, limiting its application to abridgment of rights by state officials or institutions, while exempting the acts of private citizens from its reach. This unwarrantedly narrow reading of the Fourteenth Amendment partially disarmed one of the most valuable weapons in the Blacks' legal arsenal for fighting racism.

The law was a major ally in aiding those who sought to strip the Black man of any vestige of political power that he had gained and exercised during Reconstruction. The attack on the Black franchise was made through creative legal stratagems that decimated the Black representation on the voting rolls in the late nineteenth and early twentieth centuries. Beginning with Mississippi in 1890, states in the Deep South revised their constitutions to erect difficult barriers to Black voting. Through a series of state constitutional conventions and legislative enactments, voter lists were purged of Blacks. The grandfather clause, property requirements, the poll tax, and the literacy test were all pressed into service as new legal apparatus designed to obliterate Black vote power.

This disenfranchisement effort was carried out in close connection with a campaign of violence, terror, intimidation, and lynching. At one period in the 1890s Blacks were lynched on the average of two a week. Though the violent terror tactics were extralegal in the sense that they did not represent the carrying out of any authoritative prescription, they were so widespread and enjoyed such a high level of community sanction that in another sense lynch law was in fact law—the imposition of community-approved sanctions for the violation of community mores. Lynch law and statutory law accomplished their purpose. By 1910 most Blacks in the South were no longer voting. In Louisiana alone, Black registration dropped from 130,334 in 1876 to 1,342 in 1904.

The edifice of *de jure* segregation remained largely intact from the late nineteenth century to modern times. *Brown v Board of Education* in 1954 represented the first major assault upon the 1896 *Plessy* "separate but equal" doctrine. Congress passed no major civil rights bill from 1875 to the Civil Rights Act of 1957.

There are serious questions about the amount of true change the series of modern civil rights court victories and legislation since *Brown* and the Civil Rights Act of 1957 have been able to effect in the real-life situations of nonwhite people in America. Court triumphs and new laws often take a long time to filter down and make a difference in peoples' lives, and the process here has been further retarded by the lack of executive will in the area of enforcement, and by the racist intransigence of the majority white society in protecting its dominance—the two being not unrelated. The problem has become particularly egregious because of the retreat of the Nixon administration in the area of minority rights. The so-called "Southern Strategy" is an assault upon all the poor and nonwhite it chooses to ignore. The newly made "discovery" of racism as a *national* problem has been an occasion for the white South to attempt to escape some of the force of remedial federal power by pointing a finger northward. White racism is a *national* disease, but that should not evade the fact that the South has its own peculiar virulent forms, nor should it be permitted to support the conclusion that there should be less vigorous action against white Southern racists, only that there should be more against white Northern racists.

Throughout the past the racism of American society has been reflected in its legal system. Today, however, most explicit racial distinctions are gone from the statute books. Courts have struck down such statutes or new legislation has superseded them. Significantly, among the last to go were the miscegenation statutes. Almost all judges have ceased to articulate the rationale of their decisions in ways that explicitly involve the race of the parties before the bar. Legislatures, if they are not all passing civil rights bills, at least are no longer writing explicit racial distinctions into law. These are encouraging tendencies, but they should not lead to the false conclusion that in a racist society the law has somehow managed finally to escape that racism. The interaction between American racism and the legal system continues today in less visible but not necessarily less pernicious forms.

Blacks, Indians, and Orientals are no longer barred from testifying in court in matters involving white men, but many judges and juries accord much greater weight to the testimony of white witnesses than they do to nonwhite. When the issue is one of credibility, one white witness is often worth several nonwhite ones. Statutes no longer bar nonwhites from juries, and the courts have made it clear that systematic exclusion of nonwhite persons from juries is constitutionally unacceptable. Yet through prosecutors' use of the peremptory challenge of prospective jurors, legions of Black men and women have their fates decided by all-white juries from which members of their own race have been systematically excluded. The peremptory challenge allows the prosecutor in selecting the jury to remove a given number of members from the panel without giving a reason. Throughout the country this device is used by prosecutors to remove Black prospective jurors fom jury panels in cases involving Black defendants. While invalidating explicit exclusion, the Supreme Court has upheld this use of the peremptory strike. There is also often a wide differential between what juries will allow white plaintiffs by way of damages in a tort suit and what they will allow Black plaintiffs similarly situated. In several parts of the country, for example, a white leg may be worth $150,000, while a Black leg only $50,000.

The areas of judicial and administrative discretion also provide opportunities for covert racism. This is particularly true in sentencing, parole, and probation. Unexpressed racial bias can creep in to pollute the process without fear of being exposed or proven. An examination of the racial pattern of sentencing in a particular area, however, can reveal racism at work. Disparity in sentences given whites and nonwhites for similar offenses is often a good indicator. In this connection, the pattern of the imposition of the death sentence in this country—especially for interracial rape—shows a clear racist bias against nonwhites.

There is much about the law today that may not be racist on its face but is racist in its impact. This racism is the result of the context in which our legal system must function—a society infected by racism—and the legacy of overt societal and explicit legal racism. Failure to take this legacy into account will often cause apparently "neutral" or "objective" systems to have an untoward racial dimension. Their impact may be intended or coincidental. However, the very failure to take this legacy into account must itself be regarded as racist, for to act as if the overt racism of the past never occurred, and to design systems of law without taking it into account, is to perpetuate the historical effect of racism.

The "neutrality" of such systems is entirely false. There is a structural inequality built into our law which works to the detriment of the poor and the nonwhite (often they are the same persons, but not always) because this structural inequality represents a confluence of caste and class bias in the law. It is racist in its impact because of the disproportionate number of nonwhites who are among the poor and because of the perpetuation it represents of the historical racism which is largely responsible for their impoverishment. Systems which place or keep nonwhites in positions of inferiority or disadvantage, using not race itself as the subordinating mechanism, but instead other mechanisms indirectly related to race, are properly designated "institutionally racist." This species of racism abounds in our law.

The operation of the money bail system is an example of the institutional subordination of the nonwhite. There is a constitutional right to bail in noncapital offenses, and its only legitimate purpose is to assure the appearance of the defendant at trial. However, high bail is used by a vast number of our courts as a method of pretrial punishment —ignoring nonfinancial release conditions that are available for impecunious defendants with roots in the community or for those for whom there is little likelihood of flight. This fact has been most spectacularly revealed in the exorbitant ransom courts have required for the pretrial release of Black political prisoners, but at lesser amounts and with less well-known defendants the practice is also common.

A similar structural inequality exists in the civil law. Access to the courts is restricted along economic lines. Whereas the legal system has at least reached the point of providing an accused defendant in most criminal cases with counsel, there is no such right in noncriminal cases. Poor persons seeking to use the law as a remedy in noncriminal matters may be able to obtain legal counsel (especially if they are in an area covered by a legal services program for the poor) or they may not—there is no guarantee. In some places there is a financial roadblock to the courts in the form of the requirement of a bond before eviction proceedings can be challenged. The person without funds who is being evicted cannot post a money bond and is without legal redress. He will find his goods on the sidewalk no matter how valid his claim might have been in court, had he been able to get there.

Not only does owner-biased landlord/tenant law operate to the detriment of the poor nonwhite underclass, but the structure of our creditor-biased consumer law institutionally subordinates that class as well. The "holder in due course" doctrine in the consumer area is an excellent example of the way in which unscrupulous merchants use their legal advantage to prey upon the ghetto dweller. Typically, a purchaser will be sold some goods on an installment basis. Soon after the rug or the refrigerator or the furniture arrives, it turns out to be defective. When the buyer goes back to the store to have the seller make good, the seller disclaims all knowledge of or responsibility for the defect and tells the buyer that the matter is now out of his hands, as the installment contract has been sold to a collection agency. When the poor benighted buyer goes to the collection agency, he is told that the agency knows nothing of the defect and that the agency has no legal responsibility for it. He is informed, however, that the agency as "the holder in due course" of the installment contract does own the right to collect the $31.85 a month due and owing for the next thirty-six months, and that his regular remittance will be expected.

Blacks are no longer excluded from geographical areas of the country by law, but large-acre zoning laws in the suburbs accomplish the same purpose, spreading a white noose around the inner city. Blacks are no longer formally excluded from participation in the political process, but laws which govern the political units in which nonwhites vote, through design or otherwise, often have the effect of cancelling out their vote. At-large voting systems often fall into this category. In Boston, Massachusetts, for example, the five-person School Committee is elected at large. Over the years this has resulted in the systematic cancelling out of the votes of Roxbury, the Black section of Boston. Statistically, it is as if Black residents of the city had not voted at all. Entrenched white political power has resisted all efforts to district the city to assure Blacks of effective participation in the political process. Under the current system Blacks are close to politically powerless on education issues. The Thirteenth, Fourteenth and Fifteenth Amendments were designed to make Blacks part of the polity. The mere right of an individual Black physically to place his vote in the ballot box does not accomplish that purpose. The Fifteen Amendment contemplated *effective* participation in the political process. Boston is not unique in having laws which create political units which operate to dilute or cancel out Black voting strength. The special importance of that city stems from the legal challenge to that system, based on its alleged institutionally racist effects, that has been mounted by the Boston Black community.

Further evidence of institutional subordination is found in the administrative process. Governmental officials who are entrusted with the obligation of carrying out the law often do so in a discriminatory fashion. One of the most egregious examples of this is the conduct of many policemen in minority communities. Some of the most lawless elements in our society can be found among law officials in our minority communities who daily inflict summary punishment upon minority citizens without benefit of a trial, and in other ways blatantly ignore their legal rights. The rules of the agencies themselves often reflect a societal bias. Welfare workers in the area of public assistance are permitted to assault the privacy and the dignity of recipients in ways which would never be countenanced if the public officials concerned were dealing with middle or upper class persons.

This bias is further exemplified by standards of procedural due process in administrative law. The measure of due process protection is considerably lower when what is at stake is the right to public assistance benefits, the right to a public education or of entry into public housing than it is when government is acting to substantially affect some business or commercial interest. Governmental agencies are required to follow a much more rigorous standard of fairness when they act to affect a corporate

interest than they are when they wish to cut off welfare
payments, expel a child from public school, or evict a
family from public housing. It is only very recently that a
divided U. S. Supreme Court held that a public assistance
recipient was entitled to notice and an opportunity to be
heard before welfare payments were cut off. Though nowhere in the scheme of administrative law and regulations is there a statement that there is a felt need for fewer
safeguards to protect a poor Black mother's right to feed,
clothe, house, and educate her child than there is to protect propertied interests, the institutional arrangement is
such as to make it clear that this is plainly the case.

The Kerner Commission's discussion of this society's
racism should have raised the critical question of whether
the law, or any institution in this society, can transcend
that racism. Clearly, the law has not. Rather it carries the
scars of a racist national past, while assuming present-day
postures which can only promise a racist future. The law
cannot be viewed in a vacuum, however. It must be seen
in the context of a society of inverted priorities, misallo-
cated resources, and inhumane values, run by men and
women who have drunk deeply of the heady myths of
Western superiority, and now, imbued with their own
sense of white worth, seek to impose their wills and their
visions upon weaker nations abroad, and the darker
brother and sister here at home. The law will change
when men who make the law change—or when we make
new men. Until such a time, if indeed there is still reason
to hope for such a time, those who examine the question
of racism and American law will continue to find racism
in American law.

Brown v Board of Education: The Court's Relationship to Black Liberation

*by Howard Moore, Jr.**

Racism and reform are not mutually exclusive. In the American situation, racism and reform are intertwined in an extremely complicated and important dialectical way. The 1954 decision by the United States Supreme Court in the school desegregation cases has aspects of both. *Brown v Board of Education* constituted a major revision or reform of American jurisprudence on questions of race. It also modernized the racist ideology of white supremacy. Under the guise of integration, a legal basis was created for the relaxation and adjustment of racist practices with respect to public education, transportation, parks and playgrounds, and hotels and restaurants.

In the post-World War II era, continued strict observance of the grossest forms of racism in places of general public intercourse had become inimical to America's internal security as well as its hegemony as the world's strongest imperialist power. *Brown* was a judicial attempt to deal with the apparent contradictions and conflicts between the much-touted melting-pot theory and the actuality of enforced racial separation—without disturbing the sway which the ideology of white supremacy holds over the nation's institutions.

The school desegregation cases came before the Supreme Court for the first time in the 1952 term. The Court took no definitive action on the cases at that time, but did propound questions which required further briefs and oral arguments. The cases were reargued during the 1953 term.

The records in the school desegregation cases, particularly in *Brown v Board of Education,* showed that in every measurable factor Black schools were equal to those for whites. Confronted with a record barren of any measurable inequality in school accommodations, the Supreme Court should have been constrained to go the next step. But it was not and did not. Enforced racial separation in public education could have and, in the opinion of the late Edmond Cahn, should have been declared unconstitutional for no other reason than that it was an impermissible restraint on personal liberty. But the Court did not depart from its customary jurisprudential approach whereby evidence of differential treatment or effect alone determined its decisions in cases involving the thorny problem of racial discrimination or segregation. In the prior school cases, the Court had based its decisions on evidence of the existence of measurable inequality, which in the previous cases had been tangible. It could easily be demonstrated that if Black graduate students were separated from others of their prospective profession they would be denied some important professional advantages; clearly, racism invidiously limited professional opportunities available to Blacks. However, had the Supreme Court departed from its customary approach, it could have met the problem of enforced racial separation in public education head-on.

In *Bolling v Sharpe,* the Court almost did make the

declaration Cahn suggested in its statement that racial segregation in the public schools of the District of Columbia "is not reasonably related to any proper governmental objective, and thus it imposes on Negro children . . . a burden that constitutes an arbitrary deprivation of their liberty in violation of the Due Process Clause." On the other hand, *Brown* approached the question as though it were a mixed one of law and fact. This treatment may yet result in the judicial restoration of the infamous *Plessy v Ferguson* (1896) dictum that *enforced* racial separation is a badge of inferiority "solely because the colored race chooses to put that construction upon it." If *Brown* may be read as grounded only upon a factual showing of demonstrable injury to Black children, the appointment of justices with a decided anti-Black animus could lead to the resegregation of Blacks and a national disaster in race relations—for that factual predicate is not well established.[1] Kenneth Clark's finding of damaged personalities in racially segregated Black school children has not been isolated "from the total social complexity of racial prejudice, discrimination, and segregation."[2] The inferiority attributed to Black children attending all-Black schools is as much the product of Black children's upbringing in a racist society as it is the product of separate schools.

Notwithstanding the null hypothesis that separate schools breed racial inferiority, the Supreme Court found that such separation damaged Black children. In one of the most humanistic passages in American legal literature, the Court rhapsodized, "To separate them from others of similar age and qualifications solely because of their race generates a feeling of inferiority as to their status in the community that may affect their hearts and minds in a way unlikely ever to be undone." Yet, the Court lacked the mettle to order the immediate remedy of so monstrous an injury. There was absolutely no constitutional warrant for the gradual, rather than immediate, implementation of the Fourteenth Amendment in the area of public education. It was a rank concession to white racism.

The successes in the area of public facilities and accommodations which quickly followed when *Brown* gave impetus to the relaxation of racism made it virtually impossible, if not treasonable, to find fault with that decision. But circumstances now compel a realistic assessment of *Brown*. Primary among these circumstances is the emergence of Black Power in June of 1966. Black and Blackness are no longer pejoratives. They are now sources of great pride. Not only is Black Beautiful, but it is also "So Beautiful to Be Black." Black people have radicalized their thinking about themselves and their experience. It is clear now that Black people no longer accept the assumption—if they ever did—that there is nothing of value in the Black community, and that Blacks can create nothing of value. A fundamental change has occurred in the subjective conditions upon which the struggle between Blacks and whites will continue and intensify.

The fault in *Brown* is the same as that in *Dred Scott* and *Plessy v Ferguson*. Each of these decisions assumes that whites are racially superior to Blacks. *Brown* is bottomed on the assumption that white schools are superior to Black schools, and that Black schools cannot even be *made* equal to those attended by whites. *Brown* accepts without question white domination of the institutional life of the nation. The measure of justice under *Brown*, as it was under *Plessy*, is the equal treatment of Blacks on the basis of white standards and values, not Black ones. Equality between Blacks and whites can never be achieved in this oversimplified manner, which hypothesizes a mystical racial peer group toward which all other races must be lifted. The equality to which Blacks are entitled can only be attained by dealing affirmatively with Black people on the basis of their manifest need. Blacks are different from all other races and minority groups in America. Blacks alone bear the scars and still festering sores of chattel slavery. No other group in America has ever been legally relegated to the nonhuman status of a chattel. Thus to the extent that the concept of equality found in *Brown* is based upon mere racial parity, *Brown* is but the modern analogue of "separate but equal."

Both integration and enforced racial segregation are irrelevant to Blacks. However, integration is preferable to an enforced racial separation to the same extent that prolonged illness is preferred to sudden death. The fight for integration has been necessary. It was imperative that all overt symbols and manifestations of white superiority and the imposed limitations on the individual and collective freedom of Black people be destroyed. But beyond that limited goal, the class nature of the integration movement made it an inadequate instrument for the liberation of a people whose relations to the productive forces approximate those found among colonized peoples. Integration is a way of siphoning off "qualified" Blacks into white America and exploiting their labor. It gives rise to the phenomenon of "tokenism," invariably strengthening white America as it weakens and confuses Black America.

Control is and should be the paramount concern of Black people. Only by the attainment of effective and legal control over all institutions affecting their lives can Black people become social equals, equally free to enjoy and exercise their equality. Whether under conditions of integration or segregation, it is lack of control that makes for the social inferiority of the Black experience. The implications of the struggle for control are revolutionary. Without a distinct Black-led revolution, there can be no qualitative change in the Black situation, and there can be no socially significant control by Blacks without revolution. Of course, there can and will be quantitative changes of a reformist nature, more and better jobs, houses, education, health care, etc.; but the basic fact of white domination over the nation's institutions will remain unchanged.

The emerging just demand of Black people for the limited right to control the institutions within their own communities has already provoked the Supreme Court to cut back drastically the thrust toward the elimination of vestiges of the slave system. In *City of Greenwood v Peacock* (1966), the Court refused to construe the Civil Rights Removal Statute to permit the removal of unjust and burdensome state prosecutions aimed at Black protest activities, other than those which demanded merely equal access to public accommodations. *Cameron v Johnson* (1968) authorized the withholding of injunctive relief in aid of the wholly peaceful exercise of First Amendment rights to secure equal voting rights. The decision in *Adderly v Florida* (1966) went so far as to deprive Blacks of the right to assemble peacefully on public property to protest oppressive law enforcement practices. In *Sellers v Laird* (1969) the Court refused to hear the claim that Blacks were systematically excluded from local Selective Service boards and are thus inducted in disproportionate numbers. In *Abney v Evans* (1970), the Court held that a public park reverted to the heirs of the original grantor, discontinuing its use, solely in order to prevent Blacks from using it in opposition to the provisions of the grantor's will requiring segregation. Indeed, the Court has in a few recent cases demonstrated an expansive attitude with respect to racial segregation in housing, and marked impatience with continued racial segregation in the public schools. But the difference between the cases which may be considered setbacks and those considered to be advances is critical to an understanding of the direction that future Supreme Court decisions will take. When a ruling for integration will result in dispersal of the ghetto and weakening of nationalistic feelings among Blacks, the Supreme Court, by a slim majority for the next few years, may continue to vote in favor. However, if the Court can rule in such a way as to undermine white racism by freeing Blacks from subtle forms of white domination, it will, over an occasional dissent, give unfavorable decisions.

This means that the Court will become irrelevant to the Black liberation struggle, except for its negative effects. Blacks cannot and will not wait on the appointment of liberal justices nor for another period of judicially led reform. *Brown* has made it clear that, even if the Court wanted to, it could not free Blacks from their oppression. Blacks now know that only through self-reliance and solidarity in the continuing struggle can they attain freedom, justice, and equality.

Blacks do not want it this way, but their situation leaves

them no realistic alternative. They would certainly prefer the unique historical event of liberation through the creative uses of the orderly processes of an established judicial system. But the mere preference for a less arduous form of struggle does not make it effective. The force and forces of history are dictatorial. People are pushed along an inescapable and invariably cruel path, the end of which is only a new beginning. Yet, regardless of the terror ahead, Blacks, if they are ever to liberate themselves, must face that terror and overcome it once and for all.

America is not a melting pot and never has been. The relationship between people of different cultures and races is more correctly analogous to muffin pans. Each group is a separate pan on a vertical shelf in the oven. Common to all the separate muffins is the oven or crucible in which they are baked—white settler domination of the North American continent. The higher and lower oven racks reflect the class and racist nature of capitalism. Blacks are worse situated in the oven than others. They suffer from too much heat or too little heat. To put a people to the task of proving the reality of their situation is to impose upon them an impossible task. Yet in all cases, Blacks must prove that they are truly the victims of white racism if they want the Court's judgment.

To come to grips with the problems of race and law, the courts must presume that every act is a racist one, just as the judicial system has presumed in its laws that whites are the superior race. It can no longer be denied that everyone's thinking is infected by a virulent racism. It is impossible to deal on a color-blind basis. Color is the most prominent aspect of American life. Whites seek color; they trek the globe to tan themselves. Whites have long known that Black is beautiful, but they have never admitted their preference for Black. This awful ambivalence about race and color infects the jurisprudence and must be recognized. The limited progress Blacks have made after generations of litigation is intermixed with the capitalist nature of the economic system and the psychology of color and race. The psychology of racism has blinded even conscientious and wise men to the cruelty which they as judges continue to impose upon Blacks and the utter, indescribable horror of the Black situation.

The influence of the schizophrenic striving toward color-blindness can be readily seen in the laws pertaining to discrimination in the composition of juries. In 1935, in one of the Scottsboro Boys cases, the Court set forth prima facie case doctrine of jury discrimination. The rule which gave effect to the doctrine was founded upon evidence of the long and unexplained total exclusion of Blacks from jury service in Alabama. The rule, however, was no Magna Charta for Black liberation; it was little more than a rule of evidence. In operation, a situation was created in which a Black litigant could secure reversal of a conviction or a new trial by submitting evidence of the long, unexplained exclusion of Blacks from lists for jury service. Since 1935, the rule has been progressively expanded to require the reversal of conviction where evidence was presented that even though Blacks had been included on a master jury list there remained a substantial disparity between the number of Blacks in the jurisdiction eligible for jury service and those actually included. The application of this rule, however, does not require Blacks actually to serve on the juries. Indeed, the right of Blacks actually to serve on and be tried by juries of their peers was totally frustrated by *Swain v Alabama* (1965), in which the Supreme Court implicitly sanctioned the use of peremptory strikes to eliminate Black jurors. A state may still, today, legally lynch Blacks by trying them before an all-white jury if the state can show there is not too great a disparity between the number of Blacks included on a master jury list and those eligible. The short of the matter is that all a state needs to do is to show that it is color-blind with respect to summoning persons for jury service. If Blacks do not actually serve, it does not legally matter. Form is exalted over substance. The twin myths of equality and non-discrimination are perpetuated. Antagonism between promise and performance is intensified.

The needs of Blacks are fundamentally incompatible

with the central role and function of the judicial system and with that of the Court as the expositor of the meaning of the Constitution. The Court is duty-bound to protect and defend the Constitution. The Court functions within a prescription, the limits of which have been fashioned by the past. The Court must, necessarily, demonstrate a tolerance, a sensitivity, for the essential interest and well-being of the oppressors. Of course, the Court does not consciously recognize the interest of litigants before it as being those peculiar to the oppressor or the oppressed. Usually, such interests are defined and set forth as those of property and business, of the state, of dissenters, of the poor, or racial minorities. The inherent necessity to adjust disputes by demonstrating a tolerance or sensitivity for the vital interests of competing forces means that Black interests must often be rejected outright unless they can be accommodated within the prescription. The Court cannot wipe the slate clean before it speaks. Vested interests are necessarily perpetuated. However, the liberation of Black people cannot occur unless the slate *is* wiped clean and society starts afresh. The conflict between rational judicial resolution of controversies and the continued subjugation of Blacks will propel Blacks to condemn the Court and the system which it serves.

The historically dictated attitude of Black people toward the Court and the judicial system should not be understood to mean that Blacks can ignore either the Court or the judicial system. It is only in the very broadest sense of the struggle that the Court or the judicial system may be considered irrelevant. The truth is that the judicial system surely will deal with Blacks whether they want it to deal with them or not. Courts are duty-bound to preserve order and to protect property. They are established mainly for that purpose. This means that the Court must, of necessity, pass judgment upon Blacks; it has no realistic alternative.

Blacks, too, are left little choice but to prepare themselves to deal effectively with the judicial system, recognizing the essential inadequacy of that system as a vehicle for liberation. Blacks must understand the consequences of the simple fact that there is no such thing as a legal revolution. All revolutions are illegal. The very nature of revolution is transcendental; that is, it transcends the strictures of the present judicial system. Its participants risk all to gain all. No court in any country at any time has sanctioned, or ever will sanction, revolution. Revolutionaries and a revolutionary people will be dealt with firmly and summarily.

Blacks are thoroughly justified in placing the power to control their future and their liberation in their own hands rather than the Court or the judicial system. When Blacks look closely at American jurisprudence on questions of race, they find that little progress, if any, has been made after generations of litigation. Their rights nearly always turn on mixed questions of law and fact. There is absolutely no justification for placing the right of Blacks to justice and equality on the resolution of a question of fact. To do so is to indulge in the fiction that America is a nonracist society and that white Americans are capable of functioning in a nonracist manner.

Overwhelming historical forces compel the Court to adhere to rules which do little more than exalt form over substance. The only relevant approach is to demystify the law by making a complete break with the jurisprudence of the past. The break will be traumatic. It heralds woe for people and courts. But when all is said and done, and the legal system stripped of its mystique, it will be exposed as an instrument for the oppression of Black people. When that occurs, the past will no longer rule the present. There will be a new and wondrous beginning. Right on, Kojo!

Notes

1. Kenneth B. Clark, *Prejudice and Your Child*. Boston: Beacon Press, 1963, Appendixes 4 and 5.
2. Ibid., p. 193.

The Economic Basis of Law and State

*by Kenneth Cloke**

"One law for the Lion and Ox is Oppression"
WILLIAM BLAKE, The Marriage of Heaven and
Hell.

A revolution is beginning in law. Lawyers and law students have begun to organize against and protest the systematic oppression of people perpetuated, in part, by the
conscious design of those who control the means of law
(intimidation) and order (coercion) within American society and around the world. A growing understanding that
we must recognize and move against a single common
enemy whose countenance appears in Southeast Asia,
Japan, Bolivia, South Africa, Spain, Harlem, the barrios
and ghettos, and every part of the United States has
placed legal repression in an international context. Lawyers and clients have been brought closer together. The
new bond between attorneys and clients is partly due to
the lawyers' understanding of themselves as potential clients. They identify with that which they advocate in their
clients' behalf and advance it as truth; they will no longer
allow their mouths, vocabularies, and other legal tools to
be purchased at the highest price. They must avoid any

understanding of their roles and occupations which would
lead them *on their own* to rush up the courthouse steps,
petition in hand, requesting redress of grievances, while
their clients are trying to tear it apart from the rear. The
lawyers' bonds to their clients also come from a growing
realization that what is wrong with this country is so
fundamental that a change here and there in legislation cannot rectify it. Once lawyers see themselves as
"attorney-clients," once they recognize that the nature of
the problem is systemic and that the system in question
has a definite historical origin, they will understand their
own necessity and perceive, in the process, the manner of
the "system's" dissolution and replacement. Our political
history has been one of progressively decreasing alternatives. Lawyers are increasingly being forced by rapidly
changing social circumstances into becoming either potential clients or potential jailors.

The initial problem for lawyers is one of consciousness.
Lawyers have begun to recognize that part of their legitimacy flows from their objective role, regardless of their
intentions, as hypocritical apologists and propagandizers
of hope where no hope exists, or as technicians simply
making certain that the illusion of fairness is procedurally
undamaged. In merely bringing a lawsuit, an attorney
may delude the politically immature, uncounselled client
into believing he has a legal—i.e., a legally enforceable—
right of redress, even where no court would grant the relief requested for political reasons. At the same time, we
also understand that there is some political and practical
utility in bringing or defending lawsuits. In order to understand this utility, we must return to a study in depth of the
whole and the sum of its parts, of law and its actual
effects on behalf of and in detriment to systematic social
change.

The degree to which one sees fundamental social
change occurring through law depends upon the degree of
social change one believes necessary. If one's analysis is
that the fundamental problem is racism, then a certain
political viewpoint follows, which is reflected in legal atti-

tudes. If one's belief is that racism is inextricable from monopoly capitalism and imperialism, radically different legal attitudes result. What is possible from one point of view is impossible from the other; a fundamental strategic concern to one is only momentary and tactical to the other. The differences between legal theories or approaches lie not in statutes or cases, but in different attitudes toward what the state represents, how it originated, and what is required to change it. It is therefore critical to legal competence that there be political theory which accurately describes the economic basis of law. This analysis adopts the perspective which begins by defining state and law as the organized force of a social class. The law is a mechanism for governing which arises out of social contradiction in order to preserve the interests of one class in opposition to the interests of others.

When society gives rise to social classes as a result of the creation of an economic surplus, which becomes privately appropriated and therefore distributed unequally, one class protects its rights of appropriation by subjecting others to its will. This class then creates, out of a need to fix and legitimate its relationships with all other classes, a state, and with it, law. State and law thus reflect the accumulation of property as private property in the hands of the few and the demise of property as social property in the hands of the many. The law of theft dates from the emergence, on a large scale, of private, movable property and from its unequal distribution, i.e., scarcity. The law, "Thou shalt not steal," therefore is an expression of the existence of poverty and a social need to steal.

Both state and law exist as functions of the degree of contradiction between two progressively polarized social classes: those who increasingly own the instruments of production in society, and those who are forced to work at them. The mere existence of a unified system of law for two social classes which are increasingly in fundamental opposition to one another is itself oppressive. The purpose of such a system of law can only be the "regularization" of conflict between the two to insure that differences are always resolved in favor of the dominant party. Law, therefore, is an expression of the existence of fundamental inequality and exists wherever and to the extent that inequality exists. The composition of the ruling class and the methods used to uphold the interests of one class over another have changed significantly since the beginning of slavery, but their fundamental opposition has remained a fact to our day. Changes brought about in the method of exploitation have followed technological evolution as it continually altered the nature of wealth, and produced a need for new forms of social organization. The form of rule has seen numerous alterations, but it remains rule as long as human beings are divided into social classes. "Law and order" has been pitted against justice for centuries. It will serve justice when it becomes the source of its destruction, by serving the exploited and oppressed in establishing the legal order.

Law, which is of, by and for the state, is determined in general by the specific form of class contradictions in a given society, and is simply a set of rules governing social relationships and determining how conflicts are to be resolved according to the interests of the dominant class, and given effect by the organized force and violence of that class. Law is not justice, a norm, neutral principles, nor ideal social harmony. It is not truth, due process, fairness, or any other idealization. Its guiding principles are the guiding principles of those who maintain their power partly through its auspices.

Most lawyers know that not all law is statute law, rules passed by legislative bodies, but will identify case law (judicial decisions) and English common law as the two major exceptions to rule by statute. Informal law, however, constitutes a large body of principles which is binding on conduct, yet is only seen in operation and therefore only understood when it contradicts written law, and, more practically, when it can afford to use the legal process to expose the contradiction. The common practice of the cop on the beat and the social worker in the field is understood by others to bind their conduct, and is therefore law. Informal law and its enforcement agencies, establishing different rules to govern the conduct of different classes, thereby further social conflict and duress. The law is required to be color-blind, but the cop in Watts or Harlem, the social worker, and probation officer and their supervisors are not. To be color-blind in a racist environment is simply to ignore the problem.

Law, or rule-making, presupposes conflict and attempts its regulation. It does so by establishing external means of coercion through formal and informal rules which encourage internal control. In this fashion, fault or wrongdoing is always laid to the individual, who is supposed to know the law, the reasons for its existence, and understand the difference between right and wrong. The probation and parole officer, the social worker, and other institutional officials—often including the lawyer—direct the offender to examine himself, and thereby obfuscate the origin of crime, or legal wrong.

Through the individual incident or transaction, law makes individuals the basic unit of any case. Class actions exist in civil law, but numerous and growing restrictions frustrate attempts to reach basic issues. The persons who are normally engaged in legal controversy are separated out from the mass of people by the legal process and made to look special; and each case is made to appear different from others. Legal games of distinguishing precedent and restricting the applicability of rules, except where general principles may help a judge justify a decision he has already reached, do the same; social struggles and political movements are splintered into their individual components and prevented from making any stronger or more collective statements than might be made by any of the individuals involved. Yet often, the only way a judge or jury might understand motivations behind a particular act is through its collective statement. The approach to cases involving ghetto insurrections or political movements must be contrasted with the approach to cases concerned with corporate mergers and institutions: the different time given to proceedings, papers allowed to be filed, fairness in consideration of competing claims, admissibility of "motive" in evidence, and attitude toward clients and counsel are remarkable. An examination of the Supreme Court cases as recorded in *Law Week* or the legislative record, and titles of bills passed in any year by Congress, reveals an overwhelming proportion having to do with business, monetary policy, and assistance to industry, and very few concerning "white collar crime" or social legislation.

The individual is most separated from the collective conditions of his act in the field of criminal law. Yet as Marx states in *German Ideology*, "Crime, i.e., the struggle of the single individual against the dominant conditions, is as little the product of simple caprice as the law itself. It is rather conditioned in the same way as the latter. The same 'visionaries' who see in law the rule of an independent and general will, see in crime a simple breaking of the law." The legal process isolates crime from its social roots, although it may pay attention to the mother or father who drinks, or their individual lack of money. But it considers irrelevant the fact that our social system creates crime through its daily operation, sanctions the robbery of consumers by commodity producers and of laborers by employers, but not the reverse, thereby legitimizing and reproducing inequality.

A social analysis of law must proceed from an understanding of the value of legal proceedings to the parties and to society. Law begins with an occurrence, an historical event in relationships between parties which are, for the most part, historically determined: buyer and seller, landlord and tenant, debtor and creditor, etc. Legal transactions determine either the substantive rights of the conflicting parties, whose social relationships are accepted as given, or the procedural remedies available to the parties. The beginning point in either case is jurisdiction, wherein the process of legal adjudication is anarchic and almost totally immune from real planning or foresight, since it accepts all the social givens and insists upon an acceptable "case or controversy" before it acts. Thus, the major purpose of jurisdictional questions is the maintenance of established order. Both jurisdictional requirements and procedural problems which reach jurisdiction must be seen as reflecting the social need to adjudicate acceptable controversies, and to restrict the legal adjudication of problems which question the basic inequality by holding that there can be no action until a legally recognized injury has occurred.

Thus, the courts often refuse the enforcement of a right because it will "open the floodgates of litigation," or a "Pandora's Box" of questions the courts do not wish to face; or they may refuse to accept a case because it is not "ripe" for adjudication. Here, again, the procedural restriction further reduces legal rights for reasons the courts do not state. The result is that law merely follows social evolution, becomes purely defensive, and is only capable of acting when society has changed to the degree that previously unacceptable controversies are capable of moderate solution. Jurisdictional law thus demonstrates clearly that law follows social practice and merely redefines what has already occurred. Courts reach such decisions as are socially necessary to validate expectations as to how people will behave in given relationships, and ignore any social facts which contradict their expectations.

Idealism—or the definition of material reality solely in terms of model ideas, concepts, and prepackaged "reason," the belief that material reality is only ideas—can be comprehended in every legal transaction. Law begins with real acts by real individuals, characterizes them in legal terms and then concludes that they are either legal and valid or subject to penalty. The legal conclusion is affected by the ways in which similar acts recorded in past transactions have been interpreted. Law thus applies dead standards to living acts, and interprets what is by what has been. The legal process, when it interprets individual transactions, does not permit that change may occur in real relationships, except where other factors have intervened, such as legislation, political struggle, or crisis, or when a different reality becomes so manifest that the existing legal rule is clearly antiquated. Even in the latter case, reality remains unrecognized to the extent that it contradicts the foundations of the existing order.

While idealism determines the form of law, material interests, specifically the interests of private property, determine its content. The basis of all law is the real, tangible interest in rights of ownership of property, which characterizes modern social relationships in practice. Most law has to do with competing claims to wealth. Socialist law claims all wealth as public wealth and exists for the purpose of transforming large holdings of capitalists' private property into public property of the working class, and therefore continues to be law. Only when all forms of ownership of property have deteriorated will law no longer fix rights of ownership. As it accomplishes this, it ceases to be law. Most statutes, decisions, administrative proceedings, and legal actions revolve around individual claims to property, or the efficiency of the state machinery which regulates and guarantees property expectations. The major areas of law, such as contracts, property law, wills, trusts, corporations, secured transactions, torts, administrative law, and even enormous proportions of criminal law protect existing property. Most international law relates to trade and economic interests. Even "poverty law" primarily involves conflicting claims to money, including issues of garnishment, nonpayment of rent, welfare, attachments, etc. In the interest of stability, and as a result of years of militant political action, the poor were guaranteed due process of law, but the substantive rights of parties in legal transactions always reflect the inequality basic to their property relationships.

The law assists in the dispropriation of the poor, not only in its decisions, but through the cost of court action to achieve redress. A worker has a legal right only to the wages he has contracted for with the employer; he has no right to the real value he produces for the employer over and above his wages. He has no right even to the wage he gets except by fighting for it. Poor people have no legal right to food or housing or employment. Black and Brown

people and Indians have no right to determine their own
lives according to their own needs, to the land which was
stolen from them, or to treatment as human beings. The
poorer countries have no legal recourse when the United
States interferes in their affairs, expropriating their
wealth and murdering their people. There is no legal right
to do any more than protest one's slavery, and that, only if
a permit has been received and the protest is not violent,
does not block traffic, and does not present a clear and
present danger of the overthrow of slavery.

The history of law in the United States is the history of
its property relations. The courts have consistently ruled
that property is not defined by the labor which produced
it, but by who possesses it. It is valued not by its utility,
but by what it is worth in exchange. It was in the heyday
of industrial expansion that the United States Supreme
Court, in the *Slaughterhouse Cases* (1872), defined property as "everything which has exchangeable value," and
added, "The right of property includes the power to dispose of it according to the will of the owner." The sway of
property permeates all branches of law. As it is doctrine
that "equity intervenes only to protect property rights," injunctions will be issued to protect property more readily
than to restrict it. The history of the labor injunction emphasizes the social values which are built into law and
which, through law, achieve new life. Even the poor litigant must raise a money bond for the issuance of an
injunction, for claim and delivery actions to repossess personal property, and in some cases, in wage garnishment
and attachment. Labor and debt collection laws give the
appearance of fairness and justice while masking the substantive inequality which is endemic to the entire wage-
labor system. Welfare law in many cases prohibits savings
and reproduces and institutionalizes poverty. A court will
issue an injunction against union picketing because of a
rumored threat of violence on a picket line, but no court
will enjoin a company from daily subjecting its employees
to violence as a result of poor or unsafe working conditions on the assembly line. An injunction will not be

issued on behalf of a worker as a result of a breach of contract by the employer because, on the one hand, the legal remedy is otherwise held to be adequate, or, on the other hand, because employment contracts supposedly lack mutuality, and are therefore unenforceable except by a suit for moneys due for services performed. It has often been pointed out that business libels against an employer on posters or picket signs may be enjoined, while group or racial libels may not. Moreover, the cost of bringing suit and the restrictions on attorneys serving poor clients constitute *de facto* restrictions on the ability of the poor to fight back.

The procedural justification for ignoring some realities and incorporating others is also found in the difference between equity and law, two historically different procedural frameworks for decision-making. In the language of Black's *Law Dictionary*, equity is "the spirit and habit of fairness, justness, and right;" thus, the famous maxims: "equity delights to do justice, and that not by halves," or "equity suffers not a right without a remedy," or "equity looks upon that as done which ought to have been done." Historically, equity was a transitional form for the introduction of new legal rules when antiquated feudal law began to paralyze the functioning of the new commercial intercourse. The existence of equity, or informal law, is in part a recognition of the inability of the legal system to regulate conflict through its rulings alone. It is an implicit recognition that existing law has become outmoded and, to a certain extent, useless, that it is bound up in contradictions.

As feudal law was inadequate to regulate the growth of industrial commerce, today the legal precepts of the eighteenth and nineteenth centuries, which form the bulk of modern law, cannot apply to new social relationships. Recently, in outdated civil rights litigation in the South, equity allowed the creation of new legal forms, such as federal removal, petitions to transfer state cases to federal courts, three-judge federal courts, and the *Dombrowski v Pfister* injunctions against state court criminal proceedings which "chill" the exercise of First Amendment freedoms. However, when Black Power and Black liberation became the major demand, especially when the demand challenged the basic postulates of the social system, equity and law, which previously developed in opposition to one authority, are united in their inability to substantially modify the rights and relationships fundamental to both systems, such as the right to raise an army and relationships such as those of employer and employee, and rich and poor. Neither equity nor law can solve these problems now, although equity was useful in earlier periods and contributed handsomely to the evolution of the civil rights movement in the direction of Black Power. The difference is that the substitution of capitalist for feudal law merely recognized the substitution of one form of wealth for another, whereas socialism seeks to abolish all private wealth. This, equity will not do, even by halves.

The historical dialectic of equity and law can also be seen as that between discretion and precedent. In certain areas, the "sound discretion of the court" is unchallengeable, whereas in others, the slightest deviation from accepted formulas is cause for a reversal on appeal. The difference may be only one of a few years in time, since court decisions are only reflections of larger social problems, as was true in criminal procedure or civil rights law. However, precedent has the effect, in all areas of law, of ratifying existing inequalities in relationships and making challenges to their underpinnings unthinkable. As Jonathan Swift, in *Gulliver's Travels,* comments,

> It is a maxim among lawyers, that whatever hath been done before may legally be done again; and therefore they take special care to record all the decisions formerly made against common justice and the general reason of mankind. There, under the name of precedents, they produce as authorities, to justify the most iniquitous opinions; and the judges never fail of directing accordingly.*

* Jonathan Swift, *Gulliver's Travels.* New York: Washington Square Press, 1960 (1726), p. 248.

While it is true that modern law results in part from changes brought about through legislation and judicial opinion, which in turn follow changes in real conditions brought about by considerable social conflict, after a point the law becomes apprehensive of its own abolition and refuses certain change. Debt and private property cannot, under the present order, be abolished by law, although either may change hands in an individual case. Theft cannot be legalized within the existing economic system (except for corporate theft), although an individual thief may not be punished. Through individual reforms the law maintains the fiction of its adaptability. Yet the fundamental inequality which is the basis and reason for existence of all law remains untouched.

The law contradicts its self-proclaimed adaptability by also pretending to immutability: Law therefore modestly suggests that it is all-changing, yet always constant; it is both all-knowing and all-seeing, old and new combined. History is circular, it maintains, things are always as bad and as good as they ever were, except in a few cases where they may be slightly better as a result of some well-reasoned judicial decision. Law has always existed and always will; inequality has always been with us and will always remain. The rule of precedent makes legal decisions appear to be the dominant force in social history and human, economic and productive relations appear to follow. In reality, the opposite is true, while the practical effect of this fiction is to squeeze reform inside the boundaries of law, where it can be more closely regulated. The legal institution betrays its claim to be the source of progress when it insists that since all conduct is regulated by legal means, all conduct has always and will forever remain regulated by law.

Through these contradictions, the myth has been fashioned that the civil rights movement began with *Brown v Board of Education*. Ignoring for the moment what motivated the Browns and others in several states to bring this action in the first place, the sheer audacity of such a statement is beyond belief. Indeed, the civil rights movement framed its original claim as one for legal redress; indeed, it took courage with the *Brown* decision; but to give nine white Supreme Court judges the credit for exposing to Black people the nature of racial discrimination is to ignore an entire people's history, as well as developments occurring simultaneously on a mass scale which made these judges rule differently from the not-too-dissimilar judges sitting in *Plessy v Ferguson* (which established the "separate but equal" doctrine permitting segregation). What the jurists of theory and the politicians of practice worried over was a question of legal precedents, reinforcing the myth that law is based on the will, not of masses of people, but of individual judges. Because it constantly refuses to examine anything but accomplished facts, legal theory becomes synonymous with existing law, and what exists is merely a culmination of what has previously existed. The will does not derive from reality, but from previously defined categories and relationships which are circular, and may therefore simply be plugged in to achieve the desired result.

An oft-repeated aphorism is that we have a "government of laws not of men." Disregarding for the moment the fact that men make laws—which, claims to divine guidance notwithstanding, reflect their own biases—what kind of society is it that claims people exist for law rather than law for people? The servant has become the master, and the creator the slave. As commodities in capitalist society begin to be produced primarily for exchange, so law ceases to be subject to human regulation and instead subjects them to regulation. Along with this transformation of law goes the abstraction of legal ideals from reality and their becoming less real the more they become ideal. The Bill of Rights, appended to a conservative Constitution as a result of a political struggle, guaranteeing the right to freedom of speech and to keep and bear arms, has become the means by which speech is silenced and people deprived of the right to revolt. Increasingly, the reality of law contradicts its ideal; increasingly they are polarized.

Contradictions in society between what is possible, or

ideal, and eventually what is necessary, or real, makes all legal ideals suspect, producing thereby a basis for making reality ideal, and the ideal part of reality. However, neither the ideal (*de jure*) nor the real (*de facto*) law is neutral, as it claims to be, but is largely directed by the crises of the society in which it operates. Contradiction in society affects not only its basic economic tendencies, but gives rise to a halting effect throughout, undermining and making clear the inability of any part to function unless the whole is reorganized. When the social institutions of feudalism began to take on a dual character, part feudal, part capitalist, the law reflected these contradictory patterns, and legal institutions became a place where competing class forces appealed to establish their respective powers. In a period of social revolution, law, along with other social institutions, mimics the fundamental changes taking place in the mode of production and exchange. All these institutions, however, are prone to lag behind changes in the mode of production and distribution, and evolve more unevenly, thereby necessarily coming into contradiction with the changing forces of production. Moreover, because these institutions only imperfectly mirror productive relationships, and are more subject to human will, they must also come into contradiction with themselves.

The emergence of new institutions out of antedated and excrescent social forms is part of every revolutionary process. Law in the present period increasingly demonstrates a dual character similar to that in the transition from feudalism. It is affected by the necessity for a new form of social relations as a result of what has become possible due to the changes in the mode of production and exchange, but which is made impossible because of their private ownership. Law under capitalism, as feudal law, has been unable to plan or direct its development; it has had to be elastic, but firmly resists change in the most basic aspects of property relationships. The requirements of expediency and order thereby come more and more into opposition with those of law. The lawyer increasingly looks like a client. The abolition of poverty, which ought to be easy for the United States, becomes more and more difficult. Public policy has two faces, as does jurisprudence, as does legal practice, as does the supposed universality of due process, corresponding more and more to the two major classes of modern society.

Legal institutions, however, are so constituted as to predetermine the legal part of the battle. Law affirms both war and the principles of the Nuremberg judgments; the law of leaseholds includes the right of the landlord to usurp the tenant's rent and the right of the tenant to withhold it under certain circumstances. These apparent contradictions are not really in the interest of the tenant or the war-protestor, but in a particular class interest in maintaining order. By withholding rent, the tenant forces the slum landlord to renovate, which partially eases tensions, raising the value of the property and thereby the rents charged not only in slums but in more habitable housing as well, benefiting primarily the larger, wealthier landlords. At the same time, to the chagrin of landlords everywhere, the new legal right may lead the tenant to demand the right to adequate housing for all, a right which the law cannot grant as long as land is privately owned and developed, social planning is nonexistent, and millions are too poor to afford privately owned land. The law is both hangman and priest, judge and prosecutor, and protector only of the rich, while it pretends to protect all class interests. Thus, law conspires against order and law and order together conspire against real social change. When this becomes known law brings about its own dissolution by its normal activity.

The dialectic of law and order, of violence and passivity, liberalism and fascism, coercion and cooptation, is the most distinctive characteristic of the legal order of modern monopoly capitalism. Yet it is precisely this schizophrenic nature which makes the continued existence of this social order impossible and contributes to its ultimate defeat. As one side calls increasingly for order and the other for justice, it becomes evident that order entails a different kind of justice, and justice a different kind of order.

Since law is produced by conflict arising out of contradictory social relationships, law will continue to exist as long as social classes exist. In a period following social revolution, law may become useful and socially creative when used by the working class state in destroying all class privileges and immunities including its own. Law can assist a general campaign against racism, national chauvinism, the oppression of women, thus becoming a weapon against itself, and the things it always promoted. When the modern socialist state, also a reflection of the existence of social classes, ceases to exist as such in a period of international reconstruction, law becomes chiefly administrative law, which is more susceptible to decentralization. It then must return to a form of rule by custom. But until the underpinnings of conflict are eliminated, that is, exploitative and oppressive conditions which daily regenerate a *de facto* need for state power, there can be no elimination of law nor can there be any real equality before law. Once there is *real* equality, there is no need for law.

The Whorehouse Theory of Law

*by Florynce Kennedy**

Ours is a prostitute society.† The system of justice, and most especially the legal profession, is a whorehouse serving those best able to afford the luxuries of justice offered to preferred customers. The lawyer, in these terms, is analogous to a prostitute. The difference between the two is simple. The prostitute is honest—the buck is her aim. The lawyer is dishonest—he claims that justice, service to mankind, is his primary purpose. The lawyer's deception

† Two important aspects of my experience have been the practice of law and participation in the Women's Liberation Movement. Sometimes an amalgamation of the two constitutes important insights. "Prostitution" might seem peculiar to feminism. One of my major political attempts has been to demonstrate the political nature of group variants. Thus, I use here the concept of prostitution in this extended, this political sense.

All oppressed people, who do not die quickly, collaborate in some way with their oppressor. Wives, for example, stand *behind* the husbands, are the powers *behind* the thrones. Prostitutes, on the contrary, are defined by those who stand *in front of:* A prostitute is an out-front collaborator. I see lawyers similarly: as out-front collaborators; they shield the oppressor.

I leave aside for the moment whether in a just society a legal profession would be necessary. This profession has always been of an essentially apologetic nature: an apology and concealment for injustices perpetrated by those in power. However, prostitutes, because they are exposed to society as oil that greases the wheel—the alternative to rape—have a special choice forced upon them.

of the people springs from his actual money-making role; he represents the client who puts the highest fee on the table.

Assuming that a concern for humanity is consistent with the person who avoids corruption, that is, the person who goes "straight," the lawyer is still a prostitute. As a law student, he is taught not only to park his humanity, but to think only in terms of money, power, and the "law." It follows that many lawyers wish to be in the pay of the business and government "houses." That is their highest aim—to be in a house where the richest johns come.

These are the clients who demand and get the best services the prostitute can offer. They are also the most racist, the most genocidal, and the worst polluters of the environment. The more delinquent the business or government client, the greater the employment opportunity for lawyers. Some of the two-bit-whore lawyers have spent lives of great disappointment because they have not been recruited and raised to "call girl" status in the major Wall Street firms or the MICE—Military-Industrial-Complex-Establishmentarians.

I think that where oppressed people are involved, it is customarily the guilt of the oppressor that is projected into a microcosmic corner, as it were, and made to apply only to the victims. The narcotics addict and the person immediately above him, the pusher, and other examples of society's projection of guilt and anger, while the Turkish farmer who grows the opium and the international racketeers who distribute the product are the greatest beneficiaries of the laws, protected by the whores in the Bureau of Narcotics, customs courts, and other government agencies. This contradiction is quite consistent at all levels of our society. The victim of society's attack is always the victimized!

Of course it is true that other professionals and most businessmen, and perhaps especially those in the medical profession, could fit the whorehouse characterization. Our history and literature are sprinkled liberally with "professionals" who have gone "straight" and revealed the numerous ways that they have sold themselves and their professional services for the almighty dollar. But the legal profession outdoes the other fields. For it is through the principles of law that men and women lose their liberties, and thus their lives.

The question arises, in discussing the generic sense of the whorehouse as representative of the whole legal system, whether all lawyers are the same. This is like asking whether everything that gets into a sewer is garbage. Because the shit is in the sewer means that it is garbage, of course, although distinctions can be made between better quality or lesser quality garbage.

The Wall Street lawyer, for example, services and represents, in my opinion anyway, the most delinquent johns in our society, whereas the average lawyer for hire just uses the law as a hustle. The typical lawyer represents either side: for example, the wife or husband in a matrimonial case. It is the *gelt* not the guilt that determines whether the client is acceptable in most cases. In that sense, the law is a hustle. Since this particular kind of lawyer does not represent the largest or most delinquent business people, a "hustle lawyer" is naturally less a menace because his hustle is to protect less powerful and less influential people. He is less infectious to the general community, less a shield for the carriers of the white plague of racism, war, poverty, and imperialism. And less often is there an Establishmentarian interest in his clientele. If a man and wife appear before a judge—the madam, if you wish—the dispute is not one which directly damages the whole society, except to the degree that the institution of marriage is institutionalized slavery.

People ask me whether, as a lawyer, I am not, in my own terms, a whore (especially since I'm a woman). The answer is, "of course." I have described my practice as a hustle ever since I discovered that the practice of law had much more to do with money-making than justice. I try to tell it like it is. But whether the hustler in a small, private practice tells it straight or not, this lawyer tends to be a less virulent prostitute than a major law firm that services the MICE.

The MICE are the clients that decimate the society and

threaten the world. The MICE are the genocidal developers of biological and chemical warfare, the makers of the planes which siphon off the money from the hospitals and schools and divert it into the building of airplanes to be deposited in the rice paddies of Vietnam, Cambodia, and Laos.

The MICE, of course, also include people who do not actually contribute to the war arsenal. They are the makers of tomato paste, dog food, bird chow, and the shit-on-a-shingle that the GIs eat in the rice paddies, and which ghetto Blacks buy overpriced. The MICE are the national advertisers who conspire with the Madison Avenue fifteen percenters to repackage a box of crackers so the people can't get into it without a crowbar. The MICE observe with approval and/or subsidize the "soul" stations' radio format, whose white owners beam sugar-coated bullshit to the Black community on the theory that "that's what *they* want."

Since the MICE are in alliance with the most delinquent business people, they must have a confederacy with lawyers. The whole legal-government-business community is analogous to a National Association of Whorehouses (NAW). The legal whores in NAW include the legal departments of the television and telephone companies, whose committees are humping it with the state and federal regulatory agencies such as the F.C.C. (Federal Communications Commission), the state public utilities commissions, and members of Congress who are former customers or inmates of the NAW "house." The regulatory agents are also former inmates in, clients of, or presently housed in a NAW "Affiliate House" (AH!). They tend to be bought-off political hogs in retirement from various NAW installations throughout the country, such as members of the supine New York Public Services Commission, who in the late sixties and early seventies were entertaining pleas of "Don't whip us" from the public utilities community, such as the New York Telephone Company and Consolidated Edison, when those companies projected multimillion-dollar rate rises.

Whereas the wealthy legal whores of NAW and AH spread their disease to millions of people, screwing them on a daily basis, the prosecutors and district attorneys, bodyguards for the MICE, are poorly paid, highly infectious two-bit whores. They prosecute people who are usually the victims of the pathological system of oppression. Their sadistic role is to cage and isolate their victims for cruel and inhuman punishment. Although not members of NAW, they are still held in high esteem, mostly for their screwing ability and high batting averages. They usually have a good chance to become criminal court judges or madams.

Every whorehouse has its madam. In a law firm the madam might be the senior partner. In state government, the attorney general usually plays that role. In a corporation, the chief "house counsel" assumes the position, obviously. But the superintendent of the entire national red light district, the superlawyer of them all, hence the superwhore, clearly has to be the United States Attorney General. Why? Because he is the apologist for the MICE *in toto*. He is the protagonist for the death-dealing Pentagon. He is chief counsel for the slickest of all the dicks, and the thumb-sucking FBI. He is supermadam, supersuperintendent of the National Association of Government houses (NAG).

It is he who decides that certain select "outside agitators" who want to close down the whorehouse will get hassled, rolled, bounced, or smashed. He assigns the lesser madams to NAG houses of "justice" where the rolled victims, the war protestors, draft resisters, hippies, Blacks, or Yippies try to fight back as best they can against overwhelming odds. This particular supermadam infects the country like an epidemic within the judicial whorehouse.

A whorehouse is where one finds it: the smell of injustice is unmistakable. Injustice floats in the air like incense in a bawdy house, or like Chanel No. 5 in a "respectable" house. When a lawyer and tenant-client visit a cheap whorehouse like the local landlord-tenant courthouse where the practice of high-paying landlord favoritism and corrupt tenant sellouts is the daily routine, the heavy odor of cheap incense is pervasive. Easily recognizable in the unaesthetic criminal courts is the strong odor of law and order and the cheap smell of racism and repression. The illusion of efficiency is ritualized and formalized in these courts by the judge or madam in his or her granny gown, surrounded by the uniformed attendants who are paid to keep the victims in line.

The greater the injustice, the greater the attempt to make the atmosphere acceptable. Accordingly, the greater the injustice, the more genteel the surroundings. In the higher courts, such as the state or federal "houses," it is always said that the "practice is cleaner" because it is here that one would expect that justice would be most seriously considered. But the whorehouses that are well-decorated, that smell wonderful, that make the litigants feel comfortable and welcome are the dangerous death-dealing houses. Not only are the millions of workers ignored and their impotency legalized, but the Ku Klux Klan has been legally protected, without serious challenge, for a hundred years. These "respectable" houses of the higher courts present a humanitarian front, but their real aim is to keep a good business from failing.

Lawyers, being practical people, may be forgiven for following the practice of getting in on whatever corruption they cannot stop. Likewise, it seems safe to assume that every person has a humanitarian impulse with an inclination to follow it if a viable, decent choice were available. Many lawyers, in fact, have begun to reject the quid pro quo—money—with scorn. The pervasive corruption throughout society has given rise to a new kind of lawyer, especially in the last few years.

The so-called poverty lawyer represents clients in poor neighborhoods, frequently in civil matters. Civil representation includes landlord evictions, family court cases, and consumer fraud situations. There is also the old-style poverty lawyer, sometimes called the legal aid lawyer or public defender, who defends poor people in criminal courts. The service in either case is sporadic, mechanical, and of very poor quality. Nevertheless, these lawyers are trying to go straight in a whorehouse society.

Predictably, poverty lawyers usually practice out of ugly, small offices. In a half-assed attempt to "service the community," the federal government sets up offices in storefronts, which resident indigents occasionally burglarize to the perplexed horror of the supersincere staff. These law offices are actually vaseline dispensers. The staffers comfort the rapees, but they cannot stop the screwing. They cannot stop the system that fucks people over. They have to operate by what I call the "ass-by-ass" technique. They get one ass out of the wringer at a time.

The whole legal system is devoted to the ass-by-ass approach to injustice through which the law forces people to back into a wringer. The poverty lawyer is then permitted to "get them out," thereby achieving a victory. Then the wringer starts up again or continues. The ongoing pressures of racism, materialism, war, greed, and poverty then force innumerable others back into thievery, drugs, unfair rental arrangements, larceny by banks and merchants. Poverty lawyers actually earn their living by allowing society to operate as a screwed-up washing machine from which the results are never clean. This failure of the societal washing machine constitutes a system of oppression. Oppression is a by-product of the malfunction.

Since the role of almost every lawyer is to perpetuate oppression in a corrupt, unjust Society of Whorehouses (sow), it seems to leave very little alternative to the law students or young practitioners. They don't want to be whores, and they can't survive as virgins. What are the alternatives when practically every house worth entering has a NAW or AH member, a two-bit whore or corner hustler? It's very hard to find a shelter which is not a part of the prostitute system, and this is why the young people talk about bringing down the town and all the houses in it.

Yet the lawyer or law student may go "straight" without ever becoming a whore, in my opinion, by literally battling the system. It is simply not enough to walk away and per-

mit the society of whorehouses to continue to wallow in
filth. There are obviously fewer whorehouses than whores.
Long lines of law school applicants are waiting for an opportunity to get in on the corruption. Walking away
simply leaves a place for someone else, who will probably
do a better job. Whorehouse madams breathe a sigh of
relief when they see ill-suited virgins or ex-whores quietly
walk away. They really don't want a bunch of nervous
Nellies in the house, because they will just upset everything.

The way to begin upsetting the daily routine of the
whorehouse is by accepting, for the most part, those clients and those cases that are clearly anti-SOW, anti-NAW
and anti-MICE. One way to survive while battling the system is practicing as a lawyer-hustler. A part of the whorehouse mystique is that a person must be abnormal, and
cannot possibly earn a living, if he or she remains outside
the whorehouse. Yet a lawyer-hustler whose primary purpose is to effect justice by disrupting or exposing an unjust system is not a contradiction.

For example, if a client opposed the war machine
through some direct action, and especially if the case is
not an "ass-by-ass" rescue but one which could theoretically expose a part of the war machine, then the lawyer
who takes that case is a "straight" or "right on" attorney.
In no sense is that lawyer a whore in my terms, even if
paid. One of the differences between rape and a honey-
moon night is consent. The abandonment of appropriate
concern for oppressed humanity is what makes a lawyer a
whore. The "straight" lawyers who best confront the Establishment, who best threaten the whorehouse system,
are those who protest the conditions of the most oppressed
in society as they reject the system.

Obviously, it would be desirable for those who have
been oppressed to become "straight" lawyers, say Black
lawyers for Black people who resist, women lawyers for
women activists. Alas, this cannot happen so easily, because a well-institutionalized oppressive society aims to
make prostitutes out of "upward mobiles" from the op-

pressed groups. It by no means follows that because one has been oppressed, one will fight oppression. Widespread notions to that effect notwithstanding, one has only to note that mostly white lawyers represent the Black Panther Party prisoners, to note that lawyers for an oppressed group are not always of that group. Activist women would prefer women lawyers. But they often find that although women lawyers are not wholehearted participants in the quid pro quo of corruption, which is money, they are too often completely dedicated to getting a chance to be agents for the oppressors, to join a NAW, SOW, or AH.

Lawyers who are analyzing their roles in anti-Establishment terms are saying that their disinclination to affiliate with SOW, NAW or one of the other houses is not personal, but social and political. In the generic sense, they know that as whores, they may be well-housed, well-dressed, and walking evidence of conspicuous consumption, but they would not be happy. One of the reasons the government, at the insistence of the MICE, has become even more repressive than before is because it is unable to make others happy; it is, therefore, very easy for the leaders to punish people without too much discomfort. It's part of their way of life—to divorce themselves from an honest concern for humanity. It is not so unusual, therefore, for most lawyers who regard themselves as "relevant straights" or anti-Establishmentarians to see themselves using the law as a weapon against Establishment repression and against the system itself.

Of course, my attempts to accomplish that end have made me feel like I was trying to level the Pentagon with a wet noodle. I feel that the courts and the legal system are so thoroughly a part of the whole system of prosecution, persecution, and prostitution that an anti-Establishmentarian hustler like myself might be as well off simply using the law as a source of income, and disrupting the Establishment whenever my laziness and timidity permit. It's more fun that way. What's the revolution going to be for, if it's not going to bring more fun, anyway?

The Education of the Capitalist Lawyer: The Law School

by David N. Rockwell *

In the early spring of 1970, Harvard Law School held a schoolwide meeting to discuss the disciplining of five Black law students who had participated in the takeover of university buildings as a protest against Black workers' exclusion from university construction. Speaking against the demand for amnesty, one of the law professors present summed up the reaction of many of his colleagues in the emotional statement, "Fidelity to the law is a precious heritage. If we [the members of the law school "community"] don't hold on to it, who does?" [1]

The professor's euphemism indicates the similarity between certain law professors and politicians mouthing platitudes about the need for "law and order"—both call for the repression of challenges to the established order and authority, even nonviolent and symbolic challenges. Such frank reaction in the context of the law school is particularly fitting, for the law school is one of the primary institutions for the defense and preservation of those economic and political interests which control American society.

Legal education trains people to fill the needs of the legal profession. The legal profession in turn has its needs defined by those interests which pay the highest price for the services of the profession. One of the primary functions of the legal profession is to support and defend the power and control of corporations and business interests. The top lawyers, in effect, represent the groups most concerned with the preservation of the status quo, that is, the protection of property and wealth. Besides this function, the legal profession, in cooperation with the legal system as a whole, operates in the lower economic and political levels to maintain the smooth transfer and accumulation of wealth without upsetting the essential quality of its distribution. The criminal justice system, for example, devoted as it is to the preservation of order, concentrates most of its energy in the fight to keep property rights secure. Those who suffer most in the criminal court process are those who own the least. Making courts more efficient is proposed by reformists as a cheaper remedy than revising the social and economic institutions that are responsible for poverty, slums, and racism. Price-fixing and deceptive advertising, untouched by industry-dominated regulatory agencies, leave consumers virtually undefended. The lawyers' role in these matters, of course, has been crucial to the well-being of the corporate interests. Even with such significant and difficult problems arising from the growth of corporate capitalism and the concentration of wealth in corporate hands, the bulk of the legal profession continues to devote its main efforts to the protection of the social order, not to the development of meaningful and effective solutions.

The concerns and responses of the legal profession are reflected in the law schools. As long as corporations are the highest bidders for legal talent, the principal product of the law school will remain the lawyer who can best fulfill the needs of the corporate world. The law student, as a commodity, is thus expected to master not only the fundamentals of corporate planning, contract, and property law, but also the intricacies of antitrust law (to help the

client steer clear of trouble and still achieve the desired
goal of market dominance and stability), taxation (to lo-
cate and, in some circumstances, actively lobby for attrac-
tive loopholes and advantages in tax codes), and labor law
(to satisfy the desires of both management and labor to
maintain stability within their own framework of competing interests and yet not abandon maximum profits or
wages). In addition, those who reap the financial rewards
of the economic system determine the priorities of legal
education in order to preserve their benefits; so law
schools emphasize courses dealing with wills and estates.
In short, the system of legal education, like the legal profession in general, has adapted itself to the demands
of omnipresent and omnipotent corporate interests.
Through, for example, specially trained and selected law
professors, authoritarian teaching methods, the use of the
"casebook" as the primary textbook, the limited nature of
the curriculum, and the choice of persons who attend law
school, the legal system ensures the preservation of the
economic and political system.

At least two factors arising from the nature and limitations of the legal system also have a profound effect on
legal education. First, only certain types of disputes, involving, for the most part, a particular class of disputants,
receive a fair hearing and are resolved within the legal
process. Law schools reflect this selection of disputes and
disputants made by the legal profession and by the courts.
The priorities of legal education are determined more by
this distribution than by the pressing need for representation of classes which now receive little or no legal help.
Second, as the implicit purpose of the legal system is to
maintain the social order, no change which overturns existing power relationships is possible through use of the
legal system. Whatever the legal method, it will always
reflect a greater concern for the safety of institutions and
power structures upon which the stability of the present
society depends, than for the creation or restructuring of
new or radically different institutions. There is an inherent resistance to sweeping—and often necessary—change

and innovation implicit in legal education. The effect of these two factors on legal education in American society is clear. Given the current distribution of legal talent in this society, where the vast majority of lawyers traditionally have offered their services to business interests and the most skilled have sold themselves to the largest corporations, and given the instinct of the legal system to preserve existing institutions, the law school occupies an important place in the protection of corporate capitalism and the preservation of its economic and political power.

The law faculty—the ruling class at law schools—is composed of individuals who have enjoyed the imbalanced distribution of legal manpower favorable to corporate interests. They assume that the present economic and political system and the role of the legal process within that system are legitimate. Professors are commonly those best adapted to the law school system. The typical law professor was at the top of his class and was a member of his school's law review, an organization concerned with the writing, editing, and publishing of scholarly articles on legal issues; membership in this organization, usually the highest honorary position in a law school, is determined by grades and class rank. For some, government service provides an important training ground; such qualifications might lead to a clerkship under a judge, occasionally under a Supreme Court Justice. More frequently, the professor-to-be enters into practice with a well-established law firm of the Wall Street or Washington variety before he is invited to teach law.[2]

The career pattern ending in a professorship reveals the kind of beliefs held by the law faculty member. Success in both educational and business careers is an indicator of an instructor's ideology. This success is marked by a reluctance to challenge the assumptions of the present role of lawyers in society. Willingness to conform to a standardized successful career model involves refusal to recognize the contradictions in society which permit the future law professor to succeed within the confines of his own social class.

Furthermore, the values represented in such a professional life style are transmitted by the professor to the student. He does not or cannot permit any questioning of the relationship between law and society. Thus, while acting ostensibly as a neutral who eschews any particular ethical or political judgments about the conflicting duties of a lawyer in a given situation, the law professor in fact acts as an advocate of the existing arrangement of economic and political power. This is manifested, for example, by the emphasis placed in most law schools on corporate law, and corporate values.

The ideological leanings of the professors assume a greater dimension and import in the context of teaching methods. Labeled the "Socratic method," the classroom technique of discussion favored by law professors is in fact a perversion of that method, being more an authoritarian lecture than an educational dialogue. The law professor decides what shall or shall not be discussed and determines what is or is not relevant to the discussion of law. The exclusion of material which reflects conflicting social and political conditions from class discussion amounts to a serious distortion of the reality outside the classroom. In the law classroom, where the professor decides the limits of debate, the ideological basis or social impact of judicial decisions and accepted legal principles is barely considered. When a serious problem of conflicting social interests emerges, it is brushed aside as beyond the scope of appropriate inquiry or dismissed as a matter involving the resolution of balancing interests, which can be done without wasting much class time. David Riesman has summarized this aspect of the classroom experience:

. . . [Even] where the problems are obviously real and pressing, and even where the traditional overvaluation of common-law wisdom does not stultify criticism, class debate about what is "reasonable" and how the interests should be balanced turns into a bull session. Information and philosophy are lacking on which sophisticated discussion could proceed. Discussion is, therefore, ended at a question-begging phrase about "competing social policies"

at the very point where it should properly begin. Consequently, many students tend to develop the opinion that the
lawyer does not balance the interests; he merely reflects
them. Lawyers are on the mechanical fringe of policy determination. The law is thought to follow, rather than reflect, the progressive insights of science or the drives of
class. . . . These higher domains [subjects studied in the
social sciences, for example] where the important truths
are examined and revealed are outside the province of a
mere legal technician. Thus law, which is the keystone of
the arch of public policy, is robbed of vitality and significance.[3]

Law schools have generally been quite successful in
meeting the needs and interests with which the legal profession is most concerned, and have managed to do so
without thorough discussion of social policies. Such discussion and examination of the relationship between law
and society might in fact detract from the efficient service
to those interests to which the law school and the profession have devoted themselves.

When limitations in the name of neutrality and objec-
tivity are placed on ideological analyses and detailed investigations of conflicts between social interests, the result
is that the concept of "justice" instilled in law students is
restricted and defined by the values which are taught.
Given the bias of law schools towards the solution of corporate and property problems before human problems,
justice, the ideal goal of the legal system, is seen as inherent in corporate values. Finding a just solution to a problem, within the restrictions imposed in the classroom,
means devising a remedy that will be fair in terms of
property-oriented concepts of justice, e.g., efficiency and
low costs must take priority over the rights of an accused.
An injustice such as institutionalized racism can be raised
but will not be adequately studied because the solution to
such problems is impossible in a system based on corporate law and the values which created or aggravated those
problems. Programmed nonthinking and nondiscussion
instill a passive concept of justice as the continuation and

preservation of existing institutions and social relationships.

Another fundamental restrictive aspect of legal education is the use of textbooks consisting of written decisions
of court cases. This "casebook" is used in order to gain an
understanding of some of the basic principles of a particular area of law and also, in conjunction with the so-called
Socratic method, to aid in the development of the student's ability to "think like a lawyer" through the examination of judicial opinions. This method has been the subject of serious criticism since its inception; one notable
criticism is that classroom reliance on these appellate
court decisions entails a narrowness of inquiry that is
dangerously unrealistic, unrelated to the actual practice
of law and inconsiderate of the effects which such decisions might have on society as a whole.

The stamp of reality is missing from the casebook
method. The student depends on the appellate court's decision for his knowledge of the factual situation of a case;
however, since the appellate court in turn usually relies on
the factual findings of the trial court, the discussion ignores the process of fact selection, as well as the legal
process at the trial court level. The emphasis placed on
the study of appellate decisions omits consideration of the
actual problems of trial work, such as the prejudices of
judges and juries, the deals which are made in criminal
courts, or the political forces affecting various classes of
interested parties, such as tenants. This coincides with the
insistence of many law schools that emphasis be placed
on a supposedly value-free theoretical approach to law. In
practice this means that law students draw only from theory heavily tinged with corporate values. They will thus be
able to offer solutions for corporate problems, but not for
the problems posed by injustices in the judicial system or
other injustices caused by corporate interests.

The use of the casebook also tends to discourage an
analysis in which each decision or at least each major
doctrine is given the context of its relation to other aspects
of the social order. Although some casebooks include a

sprinkling of articles that deal with the sociological or economic aspects of the particular area of law, these are usually superficial and at any rate offer only token representations of such areas of analysis.

Problems currently in litigation cannot be included in the casebooks; cases are selected because they can be discussed in terms of prevailing legal doctrine or interest. Insufficient distinction is made between the historical situations which gave rise to those doctrines and the modern conditions requiring great modification, if not the complete invalidation, of such theories and their bases. In property law, for example, landlord-tenant law is examined, but in the framework of commercial property and leases, not of urban slums. The discussion of zoning laws more typically concerns a suburban homeowner suing a neighbor whose home has a different type of front porch than the barricading of minority groups into ghettos through the use of both written and unwritten zoning laws. By ignoring such areas of reality, casebooks, as well as most of the other teaching methods used by law professors, contribute to a disastrous type of tunnel vision in which vital problems of human survival are peripheral and the focus is on the orderly transfer of property and wealth within the same controlling group.

In the past, the typical law school curriculum offered little to those students not interested in working within the business sphere or the system of corporate values and, to a great extent, this has not changed. Courses regarded as basic include, for example, corporations, taxation, contracts, criminal law, property, accounting, and constitutional law. Catalogue descriptions of these courses have been changed recently to suggest that the subject matter of these courses can be adapted to the needs of the poor or the nonbusiness clients. In the actual courses, however, these needs are rarely discussed in any but a superficial manner. Contract courses gloss over the fact that not every party to a contract is able to bargain at the ideal "arm's length" and from a position of equal strength; and students rarely hear the side of the low-income consumer who is the victim of an unconscionable sales contract. Courses dealing with corporate law are said to be necessary for the idealistic lawyer so that he or she can help set up nonprofit community corporations or promote private business in economically depressed areas, e.g., promote Black capitalism. Even for the student planning a career in criminal law, a knowledge of corporate law is essential if he is ever called upon to defend a corporate officer.

Law school curricula reflect the narrowness of inquiry found in almost any trade school, as if the practice of law were a specialty which had little relationship to other disciplines. In the spring of 1969, first-year students at Harvard Law School received a memorandum on second-year course requirements, with an explanation of the faculty's recommendation that all students take the "Big Four": Corporations, Taxation, Accounting, and Constitutional Law. "The case for a basic course in Corporations is a simple one: The corporate form of business enterprise is central to the economic system of the free world." Taxation and Accounting help in understanding and employing this "central" form. Constitutional Law is not only concerned with the rights of individuals but also with interstate and international business conflicts. These second-year courses are prerequisites for numerous courses offered at Harvard in the third year. Taxation is a prerequisite for the following: Advanced Taxation—The Taxation of Business Enterprise; Taxation—Corporate Reorganizations and Distributions; Business Planning; Estate Planning; Taxation—Current Issues and Problems; and Land Development. Corporations is required in order to take the following subjects: Business Planning; Securities Regulation; and Corporate Planning and Counselling. Accounting is a prerequisite for Business Planning. The extension of these basic courses into the third year shows the training of a business-oriented professional specialist; no courses are required to help the student develop a continuing concern for humanitarian needs.

The curriculum of a law school thus remains basically concerned with the protection and expansion of personal and corporate property, to the detriment of the problems and needs of people who do not have even the wealth to feed, clothe, or house themselves, who are not free from discrimination, and who cannot protect themselves in court. Although the subjects taught in law schools have recently been advertised as equally applicable to all problems of society, at best this advertising is misleading. A student has little opportunity to exercise his skills in the different contexts suggested by the course descriptions— whether the application of his talents to those other problems would even be effective is another question. The few available positions offering work in such areas do not compete financially with normal corporate practice for legal talent, and graduating law students are not noted for their altruism.

The character of the average law student has also contributed to the present quality and form of the legal profession. Generally speaking, law students have been content to accept the type of education offered in law schools, fully aware of the future rewards. Moreover, they, as their professors, exhibit a marked unwillingness to explore or question their position or the role of the law in society. Many of them have in fact made such an examination, found the results to their liking, and have enthusiastically embraced the social and economic meaning of membership in the profession. The study of law represents the opportunity to become a professional, the fulfillment of middle class dreams. Law school offers the key to membership in a generally respected elite group, with specialized, seemingly mystical, knowledge and technical skills which, because of the power symbolized in the mastery of the law, set the lawyer apart from and above the general populace. Although to some the potential intellectual challenge is significant, to most law students the promise of great—and easy—monetary reward offered by the legal profession is the persuasive factor in their choice of career. Admission to the legal profession is also an asset in some students' ambitious advance through various structures of power, political parties, governmental bodies, and the business world.

The law school might seem an ideal place for training

those interested in social reform, especially if they are
prepared to work in some of those established frameworks
of decision-making, such as government service or political parties. However, the elements of the standard legal
education deny this group adequate tools for even the recognition of urgent social problems, and leave them help-
less to remedy those problems. Many of these students,
after enduring three years of continuous attention to the
problems of corporate entities instead of the problems of
human beings, undergo a gradual metamorphosis. The
student who graduates with his social commitment intact
is rare. Even those still interested in being servants to the
people assert themselves instead as leaders who, pos-
sessed with secret and omnipotent knowledge, attempt to
define both the people's problems and the solutions. In
fact, as officers of the court their ideological indoctrination and limited training lead them to see the law and the
legal process as the primary means for social change so
that they are of limited use in cases where movement toward freedom has been blocked by the legal system.

Law schools have begun to respond to mounting tensions and contradictions within the legal profession and
society generally. As a result of the civil rights struggles
during the late fifties and early sixties in the South, a
number of law schools instituted courses related to the
legal issues raised in civil rights cases. In the mid-sixties
and at the turn of the decade, insurrections in Black
neighborhoods and the growth of a broad, though diverse,
student movement forced the government—in response to
corporate pressures—to use the legal profession as one
way of containing the resistance. Opportunities for young
lawyers in the poverty field increased; schools were encouraged to train lawyers to work in poor neighborhoods
on civil matters; resources for the training of public defenders in criminal cases were increased. Despite these
encouraging signs in legal education, such responses have
not been substantial and it is doubtful that they can even
endure, especially since most of these programs are gov-
ernment-controlled and financed.

Nevertheless, law students have demonstrated increasing interest in such work, and law firms have reacted by advertising their own importance. Salaries for first-year associates in firms have risen considerably in the last few years and law firms all across the country have begun to expand the opportunities for their lawyers to perform *pro bono publico* work, such as manning a neighborhood legal assistance office one afternoon a month. Such activities are supposed to relieve anxieties caused by any sense of moral obligation which survive three years of law school. Statistics on Harvard Law School graduates have not shown any significant change in their choices of jobs. The table on page 102 illustrates this point.

The director of the placement office at Harvard stated, "They put up a big fuss that they are different now, but they're not. . . . Students are much more serious about interviewing this year. And they seem to be doing more of it. Perhaps it is a reflection of their worry that firms may not be hiring as readily as before." [5]

Reflecting the trend in other institutions, a number of law firms have stepped up recruitment of Blacks, after decades of lily-white offices. The demand for Black students by law schools has increased correspondingly. However, only a few law schools have taken a meaningful step to increase the ridiculously low number of Blacks in the profession—Rutgers is an outstanding example through which the beliefs and cooperation of an obviously exceptional faculty and student body implemented a program whereby one-fourth of its entering class in 1969 was Black.

Women are also underrepresented in law schools. The general attitude among law firms is that women are not capable of practicing law as well as men. In 1965, the Dean of Harvard Law School announced that five percent of the student population were women, and that he regarded this as about optimum. That percentage has not increased significantly. Women are often discouraged from applying to law school on the grounds that they will never find employment when they graduate. Some

PERCENTAGE OF EACH CLASS ENTERING GIVEN FIELDS 1955-1970

	1961	1962	1963	1964	1965	1966	1967	1968	1969	1970*
Law Offices	54%	48%	49%	50%	50%	49%	44%	44%	49%	58%
Business Concerns	2	4	4	2	3	2	4	4	1	2
Government	9	9	9	6	8	7	8	8	6	3
Judicial Clerkships	8	11	10	12	14	13	12	12	12	19
Banks, Accounting & Insurance	1	1	2	2	1	2	2	—	2	2
Teaching	2	—	1	—	2	2	3	5	3	1
Research & Study	10	5	8	8	6	4	2	2	4	1
Legal Services	—	—	—	—	—	1	2	3	4	1
Fellowships	—	—	—	—	4	5	2	2	1	2
Peace Corps	—	—	—	—	—	3	1	—	—	—
VISTA	—	—	—	—	—	—	—	1	2	—
Miscellaneous	—	—	1	3	1	1	—	1	1	1
Number in Class	476	468	489	514	515	515	513	517	520	381

* 1970 statistics are not entirely comparable because, unlike the other years, they are based on the activities of the class immediately after graduation instead of one year later. For this reason, the 1970 statistics are based on only 77 percent of the entire class while figures for the earlier years are based on substantially more than 90 percent.[4]

women's organizations are being formed at law schools now, and one of their primary targets is discrimination at the placement bureau. Both women and Blacks have been pressing for courses on the law. Blacks have generally had more success with this demand than other minority groups. It is not surprising that law schools have been among the last educational institutions to experience dissent, given the general composition of the student body and the intimidation to radicals in the form of each state's bar character committee. To gain admission to the bar, one must not only pass the bar examination, but be found acceptable by a character committee, which functions as a powerful and efficient entity to "chill" First Amendment rights, since its standards are vague and unevenly enforced. The character committee's chilling effect extends even to the undergraduate level, for students who consider entering law school must realize that three years of time and money might be wasted if they join in militant tactics against the increasing repression in this country. Faced with a choice of remaining quiet for three years or challenging the character committee and risking the loss of three years' work, many radicals prefer to keep fighting outside the school, not caring to waste those years in an activity whose benefits are doubtful.

It is this despair of achieving any meaningful change through the legal system that makes most radicals shun law school. An assessment of the role of the legal system in maintaining the existing social order would confirm this viewpoint. Designed for and chiefly implemented by capitalist interests, the legal system will never allow more than insignificant changes; substantial and effective challenges to the established order can never be mounted through the legal system, the guardian of that order. The law schools, identifying as they do with the legal system —existing within the heart of the monster—will be just as resistant to any change which threatens the structure and stability of this society.

Notes

1. Harvard Law School *Bulletin*, Vol. 21, No. 4 (April 12, 1970), p. 12.
2. "Of about 54 full time professors at Harvard Law School, more than half have worked in law firms, most of which were engaged in corporate law and taxation and related work: about two-thirds of these firms were large New York or Washington law firms. Almost half of the professors at Harvard Law clerked for judges before coming to the law school to teach; more than 90% of this group clerked for Justices of the United States Supreme Court. In addition, 60% have held (non-military) governmental positions, both before and during their law school careers." See *Harvard Law School Yearbook*, 1970 ed.
3. David Riesman, "Law and Social Science: A Review of Michael and Wechsler's Casebook on Criminal Law and Administration," Vol. 50, *Yale Law Journal* (1941), pp. 636, 657.
4. *Harvard Law Record*, October 29, 1970, p. 4.
5. Ibid., pp. 4–5.

Women's Servitude Under Law

*by Ann M. Garfinkle, Carol Lefcourt, and Diane B. Schulder**

*We now present to you
the lady lawyer crew.
In court we have to flirt
and wear a mini-skirt.*

*Whenever we're before
a judge, we must play whore.
If we do not act cute
we cannot win a suit.*
—from the "Short Skirt Shuffle" Law Day, April
30, 1971

The legal profession, a bulwark of conservatism, can be seen as a caricature of male society's attitudes toward women. Embodying existing social values and power relationships, the law not only reinforces but enshrines woman's secondary role in society. Now women are examining the nature of their own oppression and challenging its manifestation in the law. The women's liberation movement and law workers themselves—lawyers, secretaries, researchers, and others—have begun an attack on the legal profession and the laws which men have created.

Historically, women have been excluded from participation in or control over the legal system, except for suffering penalties imposed by it. In an opinion that might sound to some like a parody written by women's liberationists, the United States Supreme Court in 1872 ruled on the challenge by a married woman from Illinois to a state law that forbade women from practicing law. The Court's answer was in no uncertain terms:

> The claim that [under the Fourteenth Amendment of the Constitution] the statute law of Illinois . . . can no longer be set up as a barrier against the right of females to pursue any lawful employment for a livelihood (the practice of law included), assumes that it is one of the privileges and immunities of women as citizens to engage in any and every profession, occupation, or employment in civil life. It certainly cannot be affirmed, as an historical fact, that this has ever been established as one of the fundamental privileges and immunities of the sex. On the contrary, the civil law, as well as nature herself, has always recognized a wide difference in the respective spheres and destinies of man and woman. Man is, or should be, woman's protector and defender. The natural and proper timidity and delicacy which belongs to the female sex evidently unfits it for many of the occupations of civil life. . . .
>
> It is true that many women are unmarried and not affected by any of the duties, complications, and incapacities arising out of the married state, but these are exceptions to the general rule. The paramount destiny and mission of women are to fulfill the noble and benign offices of wife and mother. This is the law of the Creator. And the rules of civil society must be adapted to the general constitution of things, and cannot be based upon exceptional cases.[1]

Not only were women totally excluded from the practice of law as lawyers until the present century, but they were also excluded from the whole legal apparatus—as judges, jurors, and litigants—by the same rationale. The rule of common law was that juries consisted of "twelve good men." One exception was made: when a pregnant woman faced execution, a jury of twelve women was convened to decide whether she should be executed before or after giving birth to her child, and to consider questions of inheritance.[2] Some commentators add that a jury of twelve men was convened simultaneously to stand by and make sure the women reached the right decision.

In many states today, women still do not play more than a token part in jury duty. Fifteen states allow exemptions to women on the basis of their sex alone, while twelve more allow exceptions to women for reasons not available to men, such as child care problems or lack of ladies' rooms in the courthouse. Three states require women but not men to register at the courthouse if they wish to serve as jurors, and in 1968, South Carolina and Mississippi still excluded women from state court juries entirely.[3] Although one federal court has ruled that the total exclusion of women from state juries is discriminatory and unconstitutional,[4] in actual fact there are often very few women jurors in states where jury statutes treat women differently from men. To the woman criminal who faces an all-male jury in such a state, assurances that her constitutional rights are being protected may offer little in the way of consolation. Take, for example, the case of *Hoyt v Florida,* in which the United States Supreme Court said:

> At the core of appellant's argument is the claim that the nature of the crime of which she was convicted peculiarly demanded the inclusion of persons of her own sex on the jury. She was charged with killing her husband by assaulting him with a baseball bat. . . . The affair occurred in the context of a marital upheaval involving, among other things, the suspected infidelity of appellant's husband, and culminating in the final rejection of his wife's efforts at reconciliation. It is claimed, in substance, that women jurors would have been more understanding or compassionate than men in assessing the quality of appellant's act and her defense.[5]

The Court dismissed her pleas and upheld the conviction by an all-male jury. In this instance, the Court found it convenient to minimize differences between men and women (as jurors). The Court justified its ruling in the above case by saying that "woman is still regarded as the center of home and family life." [6]

Until recently, women were also totally excluded from law-making bodies; it follows that they have had few, if any, rights under the law. They were considered merely appendages to their husbands. Under the English law of "coverture," the husband and wife were "one," and, as Justice Black reminds us in *United States v Yazell* (1966), "the one is the husband." [7] According to historical doctrine, the woman lost her legal existence upon marriage. She not only lost her name, but also the right to sue, to sign a contract, and to manage her property. It is useful to recall that women in the U.S. did not receive the right to vote until 1920.

In some parts of the United States sexual discrimination in legislation and case law still countenances the "passion shooting" of a wife by a husband. The reverse is known, of course, as homicide. In 1968, Italy abolished a law under which a woman could be jailed for adultery for one year while her husband could be unfaithful with impunity. In 1969, the United States Supreme Court dismissed the appeal of a girl who was convicted under a 1905 Connecticut law authorizing imprisonment of young women if they are "in manifest danger of falling into habits of vice or leading a vicious life." [8] "Juvenile delinquent" status for girls often relates to sexual activity or potential activity; for boys, it is the commission of substantive crimes. Thus sex discrimination is involved even in the definition of crimes. Different state laws also provide for disparate lengths of jail sentences for the same crime, depending on whether the perpetrator is male or female. One dubious advantage of teenage girls, for example, is that they receive less severe punishment than teenage boys when minor infractions of the law are committed, as in demonstration cases. The rationale for this inequity is probably that the girls didn't know what they did or were duped into the act.

Laws and the courts, therefore, act as male protectors of the status quo, maintaining the image of women as meek, feebleminded, childbearing creatures. When women clients and their women attorneys appear before a male judge, both women are often subjected to the patronization of the court. All women attorneys have on occasion been referred to as "lady" or "ma'am"; rarely are they referred to as "counselor," as are their male counterparts. Women in law schools are generally discouraged from completing their education. Only a few years ago, women in Brooklyn Law School were assigned seats in a corner of the room; the professors generally addressed the class with "Good morning, gentlemen"; occasionally there was a "Ladies' Day" so that all the women, usually four out of one hundred students, would recite on the same day. The law library, perhaps in a moment of Freudian honesty, placed its literature on women between that of mental incompetency and children. The perpetuation of these attitudes in the minds and acts of the present male-dominated courts, and the application of oppressive, outdated laws still on the books, make the law and legal institutions a regressive and stifling force.

One of the most frequent complaints of women involved in matrimonial disputes is the all-male roster of characters in court. Whether in a state supreme court for divorce (the middle and upper income courts) or family court for support or protection matters (the poor people's arena), the woman is usually faced with a male judge, male court clerks, her husband, his male lawyer, and her own lawyer, invariably another man. One woman, when seeking protection from her ex-husband who was harassing her, was told by the judge that she was lucky to have a man interested in her at all. Absolute silence followed the judge's admonition, unbroken by the woman's male attorney.

The relationship between the female prostitute and law enforcement agencies illustrates not only the abuse of power by male-dominated institutions, but also the unequal application of laws by these "neutral" bodies. In most cities male policemen actively entrap women and charge them with the crime of prostitution, or force the women to make "protection payments" so as to avoid arrest.[9] Although New York State law technically considers both prostitutes and their customers guilty of crime, a male criminal court judge in a recent pronouncement characterized women prostitutes as "hardened criminals" and said that "one could not equate their activity with that of their customers." [10] The local district attorneys, also primarily male, of course, never choose to prosecute men customers. The final indignity of a white male-dominated New York legislature which recently increased penalties against prostitution with white male judges usually imposing them, would be all the more ironic if the facts were known about the frequency of the lawmakers' visitations to the women from whom they seek their own pleasure and against whom they reveal their hypocrisy.

In addition to the male domination of legal institutions, the indignities which all women must face in the everyday life of the law schools and the courts, and the unequal application of law enforcement, today's laws continue to subject women to a secondary place in all social relations. Of these the laws surrounding marriage and the family are probably the most oppressive.

Birth control and abortion statutes still take the choice of childbearing from woman and put it in control of the state. The state, by regulating birth control and abortions, channels women into child rearing. Women are forced into the role of mothers by the whim of male-dominated legal and medical institutions.

After being refused an abortion and proper contraceptives, the woman who may be psychologically or financially unprepared or unwilling to care for a child learns that the state takes no formal responsibility for child care service in state institutions. Since the state is, after all, governed by and for men, the woman is criminally liable if the child is not cared for properly or gets into trouble in school. The "troublesome" child, especially from a poor family, will be sent to some variation of a reformatory, the only kind of institution the state provides to take care of its children.

Finally the law discourages the banding together of women for socialized child care. The health and education regulations for cooperative centers are stringent, arbitrary, and inflexible. These restrictions illustrate the essence of state control over real estate and the education of children, as they foster the family unit. For example, New York City housing is commercial and one-family-unit oriented; no zoning areas or buildings are available for group efforts. Although city schools rarely meet building or health standards, this is required of community groups who cannot afford compliance.

Marriage and raising a family are encouraged and are the state's traditional means for the subjugation of women. In all states, for example, tax benefits are lost if a couple remains unmarried or if people live in communes. No joint tax returns are permitted, higher income brackets result and deductions for dependents are difficult to obtain. If one person in a commune dies the others have no right to the estate unless the deceased was married or related to another member. Separate contracts or wills can be drawn, but the normal assumption of the law is that marriage and children are the only proper way for property to be passed on.

Alimony laws, a middle and upper class phenomenon, have often been described as oppressive to men. A different perspective becomes obvious when alimony and the laws surrounding it are viewed in the context of a woman's role and her options in our present society. Having been reared by her family, the school, and peer groups to believe that her identity and fulfillment lie in giving physical and emotional support to a man, a woman "willingly" enters the beatific state of marital harmony. For ten, twenty, or thirty years, she cooks, cleans, runs a twenty-four-hour child-care center, nurses her family, chauffeurs them, runs errands, and gives psychic support to her man. His role as the family supporter may seem to be a compensatory one in certain respects, but it is not in fact, as it excludes the woman from participation and guarantees her a permanently secondary position in the larger society. When the marriage dissolves, she has lost her "job" as surely as a man who has been fired from his. When alimony and support are granted, it is not a "victory," for it perpetuates the woman in her established role, and also as a parasite. The husband is not expected to spend half his time with the children and do the household chores which that responsibility involves. A woman, trained only for household tasks, can hardly be expected to earn a decent wage, especially since wages for women are lower than for men.[11] No undeserved windfall, alimony serves as severance pay or back wages and, perhaps, a pitiful gesture toward reparations for the stunting of the woman's potential for growth and development.

The courts, of course, take a different and, predictably, more paternalistic view. They insist, in most cases, on the outdated Common Law notion that alimony is an extension of the husband's legal duty to support his wife and children. Alimony and support, when granted on these grounds, tend to perpetuate the woman in her traditional role, even when she has the desire and the ability to escape it. The income tax structure favors the male and favors the marriage. A woman pays income tax on alimony payments but not on child support payments. If the woman is capable of supporting herself by working outside her home, the courts will not allow her sufficient child-support payments to cover day-care expenses, but instead will grant her taxable alimony payments to cover her living expenses and then add a minimal, nontaxable, child-support allowance. The courts make it as unprofitable as possible for the woman to make a life for herself outside her home. Thus, while a man can deduct for child-support payments, women (divorced, married, or single) cannot deduct for child care or baby sitters. Except for rare cases of great wealth, if the couple is childless and the woman capable of supporting herself, the courts will not award her alimony. If she is found guilty of adultery, abandonment, or cruel treatment, she collects little or no alimony. The man is seldom forced to pay more alimony if he is found guilty of these acts. In any case, whether or not a marriage disintegrates, and regardless of whether a legal wrong was committed by either party, the woman provides services for which she is not compensated.

Married women's efforts to become independent must include an attack on male-dominated property relations within marriage. In some states in which the property of the husband and wife is owned jointly, so-called "community property states," control often rests with the husband alone.[12] This has the absurd result that a wife is liable, as co-owner, for the mismanagement of property she has no legal right to control. In states that do not have community property statutes, vestiges of the woman's Common Law inability to own and control property still exist, as where women are not allowed to buy or sell land without their husbands' joinder in the deed.[13]

Women are greatly restricted in their efforts to acquire property within the marriage, since they cannot contract with their husbands for wages in compensation for their performance of household services.[14] Since the law commands a woman to perform such services, the courts hold that her promise to perform them in return for wages is void for lack of consideration. In the great majority of cases, women may not contract with their husbands to receive wages for work of any kind, even work in the husband's store or office.[15] Unless she takes a regular job outside her home, or has inherited wealth, the wife is completely dependent on her husband's good will for any income greater than the support allowance he is required by law to give her. And if this allowance is insufficient, even glaringly insufficient, the courts will usually refuse to interfere with the husband's judgment unless the woman files for divorce or separation.

In addition to suffering severe disadvantages in the property relations within marriage, a married woman is greatly restricted in her ability to sue for damages when either she or her husband has been negligently injured. If she is injured, her husband can sue the negligent party for loss of "consortium," that is, for loss of her services, such as sexual companionship. If her husband is negligently injured, in most states the wife cannot sue since she is not legally entitled to the benefits of consortium from her husband. Nor can a husband and wife sue each other if one negligently injures the other. The rule is not discriminatory on its face, but since most of the negligence cases that arise involve automobile accidents in which, of course, the man was driving, married women frequently find themselves permanently disabled, yet without any legal claim for damages against their husband's insurance company.

Women are also required by law to live where their husbands live; refusal to move when the husband decides to relocate the household is grounds for divorce in almost all states. In some states, a husband can divorce his wife if she commits one act of adultery, but she cannot divorce him unless she shows that he is living with another woman. To prove that his wife has committed adultery, the husband must only show that the opportunity to commit adultery existed along with the inclination. If the woman is divorced on grounds of adultery she will almost always be denied custody of her children.

For a woman without a man to support a child, public welfare often is the only choice. The alimony laws in practice have no application to the majority of women in the United States. A 1964 study of welfare law in California makes the observation that "we have two systems of family law . . . different in origin, different in history, different in administration, different in orientation and outlook—one for the rich and one for the poor." Welfare regulations are, of course, more degrading and limiting to women than alimony laws, but they are based on similar assumptions.

One of the most abusive welfare regulations for many years was the unannounced night visit to discover if a welfare mother were having a sexual relationship; if evidence of a man's presence was found in her home, welfare payments would be stopped. It was assumed that such relations were "marriage substitutes," that the man should pay support, and that a man in the house meant food on the table. The state wanted to substitute a standard "marriage" for welfare. The indignity of the "night raid" has ceased, but the basic system continues. In effect, the state pays welfare to confine the woman to her traditional role by providing few possibilities for child care or for employment. The state thus commits itself to maintaining women in their subordinate position in a family unit.

The law has shown a similarly paternalistic role towards women in the area of employment. In 1908, in upholding an hour limitation statute for working women, the Supreme Court stated:

> That woman's physical structure and the performance of maternal functions place her at a disadvantage in the struggle for subsistence is obvious. This is especially true when the burdens of motherhood are upon her. Even when they are not, by abundant testimony of the medical fraternity, continuance for a long time on her feet at work, repeating this from day to day, tends to have injurious effects upon the body, and, as healthy mothers are essential to vigorous offspring, the physical well-being of woman becomes an object of public interest and care in order to preserve the strength and vigor of the race.[16]

Hour and weight limitation laws and lower wages for women are even today defended by trade union representatives. But the courts are beginning to take a closer look at some of these restrictions. Title VII of the 1964 Civil Rights Act forbids discrimination on account of sex in employment.[17] For example, it is now illegal to discriminate against women because of a shortage of bathroom facilities or because of worker preference for all-male surroundings on the job. Now an employer can use sex as a criterion for making decisions only in cases where sex itself is a bona fide occupational qualification for the job: acting, topless waitressing, and modeling are typical.

Attacks are being made on the state protective laws which actually discriminate against the women they were designed to help.[18] Laws enforcing rest periods and sitting areas for women workers will presumably be expanded to include men. However, it is not likely that Title VII will obviate state laws which designate the maximum number of hours that a woman can work for an employer in a day.[19] Thus, women who wish or need to work longer hours will continue to be forced to take on second jobs at regular, rather than overtime, pay.

The Equal Pay Act of 1963 supposedly bars unequal pay for equal work. But it is not enforced. If the theory is that a married man must receive a higher pay because he needs it to support his wife and children, then perhaps that additional amount, instead of being added to his salary, should be given directly to the woman. All unmarried people would receive an equal salary. And those with dependents would have payments made to the dependent.

Statistics on earnings still reveal appalling discrepancies between (in descending order) the salaries of white men, Black men, white women, and Black women; in addition, the typical employment open to women is monotonous service jobs. According to 1968 U. S. Department of Labor statistics, women file clerks, secretaries and saleswomen almost all earn less than fifty-eight percent of men's wages for the same work. The exclusion of women from many fields, such as construction and various skilled trades, and token admission into a host of areas, including top executive positions in the corporate world, has rarely been challenged through the law. As recently as 1948, the Supreme Court reaffirmed its protective approach in upholding a state's right to forbid a woman to be a bartender unless she were "the wife or daughter of the male owner." [20]

Generally, our whole system assumes that even if a woman ventures out into the "man's world"—the cliché seems anachronistic—she must still have time to accomplish household tasks. Women's creativity is forgone to insure that laundry is washed, floors are swept, meals are cooked, a little family income is added, or leaflets typed. The man must be served so he can accomplish the major wage-earning or idea-formulating role. Anything the woman does outside the home is viewed as extra, however admirable. Even though more women work than ever before, their jobs are likely to be lower paying and less creative than those available to (white) men. In any event, a married woman who tries to reject her assigned role is faced with a hostile world, pushing her back to take care of her responsibilities. The unmarried woman is viewed as a kind of freak.

The unspoken law of societal norms and values, together with the written law as their expression and handmaiden, enforce the continuance of these roles by subtle ways or by outright coercion. There is no reckoning of the psychological toll these laws have taken on women for hundreds of years. Psychological, legal, and economic oppression and their consequences are rationalized to justify subservient roles for women. Men are the immediate oppressors of women, enforcing rules made by other men. Domination by the male and the division of the sexes into arbitrary roles objectify the woman and alienate both male and female. This kind of fragmentation is connected with the capacity of an entire society to view other societies as objects to be used or destroyed (the nations of Indochina), to ghettoize whole peoples (Indians and Blacks), and to exploit the masses of workers.[21]

The institutions of marriage and the family are the fundamental structures which subject women to the tyranny of a white-male-dominated society. Significantly, those once-stable institutions began to disintegrate before the emergence of organized women's movements. It is not the purpose here to analyze the causes of this disintegration— divorce, adultery, separation, marriages of convenience and habit—but it is clear that the cohesive family is becoming less ordinary. Furthermore, as long as these institutions and the male attitudes that sustain them continue, there are few ways for women to escape the traditional roles.

It is unrealistic to speak of major changes through the legal system. However, the legitimacy of the laws enforcing an antiquated status quo must be continually challenged on all levels. Part of this challenge is an attack against the male-dominated court system, the legal profession itself, and the broad set of restrictive laws. Many women have begun to dispute the authority and legitimacy of men making decisions which affect their lives. Women's caucuses, that is, small groups of women within their places of work and education, have emerged to demand greater control of institutions and the restructuring of social relations.

The nature of this challenge within the legal profession is an attack against male domination and "professionalism." Women are demanding greater participation in their law offices, whether they are secretaries or lawyers. They are demanding establishment of child-care programs at their places of work and study; they are also demanding more teaching positions and restructured curricula in law schools. Finally, they are calling attention to the need for the participation of women as "lay advocates," especially in the areas of welfare and family cases. More women lawyers, judges, and legislators, however, is not the solution to the problem of an inequitable and corrupt judicial system, although an increase in the number of women committed to the fight against the institution may help to expose its nonneutral role. The courts, however, are so class-oriented, racist, and sexist that a total attack on all fronts is required.

The fight against restrictive laws in recent years has been led in part by women opposed to barbaric abortion laws. In 1969 California's abortion statute was declared unconstitutional as an invasion of a woman's privacy.[22] Similar statutes were attacked throughout the country, with the result that a few states have now declared their abortion statutes unconstitutional. A lawsuit in New York attracted hundreds of women litigants and thousands of supporters. In 1970 the law was in effect reformed before the court heard the suit. The women had won a limited battle against the state's right to regulate childbearing. The attack on abortion brought to the surface women's discontent with forced families, bearing unwanted children, and the social stigma attached to unmarried sex.

The problem, however, had as usual gone beyond the possibility for legally resolving inherent inequalities and the solution was hampered by property relationships, unresponsive medical institutions, and lack of facilities. Insurance companies do not cover all the necessary expenses; hospitals have limited beds; the state's Medicaid program is hopelessly inadequate; and doctors' fears and conservative responses have dampened enthusiasm about the first important challenge to male dominance of the female body. Women, therefore, after challenging the specific law, are now demanding free medical clinics run by patients, doctors and all medical personnel, so as to be responsive to the needs of all, unlike the male, supposedly professionally run hospitals. The next step, unfortunately, may have to be a fight against imposed contraception and abortion.[23]

Women's groups are planning a broad series of attacks in opposition to the restrictive laws regulating marriage and the family. The legal symbol of the secondary role of a married woman is the adoption of a man's surname. Women have now begun to retain their own names upon marriage, thus symbolically asserting their own identities. Their challenge, in the long run, can have its greatest effect on male control of property relations. A challenge to the basis upon which divorces are granted, alimony is established, and support payments calculated has begun. Practical interim solutions to women's economic problems resulting from divorce or families without men must be created. For example, the law regarding alimony and child support, as it is now, uses as criteria the manner in which the couple has become accustomed to live. Instead, a woman should be compensated for her past contribution to the husband's "career" and paid for the child care and other services she must continue to provide. The fact that women have been reared to serve these roles and are left without education, training, or motivation to start a new life must also be compensated.

One women's group plans to station a member at the marriage license bureau, informing people of possible loss of rights involved in the marital relationship. It should be a requirement by law that the state or city inform people of their legal rights and obligations in a marriage contract. Women's groups are beginning to demand the abolition of all laws controlling the sexual conduct of women. Groups of lesbians marched in a public demonstration, affirming their right to private relationships. A woman arrested for indecent exposure for wearing a see-through blouse welcomed the ensuing battle in court. Adultery laws, promiscuity laws, sodomy laws, etc. are being challenged throughout the country.

In essence, the laws are a formal codification of attitudes toward women that permeate our culture. They are used as a means of coercion to obtain conformity with norms and mores. The law is not then an instrument for altering the unequal male-female relationship; rather, it is an institutional barrier to change. The change must come, therefore, from outside the law and must bring down the restrictive laws in the struggle.

Notes*

1. *Bradwell v Illinois*, Vol. 16, Wallace's *U.S. Supreme Court Reports* (1872), p. 130.
2. See note, "Courts—Women Jurors—Automatic Exemption," Vol. 36, *Tulane Law Review* (1962), p. 858.
3. See Leo Kanowitz, *Women and the Law: the Unfinished Revolution.* Albuquerque: University of New Mexico Press, 1969.
4. See *White v Crook*, Vol. 251, *Federal Supplements*, Northern District of Alabama (1966), p. 401, in which the court held that the Alabama statute which specified that only males could serve as jurors was ruled unconstitutional as a violation of the equal protection clause of the Fourteenth Amendment.
5. *Hoyt v Florida*, Vol. 368, *U.S. Supreme Court Reports* (1961), p. 57.
6. Ibid.

* Our thanks to Alice Ballard and Molly Mungar, two Harvard law students, who helped to organize the Women and the Law course at Harvard and who assisted in researching this article.

7. *United States v Yazell*, Vol. 382, *U.S. Supreme Court Reports* (1965), pp. 341, 343.

8. *Mattielo v Connecticut*, Vol. 225, *Atlantic Reporter Second Series* (1968), p. 507, held the statute not subject to constitutional attack for vagueness in use of the words "vice and vicious." See also *Mattielo v Connecticut*, Vol. 395, *U.S. Supreme Court Reports* (1969), p. 209, in which the Court dismissed the appeal for want of a properly presented federal question.

9. In New York City Criminal Court, one could observe that Black and white policemen arrested Black prostitutes, whereas only white policemen arrested white prostitutes.

10. Judge Amos Basel, *The New York Times*, January 27, 1969, p. 1.

11. For a good economic analysis, see Margaret Benston, "The Political Economy of Women's Liberation," *Monthly Review*, September 1969.

12. Arizona, California, Idaho, Louisiana, Nevada, New Mexico, Texas and Washington.

13. Alabama, Florida, Indiana, North Carolina and Pennsylvania.

14. Homer Clark, *The Law of Domestic Relations in the United States*. Minnesota: West Publishing Company, 1968, p. 227.

15. Ibid.

16. *Muller v Oregon*, Vol. 208, *U.S. Supreme Court Reports* (1908), p. 412. See also the statement of Lt. William Calley, testifying in his trial about an alleged massacre of North Vietnamese civilians: "Men and women are equally dangerous. Because of the unsuspectability of children, they are even more dangerous. Most women are better shots than men are— they fight equally the same. Children can be used as warning signals." *Boston Globe*, February 23, 1971, p. 13.

17. Title 42, *United States Code Annotated*, Section 2000 et seq.

18. See *Rosenfeld v Southern Pacific Co.*, Vol. 293, *Federal Supplements*, Central District of California (1969), p. 1219, in which the California maximum weight-lifting law for women was held unconstitutional. See also *Weeks v Southern Bell Tel. and Tel. Co.*, Vol. 408, *Federal Reporter Second Series*, U.S. Court of Appeals Fifth Circuit (1969), p. 228, in which Title VII was interpreted as rejecting the supposition that women could not safely work late at night.

19. See *Ward v Littrell*, Vol. 292, *Federal Supplements*, Eastern District of Louisiana (1968), p. 165, in which the court justified upholding such legislation on the grounds that not all women would want to lose the protection.

20. *Gossaert v Cleary*, Vol. 335, *U.S. Supreme Court Reports* (1948), p. 464. A New Jersey lower court recently held otherwise, however.

21. For a discussion of the circularity of oppression, see Florynce Kennedy, "Institutionalized Oppression vs. The Female," *Sisterhood is Powerful,* ed. Robin Morgan, Random House, 1970, p. 438. See also Erwin Knoll and Julius Heis McFadden, eds., *War Crimes and the American Conscience.* New York: Holt, Rinehart and Winston, 1970, p. 122: "When American people were asked what they would have done if they had been the U.S. soldiers at My Lai, 74 percent of the women surveyed said they would have refused to follow orders, but only 21 percent of the men would have refused." (Cited in the *Red Pamphlet* of December 20, 1970, to commemorate the tenth anniversary of the founding of the NLF [National Liberation Front], by the Committee of Women to Defend the Right to Live.)

22. *People v Belous,* Vol. 458, *Pacific Reporter Second Series,* California Supreme Court (1969), p. 194.

23. See Diane Schulder and Florynce Kennedy, "Black Genocide," *Abortion Rap.* New York: McGraw-Hill, 1971.

Lawyers for the Poor Can't Win

by Robert Lefcourt

"A power over a man's subsistence amounts to a power over his will."
ALEXANDER HAMILTON, *The Federalist.*

An attorney for the underclasses rarely escapes his pre-scribed role, which is *not* the constitutional obligation to serve the indigent. In a legal system which arrests and convicts underclass individuals more often than the crim-inals of the higher classes, and which effectively prevents most challenges to this legal oppression, the defense law-yer performs an administrative rather than an adversary role. He protects the class interest of the court structure by adhering to his assigned role. He may want to protect the accused, but his actual role, stated harshly, is to give the final twist of the knife to a person whose guilt is predeter-mined by his class and race.

The legal system creates the class role of the lawyer through its own civil and criminal structures. In criminal defense, the two primary forms of legal assistance to indi-gents are the assigned counsel and the public defender systems, both inherently oppressive in their relationships to the poor and near-poor. In civil law, a brief analysis of the so-called "neighborhood legal services" exposes the contradictions in this new form of legal assistance. Com-mon characteristics of almost all legal assistance programs include legal professionalism, intimate relationships among primary court officials, government financing, and the institutionalization of legal services. These similarities indicate the substantial degree of control which the legal system maintains over the disenfranchised.

Even though legal assistance has obvious benefits for the underclasses, such assistance will never equal the resources and influence of the wealthy; the poor cannot compete against the rich. The contest in a criminal case is really between the state (court apparatus) and the citizen. The middle and upper classes have some capacity to protect themselves, but the indigent have none.

One of the great advocates of legal aid for the poor in the first half of the twentieth century, Reginald Heber Smith, had high hopes that the legal profession would provide full assistance to the indigent. He had two propositions for the potential success of legal aid programs.

> The first proposition—which is far more important than the American people yet realize and which indeed is axiomatic—is that an independent bar is just as essential to the preservation of freedom as an independent judiciary or the Bill of Rights in our federal and state constitutions. . . . The second proposition is that there is the ever-present danger that a grant of governmental money will be followed by governmental control. To put it succinctly, if the government becomes the lawyer's paymaster, it may soon become his master.[1]

Smith argued that if legal aid programs were independently set up by the legal profession, the government would be prevented from being a party to the defense. The state is a party in all criminal cases anyway, because the prosecutor is paid from public funds. When lawyers for the poor are also paid from public funds, the indigent defendant cannot get the resolute representation required under any concept of "fairness." Yet Mr. Smith would be more heartened by the 1963 Supreme Court decision which guaranteed a lawyer to every indigent charged with a felony than he would be dismayed by the present government-sponsored legal aid swamp. For he did say in 1951, as most people now would agree, that "Legal Aid Offices and Legal Service Offices conducted by the government are much better than nothing."

Nevertheless the poor have never had a source of legal defense independent of the existing legal and political institutions. The growth of legal professionalism, of a group consciousness among attorneys, has arisen from the increasing social utility of the legal profession since the beginning of the industrial revolution. The operating basis for the law's oppression of the working class and the poor has been the relationship of the government, the courts, and the legal profession. Although lawyers traditionally proclaim their "independence" from government or other outside influences, legal professionalism exposes the class interest of attorneys in relation to their indigent clients. This contradiction is best illustrated in the predominant and oldest method of defense assistance for the poor, assigned counsel.

In 1695 or earlier, assigned counsel was used in England and the colonies for those accused of treason. Early in the eighteenth century, the colonies began assigning attorneys to defendants involved in other serious crimes as well. That the government permitted legal defense of those accused of being enemies of the state set important precedents. It provided simple justice and it halted accusations of unfair treatment. It also protected the system, since the state chose the attorneys and set the guidelines for the growing legal profession. State regulation has continued to limit the scope of professional association and concern and has increased the gap between lawyers and indigent clients. The state exerts direct control in the licensing of lawyers, and indirect control in determining "ethical" criteria for practice. Such control limits the conventional lawyers' association's deliberations on public policy, and prevents private lawyers from becoming partisans in struggles for social change.

The "professional obligation" to defend the indigent is one of the traditional guidelines set by the legal profession. Under an assigned counsel system, lawyers in private practice are appointed by the court on a case-by-case basis to represent defendants who cannot afford to hire an attorney. Until 1910, this was the only method of legal defense for the poor. At present, assigned counsel systems are the most widespread form of legal assistance, serving 2,900 of 3,100 counties in 1966. Their simple operation illustrates the inherent abuses of those they ostensibly serve.

Police in a small Midwestern county arrest two dozen teenage suspects for car thefts, possession of marijuana, burglary, vagrancy, and prostitution. Some of the suspects cannot raise the bail required for their release and sit in jail perhaps a month or more. The judge, hand-picked by the local Republican leaders, finally requests that one of the county's criminal lawyers defend the group, none of whom has money to hire counsel. The judge and the lawyer are acquaintances, perhaps recent business associates. The attorney may accept the assignment because he takes pride in defending the indigent. Or perhaps, if the shortage of criminal lawyers is acute, the judge must promise business opportunities or political patronage.

Such intimacy between a defense lawyer and the court is a basic part of an assigned counsel system. A judge chooses the indigent's attorney; in most states the defendant has no choice of his own. One system, that of the Houston Legal Foundation, even has the assigned lawyer's performance evaluated at the termination of each case *by the judge and the prosecutor*. This information is then included in the defense attorney's record for consideration in future assignments.[2]

The Sixth Amendment guarantees the right to counsel. But doesn't this right lose its meaning when the state determines who that counsel should be? When the state picks lawyers for both sides, the result can surely be predicted. The fact is that the right to counsel should mean the right to choice of counsel. Unless this is so assigned counsel is a sham.

The assigned counsel system's failure to protect the

poor reflects the legal profession's position that the law is of limited use to the indigent. While the profession offers legal services to the upper classes for every conceivable reason—preventive research, preparing contracts, and insuring many other legal advantages—it generally assumes that the problems of the poor are basically nonlegal and essentially economic, social, or psychological in character. An assigned counsel system supports this belief since, by its nature, it is neither continuous nor preventive, but simply remedial. The poor get assigned lawyers only after arrests or after property has been repossessed. The upper classes have lawyers to look after their property rights, but the poor and working class have no lawyers to see to their economic needs—job, home, social security, unemployment compensation, public assistance, health insurance, transportation needs, education. Compared to the right of a landlord to evict a tenant, the struggles of welfare groups for the "right" to a decent living have no weight in the courts. The need for adequate public transportation or an educational system geared to community interests is not the concern of assigned counsel systems. They begin their work only when an alleged crime is committed, not when a general class interest is at stake.

Legal professionalism makes impossible any affirmative use of the law to protect the economic needs of the poor. Defense of the indigent is a secondary function of a lawyer's private practice. Ironically, advocates of an assigned counsel system claim that it enlarges the role of the private lawyer by permitting him to maintain his private practice while helping the indigent. Full-time public defenders, it is argued, are really "socialized" lawyers who lose their identity and their interest in a case because they are part of a bureaucracy. The private lawyer, on the other hand, who keeps his professional position intact and retains his economic independence and status, can give more time and effort to a client. Whatever the legitimacy of such an argument, it assumes that the indigent's legal needs can be filled out of a private lawyer's hip pocket.

The Houston Legal Foundation is an example of an assigned counsel system which keeps the lawyer's practice primary and the client's interest secondary. In 1965, at the insistence of a conservative bar association, the Texas legislature rejected a public defender system and instituted an assigned counsel system run by computers. Detailed professional data about each lawyer are programmed to insure that cases are equitably distributed—3,500 cases required 2,800 different attorneys in the first year, thus assuring that lawyers, qualified or not, would get good criminal experience from handling an indigent's defense. The computerized system, like almost every assigned counsel system, takes a minimum of two days after a suspected lawbreaker is arrested and incarcerated to find an attorney for the case. The Houston program may improve record-keeping and evaluation of attorneys, but it assures that the defense of the poor remains an extracurricular activity. The principle that an attorney who provides legal services should be reimbursed is the essence of legal professionalism. Like a doctor treating a man dying in the streets, the unpaid or low-paid lawyer for the poor is doing a good deed. As a general rule, no such lawyer can prepare a case as thoroughly as a lawyer who is paid or who has enough resources himself to invest in an adequate defense, and there is now a move to pay private attorneys for defense of the indigent.[3] But payment by the state to the assigned lawyer helps preserve the assigned counsel system and the class position of the private lawyer in the legal defense of the poor. When the state pays the fee, the legal profession, not the indigent, gets the most benefit. The gulf between the lawyer and his indigent client widens.

In 1919 Reginald Heber Smith wrote, "The administration of American justice is not impartial, the rich and poor do not stand on an equality before the law, traditional methods of providing justice have operated to close the doors of the courts to the poor." [4] His call, which was heard fifty years later, was to supplement the assigned counsel method with a public defender system. Among other points, he argued that an indigent defendant had to wait long periods in jail prior to trial until the court could find an attorney willing to handle the case. With public defenders, a salaried lawyer would be available at all times, in the court, for the specific purpose of defending those who could not afford to hire an attorney. The system would be most useful in large cities, where most arrests occur.

It has taken American law over one hundred years to *guarantee* organized legal assistance for the indigent. The United States Supreme Court in its 1963 *Gideon* decision gave all indigents in felony prosecutions (imprisonment for more than one year in most states) the right to counsel. In the *Miranda* decision of 1966, the Court extended this right to the period when the accused is first arrested, technically called in-custodial interrogation. The defendant's right to obtain counsel when accused of a misdemeanor (imprisonment usually less than one year) is still unresolved. Since it is estimated that over five million misdemeanors occur every year, millions of people accused of a crime are incarcerated without the guarantee of an attorney to defend them. Recently, the Supreme Court refused to take on the question of whether the right to counsel applies in misdemeanors. But even if the courts do grant every accused the right to counsel some day, as do a few states now, the class basis of lawyer-client relationships will remain unchanged. The courts' decisions, like the emergence of public defender systems, alter only the forms of law administration.

The extension and institutionalization of legal service is a fact. In 1963 thirty-three counties of over 400,000 population had no organized public defender system. In 1968 this figure had been reduced to fifteen. This proliferation of legal aid systems, such as the Minnesota Plan (1965) and the Detroit public defender offices (1968), means that for the first time a lawyer will be present for almost every defendant accused of a felony. Conservative bar associations may view free legal services as a threat to free enterprise. The real problem, however, is not conservative resistance. Nor is it, as many argue, lack of facilities or funds for more lawyers and judges. The problem is that the indigent are strapped to an oppressive legal superstructure. Most legal service agencies are controlled ideologically as well as financially by corporations, foundations and/or the government. The Ford Foundation from 1963 to 1965 granted over six million dollars "to support a program of experiments to improve the administration of criminal justice by strengthening defender and auxiliary services required for defense of the accused in criminal cases." [5] Poverty is defined by rules and regulations; lawyers are middlemen who sell legal services; the courts fulfill their part of the operation by incarcerating the indigent. The class and race basis of the legal system has been more firmly cemented, rather than weakened, by the growth of public defender systems.

Public defender systems fail, not because they are impersonal bureaucracies and not because they are severely underfinanced, but primarily because their programs are administrative: their purpose is to process the underclass through the courts on a mass basis. The assigned counsel system masks its class bias behind legal professionalism, but public defender systems make no pretenses: its lawyers are full-time advocates for the poor. Yet the ties between the public defenders and the court hierarchy are necessarily intimate, so that class conflict is reduced to an administrative process; the cooperative effort reveals the class and racial basis of legal aid paternalism.

There are three types of defender systems—public, private, and a combination of public and private. The public defender idea was first adopted in Oklahoma in 1911. Under this plan financial support comes from the city, county, or the state. A public defender system is an integral part of the judicial machinery of the state. In private defender systems, funds to support an office come from voluntary sources, such as bar associations or individual contributors. Because of the fund-raising difficulties, it is the least successful type of operation. Many bar associations consider a combination private and public office to be an ideal solution, especially if most of the financing is private. This is just the image which the Legal Aid Society in New York, founded in 1876 and the model for many of the more recent defender programs, has projected. Unfortunately, the image has little to do with the reality.

In 1970 the Society employed about 330 full-time, salaried lawyers. In addition, it receives legal assistance from volunteer attorneys and law student clerks. Its twenty-five offices are all supported by the city, state, and federal governments. The Legal Aid Society claims to be an "independent organization" that supports "the court reform and legislative changes necessary for the attainment of . . . Equal Justice for All." The reality is that Legal Aid is as much a part of the court system as the government which prosecutes. Financially, nearly eighty percent of its support comes from the government. In 1969 New York City allocated $2,225,000, New York State $468,000, and the federal government $745,000 of a total income of $4,495,000.[6] In 1969 the head of the Criminal Division of Legal Aid was appointed to a judgeship, casting doubt on the Society's political independence as well. The Society permits fewer than two hundred lawyers to handle over 13,000 criminal cases a month, at a cost of $18 per case, thereby accepting an intolerable situation for its clients. Of course the aim of the organization is to push for more attorneys, more judges, more money, and better facilities. But its day-to-day program operates to speed the judicial process along as fast as possible. Inadequate representation for the poor cannot be blamed on the Society, but the Society is ultimately doing what it can to help the overall court system in its present form.

The policy of cooperation with the courts rather than commitment to the clients illuminates the character of both policy-makers and the policy-making process. The Legal Aid Society is run by a self-perpetuating absentee Board of Directors which decides policy. The board consists of about forty-six members—three Black, one Spanish, and four women. The majority of board members belong to the most prominent law firms in the country, firms which represent some of the largest corporations and financial institutions in the world. The board's policies perpetuate some of the most barbaric court practices and detention prisons in the country. Two such policies not only make a mockery of the lawyer's role but are in absolute violation of New York state law: the Legal Aid Society accepts the jailing of over 6,500 accused suspects because they do not have $500 to $1,000 bail to be released on their own recognizance, otherwise known as preventive detention; and the Society permits over 6,000 persons per year to sit in jail an average of more than three months awaiting disposition of their cases. Many inmates must wait almost a year on a charge that brings a thirty- to ninety-day sentence.[7] The increased caseload of the courts is used an an excuse for maintaining policies which primarily affect the lower classes and nonwhite populations.

Subtle racism and class interests are apparent not only among the predominantly wealthy, white, and influential Legal Aid Board of Directors, but in the structure of the Legal Aid program. If ninety-seven percent of Legal Aid lawyers are white and well-educated, probably more than seventy-five percent of their clients are nonwhite and uneducated. (The exact racial breakdown of clients is barred from publication.) Aside from a federal grant in 1967 to operate several additional Civil Branch offices, the Society has made little effort to relate its Criminal Branch to the Black and Puerto Rican communities. It has made only token gestures in the recruitment of women and nonwhite attorneys and in their appointments to high administrative positions and to the Board of Directors.

A Legal Aid attorney should be able to claim that his main interest is his client. But Legal Aid lawyers or public defenders are in a contradictory position. As employees in a legal aid program, their job is to defend the indigent. As employees, their first concerns are their jobs, working conditions, and salaries, all of which are valid interests. In their relations with the public, including even their clients, they serve the interests of those who run the organization, who in turn cooperate with the interests of the government, the primary financial supporter. In practice, the defense lawyers often complain about working conditions which hamper their effectiveness with clients. One of these problems is that lawyers must hold interviews with defendants standing in detention hallways surrounded by guards and other prisoners, or before the judge in hurried whispers. The result is overly hasty legal judgments. The concerned lawyers who object to such conditions have had no remedy for their complaints.

In June 1968 one of the staff attorneys, Gerald Lefcourt, was fired. He had been organizing an Association of Legal Aid Attorneys, a lawyers' union which could present collective demands for improved working conditions, and new approaches to defending the poor. When Legal Aid dismissed him, it avoided the organizing question. Instead it claimed that Lefcourt had accused Legal Aid of "pleading too many defendants guilty without studying the merits of each case and that Legal Aid was helping to foment the Black revolution because of its policies and treatment of Black people." Almost two years later, the lawyers' association did rebel against the treatment accorded their clients. They refused to handle any case until conditions changed. Although the lawyers did not directly attack the policy-making mechanism, and their strike lasted only a few days, they had given the Society warning for the future.

Coincidentally, one week after the strike, a federal judge dismissed Lefcourt's two-year-old lawsuit, concluding that the firing was lawful. The judge did say, however, that the problems raised by the suit concerning the operation of the Legal Aid Society are "real and acute, and no solution will be found short of massive efforts on the part of all concerned with the administration of criminal justice. . . ." [8]

Although not all legal aid or public defender offices are as averse to change as the New York organization, the Legal Aid Society is representative in that it derives its income from the courts and the government, and exhibits internal and external class-based structures and discriminatory relations with nonwhite communities. Legal assistance programs have never tuned in to the needs of poor communities. Lawyers have never dealt with the everyday legal problems of the unpropertied classes. People with serious problems have had nowhere to turn unless they had sufficient income to hire an attorney. So when, in the early sixties, government antipoverty programs developed programs designed to "keep the ghetto cool," the concept of neighborhood legal services was, not surprisingly, a part of the plan.

> By giving the poor ready access to lawyers when needed, a sense of respect for law . . . would begin to replace a general cynicism in the low income communities where legal institutions and processes seem alien and hostile.[9]

Respect for law and order was to grow by the "maximum feasible participation of the poor" in their own communities. With the passage of the Economic Opportunity Act and the Criminal Justice Act of 1964, federal financing became available. By the end of the decade, over 2,000 so-called poverty lawyers were employed in the government's Legal Services Program, the largest law firm in the world.

Neighborhood legal services were merely an offshoot of the public defender system designed to handle civil rather than criminal cases. Federal moneys were promised to poor communities with the guarantee that local residents would control policies and programs. These promises were never kept, government remained the boss, the lawyers were still the employees, leaving little hope of aggressive legal assault against oppressive conditions. Nevertheless, the response in poor neighborhoods to the establishment of local law offices surprised the legal profession and the government. Thousands of people demanded to know their rights in a multitude of areas; groups as well as individuals requested representation in legal actions. Affirmative legal strategy for law reform began to have some impact.

The lawyers help local residents to challenge the eviction of tenants who report housing code violations, support rent strikes, encourage welfare groups demanding more income, contest residency requirements for public assistance, initiate Supreme Court cases to grant more rights to welfare recipients, fight for increased public services, organize migrant worker groups, and establish community organizations such as tenant unions, cooperative food or housing associations, day-care centers, and school parents' groups. The poverty lawyers and their clients sometimes confront the institutions which have created impoverished neighborhoods: departments of welfare or housing, boards of education, the business community, or the state itself. In New York City, a legal services unit exposed the "sewer service" fraud in which poor persons were made the subjects of default judgments in court actions without ever having been served with a summons or other process notifying them of the court action. For the first time in many cities throughout the nation, pressures from local community groups and their lawyers were felt by unscrupulous landlords, finance companies charging excessive rates for installment purchases, school systems arbitrarily suspending students, and state governments cutting health service payments to the aged and poor. Lawyers were fired and their programs threatened with curtailment in 1969 and 1970 when they began to defend dissident groups such as the Black Panther Party in Louisiana, the Navajo Indians in Arizona and New Mexico, and migrant workers in California and Florida.

Legal challenges against institutions, however, have not resulted in substantial changes in the individual lives of the oppressed nor in their neighborhoods. Neighborhood legal offices develop programs more as a "service" to the community than as a catalyst for confrontation. Service programs are the least threatening to large institutions or the government, since they are based on a traditional legal approach in which lawyers work with poor people on a case-by-case basis. Hundreds of troubled human beings pour into a poverty office daily with relatively routine legal problems, all of which demand enormous time commitments. It is estimated that "as much as five times as much time and effort is necessary to provide the same adequate professional representation and degree of benefits to a poor person as to a middle-class client." [10] The number of lawyers needed for such programs will probably never be found. Almost none of the nationwide programs has sufficient staff to carry through the day-to-day caseload, let alone to enlarge the services by providing adequate legal services. The whole neighborhood concept involves a choice between trying to ease the massive individual injustices on a case-by-case basis, and trying to benefit as many people as possible through selective legal and political challenges against oppressive institutions. These efforts are further complicated by a conservative legal profession working cooperatively with the federal government. The hesitancy among many attorneys stems from the federal restrictions in the laws which established the legal units. But initially resistance to legal services came from lawyers who believed that their businesses would suffer and from existing legal assistance programs which operated under the leadership and control of bar associations.

The legal profession itself restricts action by enforcement of its own conservative Canons of Ethics. For example, three of the Canons refer to how far a lawyer may go in supporting a client's cause (Canon 15), the use of indirect or direct advertising (Canon 27), and the attempt to stir up litigation, directly or through agents (Canon 28). Canon 15 means that a lawyer must never assert in argument his personal belief in his client's innocence or in the justice of his cause. The lawyer must be "neutral" even though the law that caused his client harm was not. The rule against advertising is meant to free clients from pressure in the choice of a lawyer. This Canon is violated on a mass scale because of its impracticality. For many people the choice is not between one competing lawyer and another, but between the poverty lawyer, who may be advertised on a flyer, or no lawyer at all. A lawyer may "stir up litigation," violating Canon 28, if he tries to expand an individual's legal problem into a test case involving a group, without the consent of the particular individual. The real danger, in the eyes of the bar association, however, is that the attorney may challenge an institution that has some say about the continuation of the program's existence and find that Canon 28 is thrown at him by the institution under attack. The more independent and aggressive the neighborhood office, and the more dedicated it is to bringing about institutional changes, the more likely it is to alienate those very interests it needs to survive.

The restrictions on lawyers who defend the poor, whether as assigned counsel, legal aid, or neighborhood attorney, cannot be attributed merely to limitations in the type of legal assistance program. The Canons of Ethics affect assigned counsel programs as much as the neighborhood legal offices. The ties between the courts and the attorney are found in almost all government-sponsored legal programs. Legal defense systems differ in their structures, programs, and historical development, but they do not differ in the way they treat the lower classes and nonwhite population. Embedded in the ideology of any program is the class relationship between lawyers for the poor and their clients, almost all of whom are oppressed by the social, economic, and political system of capitalism.[11]

The fact is that almost all legal assistance programs camouflage their ideology by restricting their purposes. Means are promulgated as ends in the simple statement of aims, "to provide legal services for the poor." Programs differ only in how this "goal" can be achieved. The belief that sufficient funds for legal services would considerably alter the economic status of the poor ignores the harsh reality that legal assistance cannot change the existing social, economic, and political relationships. Rather, the struggle for change in legal services must be part of a strategy toward the liberation of oppressed people, not toward a mythical legal equality. For this reason, a number of programs stretch the interpretation of the ambiguous aim, "providing legal services for the poor." Some see legal aid programs, for example, as a means to unite a poor community against a particular target. In the early sixties,

New York City's Mobilization for Youth Legal Services
Unit helped organize tenant groups on the Lower East
Side to confront housing authorities and real estate interests over housing conditions. The combined community
and legal struggles, as in rent strikes, did not transform
the area into a housing paradise, but they did help to create community involvement in a class struggle against oppressive housing conditions and profiteering landlords.
There are many target areas for a people's legal services
program: schools, welfare, transportation, and housing
are just a few. Such a program must entail commitment
to a raped community's needs and give legal support to
political groups engaged in struggle. A real commitment
to the people's struggles involves understanding that the
scope of all legal assistance programs is limited by the
class and racist bias of the legal system. The people are all
too familiar with Establishment programs which promise
more changes in economic and social relationships than is
possible under their guidelines. If lawyers continue to play
the law game by the rules of the standard assigned counsel, legal aid, or neighborhood legal programs, they will
further separate themselves from the people they serve.
Only if lawyers seek their guidelines among the people
and in the conditions which need transforming can they
rightfully become part of the struggle for liberation.

Notes

1. Reginald Heber Smith, "Introduction" to Emery A. Brownell,
   Legal Aid in the United States. Rochester, New York: Lawyers
   Cooperative Publishing Co., 1951, p. vi.
2. See Lee Silverstein, *Defense of the Poor: The National Report.*
   Chicago: American Bar Foundation, 1965, 3 vols., for information concerning the high percentages of incarceration under
   assigned counsel systems.
3. Robert S. Hunter, "Slave Labor in the Courts—A Suggested
   Solution," *Case and Comment,* July-August, 1969, pp. 3–14.
   Hunter presents an argument for more fees for attorneys
   defending the indigent. The article also shows the state-by-
   state breakdown of attorney compensation.

4. Reginald H. Smith, *Justice and the Poor*. New York: Scribner's, 1919, p. 8.
5. John J. Cleary, "National Defender Project: A Progress Report," Vol. 26, no. 3, *The Legal Aid Briefcase*, February 1968.
6. *The Legal Aid Society 1969*, 94th Annual Report.
7. See Jack Newfield, "New Ideas for Old Jails," *The Village Voice*, February 4, 1971, p. 1, for some typical reform proposals which an activist Legal Aid Society would obviate.
8. *Lefcourt v Legal Aid Society, et al.*, Vol. 312, *Federal Supplement* (Southern District of New York, 1970), p. 1115.
9. *Neighborhood Legal Services—New Dimensions in the Law.* Washington, D.C.: U.S. Department of Health, Education and Welfare, 1966, p. 4.
10. Carol Ruth Silber, "The Imminent Failure of Legal Services for the Poor: Why and How to Limit Caseload," *Journal of Urban Law*, Vol. 42 (1968), p. 217.
11. Jerome Carlin and Jan Howard, "Legal Representation and Class Justice," *UCLA Law Review*, January 1965, discusses class characteristics among attorneys.

The Civilliberties Lie

*by Michael J. Kennedy**

Let's not allow phony subtleties to hide simple truths. I'm human first, an anarchist second, and a lawyer last. The first came about through chance. The second through choice. And the last through chicanery. Civilliberties is the concern of almost any humanist; the denial of their equal application incites the anger of anarchists; the historical function of civillibertarians to promote the civilliberties myth can no longer be ignored by practicing lawyers. Let's roll out the law's lie for all to see and to smash.

As an attorney of some years practice, I know the law is replete with myths. As a matter of fact, law practice is a methodology of myths. Among the most popular myths of the law are those that tell us that the Bill of Rights, as the highest embodiment of legal principles, applies to all the people. Civilliberties is championed as the essence of the people's rights over all others. It is one of the darlings of the liberal rich. It is the raison d'être of such paragovernmental entities as the American Civil Liberties Union, which fights for the rights of Communists on the Left, fascists on the Right, and the irrelevant right's issues of middle-of-the-road interest groups and individuals. The civilliberties lie can be exposed by an examination of reality; that, in fact, our political and economic system protects the rich, screws the poor, ignores the majority, and pretends to apply all laws equally to all people.

A basic ingredient of the myth of civilliberties is that the individual must accept the assumptions and rules of the American judicial system. One must not only believe the system will work in the sense of fulfilling individual civilliberties, but also believe that the assumptions, structures, and rules of the system are designed to vindicate individual civilliberties. One must further assume that there are lawyers and organizations available to assist in the enforcement and vindication of the particular rights. One must also assume the courts to be accessible. Additionally one must accept that the legal apparatus, through its judges, lawyers, and methods of jury selection, are fair and just; finally, that the government will act as the ultimate defender of all civilliberties. In this article we shall see that these assumptions are not only inaccurate, they are heinous, deluding, and cooptive.

To the overwhelming majority of people in this country, the reality of civilliberties is obvious. Most people have no access to the legal system; many who do have access don't use it because they know it won't work for them; the few who choose to confront the legal system's basic inequalities through extralegal or legal means get fucked by it.

Those who cannot afford to buy civilliberties through a lawyer-broker are denied their rights; the few who convince an ACLU-type organization to champion their cause as a "test case" and win, rarely, if ever, change existing relationships. Those who can afford to retain counsel and buy "justice" earn their right to quasi-civilliberties. The civilliberties championed is quasi at best because the lawyers involved, paid or not, are really only trying to make the system work in the usual ways—by following the rules of a fixed game and soaking in the profits, in the form of prestige or money.

Finally, we will argue that, given the nature of the system, the key role available to the people's lawyers is not only to expose the lie, but to heighten the contradictions within the economic and political system—in a phrase, to hoist the system with its own petard. In addition, what is needed is the clarification and enforcement of human rights. Not just through resistance, but through affirmative action.

It may help to define civilliberties. We can begin by noting what it is not. Civilliberties embodies neither civility nor freedom. It is not pretty, nice-smelling, or very tasty, although most desire it. Those lawyers who deal with it in earnest for very long are frequently identifiable by their sweet, sick smell of success. It does not cure social or economic ills, although we are told that it does. As a matter of fact, in spite of the screen of hope it casts, it is neither important nor relevant, although we are brainwashed otherwise. A purist definition of civilliberties is that glorious condition wherein everyone leaves everyone else alone. What the civillibertarians are really talking about is that condition wherein some select people condescend to allow other select people to leave some people alone some of the time. Or as civillibertarians paraphrase Voltaire: "I'll defend to the death your right to say anything I agree with." What civilliberties should mean is the human right of the people to govern their government and throw it the hell out if it refuses to be governed.

An historical glimpse at civilliberties may be illuminating. The Declaration of Independence is the most revolutionary American historical document. Unfortunately, between the time of the writing of the Declaration and the drafting of the Bill of Rights, the rebels became the Establishment. The last word on civilliberties, American style, is the Bill of Rights. The authors were eminently qualified to be civillibertarians—they included in their ranks slaveholders, aristocratic landowners, merchants, and pirates. They wrote the Constitution for themselves and their peers, little thinking that the words might be taken literally. The Bill of Rights—though initially felt to be unnecessary by such gentlemen as the Tory leader Alex Hamilton—was added to protect their class from the intrusions of rabble such as Tom Jefferson wanted to protect.

The people won a victory which history declared useless: the government was prohibited from passing any laws that would interfere with what the Constitution framers considered to be the people's freedom of speech, press, religion, or assembly. Freedom from unreasonable searches and seizures and from the denial of liberty without due process of law were also called for. Further, the people were given the right, theoretically unfettered by government, to petition the elected officials for redress of grievances. It is this right to petition that we will explore, because if the Bill of Rights has any significance today, it is in its concomitant, the right to throw the government out if it does not provide redress.

Now all of these rights and liberties read very well in the abstract. The problem is that the government—through a conspiracy of the executive, judicial, and legislative branches—defines what these rights and liberties mean and when they should be enforced. To no one's surprise, least of all the civillibertarians, the government's definitions are self-serving and designed to further aggrandize the government's power position by preventing any threatening form of antigovernment activity. Hence, freedom of speech means the freedom to say anything one wishes so long as it is sufficiently inane as to be inoffensive to the government. Freedom of press is the liberty to write anything at all provided it is not overly critical of the government. Freedom of assembly protects sewing bees, Girl Scout picnics, and American Legion parades, but does not protect a gathering of dissidents bent on necessary social change. Freedom of religion has meant the protection of those religions which best served capitalist interests. Outrageous conclusions? Tell that to the massacred Indians, the Black slaves, the abolitionists who fought for the end to racial inequality, the people opposed to the Spanish-American War, the immigrants at the turn of the century, the pacifists in both World Wars, the workers who fought the early union battles, the religious advocates who tried self-education instead of state education or who viewed the family unit as harmful to the best interests of the larger community, the Communists and liberals during the McCarthy period, and the Black and white radicals in the present era of civilliberties non-enforcement.

Presumptively, however, one is allowed to worship and defend the government with impunity. The gravamen of these ramblings is, then, that as long as the government decides when to enforce and how to define civilliberties, the enforcement and definitions will be decidedly progovernment and antipeople. Which is to say that civilliberties means governmentrights. From this notion, it follows that civillibertarians are protectors of governmentrights.

Lest we get hung up on Social Democratic rhetoric, let us lay a few questions to rest. Who is to determine what constitutes a grievance? Who is to determine what constitutes appropriate redress? Who is to enforce the redress and prevent reoccurrence? The answer is them or us. The government or the people. When the government is the aggrievor, the government is totally unfit to make any determinations. As we have seen, the government will halt, control, or fault anyone and everyone but itself. It even insists that its three branches still have internal checks and balances which prevent an imbalance of power in one branch. Factually, it has become a monolith of self-perpetuating bureaucrats. The executive branch harbors the most conspicuous aggrievors, especially the free-wheeling power of the President. The judicial branch, appointed and controlled by the executive, affirms the power of people's rights only in rare historical moments. The legislative branch, once the people's voice, has defaulted to the executive, and is completely incapable of making any but progovernment self-preserving decisions. These three parts equal the (w)hole that is government. The government may be fit to govern bureaucracies, but it is clearly unfit to govern people.

Now that we know where civilliberties is at and who the civillibertarians are and work for, let's see where it ought to be. What this country needs is a good propeople, antigovernment conspiracy to redefine, protect, and enforce people or human rights.

How? We can steal a phrase from the government's Bill

of Rights. The people have the right to petition the government for redress of human grievances. What are the people to do if the government doesn't hear or refuses to listen? Kick the government the hell out, what else? Let us begin by first honing up the kicking leg and next enlarging the boot. Then we get the government to bend over a bit. The rest is simple coordination.

The people's kicking leg is somewhat weak and out of shape. This is due in part to a human addiction to governmental paternalism and the promises of similar political parties. We suck up all the patriotic pap and placebos each party feeds us. The people should reject out of hand the illegitimate authority of unresponsive government by beginning to exercise their legs. This exercise will strengthen the natural, incontestable human right of the people to control their government and not vice versa. The boot is the fundamental human power to compel the government to redress grievances. The kick will be the reflex action of an angry, coordinated, and exercised people. The decision to kick is the people's, like it or not, want it or not.

Who are the people? They are not the government. They are as hard to find as the middle class, working class, or "silent majority." Like "society," the people probably don't exist. In a search for the people, one can only come up with individuals, no two of whom are alike in all particulars. Thus, each individual in a mutual interest with other individuals must decide what is a grievance and what is its appropriate redress.

Inasmuch as most individual rights are abridged by government, either directly or indirectly, those situations in which people claim rights to have been abridged by others' exercise of rights are not crucial to this discussion, nor are they a source of much dilemma. Most crucial situations involve human rights versus property rights. Clearly, the human should prevail over the property. Where one is faced with conflicting human rights, the natural priorities of time, numbers, merit, and competition will resolve the conflict. The people should avoid submitting the conflict to government for resolution, for government will only fuck it up! That is as it should be. As it is, government has more power than an individual, and being antithetical to people, government uses its power to put down the people and build up government. This is where the boot comes in.

If one or more individuals determine that they are aggrieved by government, they should "inform" the government of the grievance and specify the redress (e.g., get the hell out of the war in Southeast Asia). This is the demand/request stage of the enforcement of civilliberties. It should be noted again that only the rich and/or organized even bother with this step. If government does not respond, it may be because government did not hear, or hearing, did not understand. In which case, the petition should be sharper, closer, and simpler (e.g., file suit to get the government the hell out of Vietnam, petition Congressmen, etc.). Again, a "right" reserved to the rich and elite. If the government still fails to respond, the aggrievees have no choice but to take on directly the government's illegitimate authority (e.g., refuse military induction; if inducted, refuse to serve; counsel, support, and incite others to do likewise). This step involves negative or passive attacks on the government and its illegitimate laws. At this step we lose most, if not all, of our "civillibertarians." Also at this step we can count on a government response: repression and intimidation. The government has not only refused to redress grievances, but also compounded the grievances by trying to repress the aggrievees. The lines are drawn; the issues between the goverment and the people are clearer. The options available to the aggrievees are: cave in or fight on. If the people cave in, the penultimate goal of government is achieved: fascism! So the people, in an effort to remain human, have no choice but to fight on.

The level of petition must now include affirmative, positive, and active attacks on government and its exercise of illegitimate authority (e.g., through massive student, servicemen's, and poor people's strikes; through the seizure and/or destruction of the government property used to aggrieve: draft records and draft buildings, ROTC, and other military structures). At this level we lose the few remaining "civillibertarians" and all others who consider "property" an inviolable human right. This is essentially the level which the antiwar movement reached after the U.S. invasion of the countries surrounding Vietnam in 1970.

It is not enough to say—as no civillibertarians will say —that these activities are constitutionally protected human rights. It is necessary to note that these antigovernment activities are made necessary by the government's conduct and are absolutely essential if people are to survive government. To assuage the shock, if any there be, one need only look to the forces of the antagonists. The people are not killing anyone. The government is murdering people here and in Southeast Asia. The people are not jailing anyone. The government's jails are so filled with aggrievees (i.e., political prisoners) that the government is forced to refurbish its concentration camps. The people are not conspiring to suppress the people. There may be individuals who are robbing, beating, cheating, and lying to the government. These are coveted pastimes of individuals traditionally contemptuous of government authority. What the people are doing is threatening to take away, and/or destroy, if necessary, the government's property. That is, the government's arms, buildings, and bullshit papers. Presently it is mostly threat. But if government does not respond to this threat, the people will be compelled to carry it out. And those who dare to place property rights above human rights—as does the government of the United States of America—will justifiably lose the most. It is this threat that will help cause government to bend over. Being aggressive and repressive by nature, the government will expose its ass by coming down harder and harder on the resisters.

Thus, if the human right to petition for the redress of grievances in the First Amendment has any meaning, it is its recognition of the most fundamental human right of the people to dismember and overthrow an inhuman, unresponsive government.

Even Lincoln caught this historical imperative. In his inauguration address of March 4, 1861, Honest Abe came on honest for once with:

> This country, with its institutions, belongs to the people who inhabit it. Whenever they shall grow weary of the existing government, they can exercise their constitutional right of amending it, or their revolutionary right to dismember, or overthrow it.

Well, the people do grow weary. And if this government continues its crimes against Humanity, Humanity is, by God, going to burn it down.

So the human leg is exercised, the boot is honed, and the government's ass is bared.

Kick on, People! Kick on!

What does all this rhetoric mean to lawyers? Simple. We must decide whether we are going to join the kickers (revolutionaries), the kickees (government and paragovernment), or stay in the middle and be kicked from both sides.

Being a lawyer for the kickees essentially means working for the ruling class, be it in Wall Street or in the Justice Department. People's lawyers have no business here unless it is to infiltrate and destroy from within or to steal money and power and to vest them with the poor and powerless.

In the middle, being kicked, is where most of us lawyers are at. Trying to make the system work, rather than trying to change it and ourselves. Legal reform, rather than legal revolution! Getting caught in our contradictions rather than hitting the courts with theirs. Being an "officer of the court" and a criminal defense or matrimonial lawyer simultaneously—and doing both half-assed. Making money instead of giving it back to the people's struggles. Lauding the system when we win and apologizing for it when we lose. Allowing the law schools to teach us creditors' rights instead of debtors' rights, landlord law instead of tenant law, insurer's law rather than insured's law, producer's rights rather than consumer's rights, constitutional law from the standpoint of the government rather than the governed, permitting a marriage to precedent rather than to progress.

In the middle we lend credence to the legal system. Rather than stay in the middle, we should either drop out and grow sweet peas or turn left and fight.

Working with the kickers is practicing "legal insurgency," collectivized law, and politics. It means less defensive and more affirmative attacks—prosecuting government, cops, big business, polluters, landlords—wherever we find them slipping. It means that fighting in (and against) the courts is more important than winning or losing. Neither the win (the system works!) nor the loss (the system sucks!) can change the system as much as the fight. It has more to do with who the real criminals are and the whys of so-called antisocial, criminal behavior than it has to do with plea copping and making an extra buck. It means unswerving allegiance to a political client first and being an officer of the court last, if ever. It means helping to structure a public forum for a client's antigovernment goals. It means training people to represent themselves. It means giving freely of one's time and talents to the movements of the poor, nonwhite, and powerless. It means taking (making) the courtroom into the streets and the streets into the courtroom. It means understanding that imperialist wars keep the system thriving, pointing out who the warmakers are, and thus demonstrating that our clients are not just political prisoners, they are prisoners of war. It means exploiting the contradictions of the system and heightening them until the courts are forced to vindicate human rights, expose their hackish fascism or be hoisted with their own petard.

So kick, brothers and sisters! Hoist, revolutionary lawyers!

Law, the Breakdown of
Order, and Revolution

by Stanley Aronowitz*

Repressive violence is no longer an occasional tool employed by the state to quell political dissenters. It has become a pervasive and a routine feature of bourgeois rule. Its deployment is so widespread, the number of persons murdered, in jail, or awaiting imprisonment as a result of political and social acts deemed dangerous to the prevailing system of power is so large that the time has come for reassessing its significance.

Of course, political and social repression is rooted in the institutions of capitalism. Repression has always been a weapon used by the ruling class to protect its property or to reinforce the legal system. But the contemporary situation suggests that, far from being just another weapon in the arsenal of class rule, repression is fast becoming the central adhesive for disintegrating political and social institutions. For the victims of state repression and others concerned with the preservation of traditional liberties, there has been a qualitative shift in the modes of rule, lending legitimacy to talk of a fascist or "authoritarian" country.

The use of violence as a mode of rule is a sign of profound weakness. Otherwise the mediations between consciousness and real social relations would remain effective. But it is precisely the inability of ideologies and institutions to disguise corporate control over all property and resources which has required the large-scale deployment of armies, police, and the courts to thwart popular movements contesting the prevailing organs of power.

This is not to claim that the revolutionary project has gripped the consciousness of large sections of the underlying population. On the contrary. Yet even though the struggle remains within the institutions and has not succeeded in transcending their limits, the feebleness and disfunctionality of all the primary social institutions are such that even attempts merely to wrest concessions threaten the fabric of social life.

The notion that advanced capitalist societies, owing to their surfeit of resources and technological capacities, can coopt any demand for sectoral reform seems to be losing its force in a period when the fiscal crises afflicting major social welfare and educational institutions have created severe limits to the options available to bureaucracies. It is important not to overstate the case. It is still true that any individual challenge to a particular institution can be granted if the pressure mounted is sufficient to offset the political deficits of denying another sector. But massive concessions seem no longer possible. A general challenge to the resources of institutions is no more likely to be met with substantial concessions than a challenge to their juridical and moral legitimacy. We are experiencing the merger of these challenges; that is, the distinction between the struggle for more resources and the struggle for power within institutions is disappearing.

The rise of repression in America cannot be separated from the disintegration of the institutions of daily life. The breakdown has reached crisis proportions, the most significant of which is the ideological crisis, the demystification of morals, values and norms. Ideology is more than a series of rationales for legitimating existing property and power relations. It is not merely false consciousness. To the extent that ideology is transformed into social and personal conduct, to the extent that ideas such as laws, having been produced by underlying social relations, become guides to practical action, they become part of social reality. The ideological crisis undermines the capacity of institutions to perform their assigned roles. Moreover, the tenuous state of ideological apparatuses has produced a void for the ruling class. Repression in its ideological cloak, law and order, has attempted to fill that void. This is the basis of the rise of authoritarian modes of rule in our society.

The law is but one moment of the codes of conduct governing social intercourse. More generally, it is part of the social norms which arise from the divisions within society —the division between public and private, rulers and the ruled, ownership and nonownership of property. Insofar as social divisions exist, the law serves as a regulator of social and economic relations. The mutual contract, including the labor and marriage contract, is the formal expression of the division of labor and provides a universal code to guide various transactions within the system of production and exchange. The rule of law insures social order, the smooth operation of all social institutions resting on class divisions. Its effectiveness presupposes its legitimacy in consciousness.

Law must retain its independence of the interests of any sector of the capitalist class if it is to remain the final arbiter of all social conflict. The universality of laws derives from the laws' alienation from real production relations and their autonomous form. As one of the most important ideological apparatuses of the state, law appears as an independent force standing above all institutions and the sphere of production and exchange. Its autonomy is the condition of its permeation into all social spheres.

The hidden hand of law is embodied in moral codes, administrative rules, and institutional values. More than laws which are mandated by the state, these norms constitute the ideological underpinnings of all social relations. Children are socialized to specific standards of conduct, systems of moral behavior, and respect for hierarchical authority through the family and the school. Although the legal institutions of the state provide public sanctions for the institutions of civil society which govern everyday life, no system of law actually encompasses everyday behavior. Yet the institutions at the base of society, those dealing with family, education and work, impose norms which are consistent with those of more formal legality. The laws governing institutions, in short, are not confined to the ideological or state spheres. They operate as morals, rules, and values in the institutions of everyday life.

The challenges to the division between public and private, to the authority of the state and the institutions of civil society, and more profoundly, to the ideas which maintain the legitimacy of prevailing hierarchies within these institutions, have become the greatest threat to the viability of capitalist society. This does not mean that the hegemony of ruling class ideas and capitalist institutions will necessarily be challenged, even if the society experiences profound economic crisis. On the other hand, in the 1960s and early 1970s America underwent profound social crisis amid relative economic boom. The social crisis consists precisely in the challenge of sectors of the ruled classes to the legitimacy of social institutions, including the state. College students are challenging the power of school administrations to determine curriculum, the hiring and firing of teachers, and the use of facilities. High school students are refusing to observe even the elementary rules of decorum. Blacks particularly are demanding control over public education and a greater influence in determining the policies of colleges which exist adjacent to ghetto communities. Health institutions, especially hospitals, face demands from consumers of health services for a voice in, if not sole determination of, hospital policy. It is doubtful whether these demands would be made if the costs of medical services had not become prohibitive to working class people or if the quality of the services was not deteriorating rapidly. But the demands of health groups have gone beyond simply asking for expansion of health care. They are demanding representation on hospital boards. More important, they are evincing distrust of the sanctity of medical authority.

The crisis of institutions is the objective side of a revolutionary process, the crisis of bourgeois culture and ideology the subjective side. Together they constitute the necessary, but not the sufficient conditions for the emergence of a revolutionary situation. Revolutionary action requires the development of new social relations within the old society, a new hegemony of ideas, values and norms—a widespread belief among the ruled class that the old institutions and ideologies have lost their legitimacy.

The demystification of the law, in this respect, goes deeper than the beginnings of revolt by radical lawyers and clients against legal institutions or of law students against their education and indoctrination. Rather, the revolt of ordinary people against all forms of legitimate authority controlling the institutions of daily life and their simultaneous efforts to establish their own authority over these institutions takes the law from its position of preeminence in society and reveals it as an arm of class rule.

The process of demystification is complex and contradictory. Often the revolt remains confined to a single sphere of social life. Popular consciousness is often unable to transcend the concrete conditions within a particular institution and penetrate the universal character of all institutions. In other words, the challenge to institutions has not yet reached class consciousness, if we mean by this the capacity of workers to join the alienated conditions of their own labor and the struggle against a particular employer to the general class essence of domination in all social institutions.

But the demand for popular control itself poses all the questions about the neutrality of law and the legitimacy of bureaucracies and hierarchies to manage our lives. If law is not merely an ideological apparatus of the state for the coercive preservation of external social relations but rather permeates all aspects of public conduct, then the challenge to the institutions is the challenge to patterns of ordinary life and the legitimacy of those institutions which govern it. The breakdown of institutions is the breakdown of their legitimacy and consequently the breakdown of the legal order and its functional efficacy.

Capitalism depends on three kinds of institutions to enforce its hegemony over society. These institutions are: first, the work place itself and those institutions which organize the division of labor, the conditions of work, and the production and distribution of commodities. The corporation is the decisive form of organization in contemporary capitalist society. Within its framework, the relations of capitalist production and exchange are mediated. The trade unions act as a disciplinary force among the workers and serve as a contractor of labor according to an established price.

Second, the coercive and administrative institutions of the state, particularly the police, the army, and the social overhead or public service institutions. In contemporary American society, many of these services, particularly power, transportation and communications, are owned directly by the private sector but regulated publicly. The same condition applies to health and education.

Third, the ideological apparatuses, which include law, education, trade unions, and cultural functions. Here one can observe a great deal of overlap with other institutions. For example, educational institutions are both administrative and ideological apparatuses of bourgeois society. Law serves a regulatory function in all institutions and an ideological role as well. Trade unions are important ideological apparatuses because they provide legitimacy for the prevailing political parties as representatives of the working class; they support the principle of private ownership and state intervention into institutions of class conflict; and they appear as instruments of class struggle because of their bargaining role.

Historically, the separation of the state from the underlying economic and social relations has facilitated the illusion of popular sovereignty. To the extent that civil society remained sharply demarcated in form and function from the state, the ideology of popular control and representative democracy was consistent with the notion of the bourgeois state. Within civil society, the system of private appropriation of the means of production was legitimated by the doctrine of individual liberty, and its corollary, free competition.

The corporations have destroyed the whole ideological and institutional foundation of their authority. By taking over and "colonizing" civil society, they have plunged the third group of institutions necessary for the preservation of their authority into crisis. Capitalism does not merely rely on its force or its administrative capacity for survival. Equally, it requires ideological apparatuses to diffuse and channel social discontent and to return industrial and social discipline. The rebellion which transcends established channels of negotiation is a sign that institutions created as buffers between the subject and the dominant classes have lost their legitimacy, at least temporarily. The challenge to institutions has exacerbated the crisis.

The crisis is manifested most sharply in the disintegration of the structures of everyday life, especially the primary institutions of acculturation and socialization, the first of which is the family. The rise in the divorce rate, the breakdown of family solidarity in wide social strata and classes, and the spread of common law marriage are all symptoms of the decline of the authority of the family and its growing disutility as an instrument to successfully integrate children into the prevailing norms, values, and rules of conduct.

Law sanctions sexual relations between men and women under specific conditions, that is, provided that people agree to reproduce a new generation of workers. For example, the law requires children to attend school. This requirement arose historically from capitalism's need for a highly trained labor force. The state, representing the general interest of the capitalist class, was invested with the responsibility of training the new labor force, by transmitting technical knowledge required as a prerequisite for productive labor and by inculcating approved social values and norms to the new generation.

The family is the only legitimate form for cohabitation between men and women, although the state will tolerate other forms as long as these do not materially threaten the existing social norms. In advanced capitalist societies where there is chronic overproduction of the work force relative to the capacity of the forces of production, the degree of social toleration of "deviant" sexual behavior is greater, although subject to more or less repression depending on social and political circumstances.

The disintegration of the family threatens contemporary capitalism not because a new labor force is not being produced, but because the family is the chief instrument for the transmission of approved values. The habit structures of the individual are formed within the family. Work discipline may be enforced in part by the material requirements of human survival; indeed, the slogan "He who does not work, neither shall he eat" applies to every working-class person. But industrial discipline is not sufficient to insure proper adaptation to the world of work. Indeed, discipline involves at least two elements: the capacity to perform sustained work over the prescribed length of the working day, and respect for authority, the ability to act on external command, to internalize the legitimacy of the prevailing hierarchy.

The family is among the authoritarian institutions of capitalist society and is organized on principles which mirror the hierarchies of all institutions. The male "head of household" reigns as "lord of the castle." The position of the working class man at the head of the family serves the dual role of preparing children for industrial labor and mediating the alienation of the worker at the work place by restoring his sense of personal, if not social, power. If the man's position in the family teaches children the inevitability of authority supported by financial power and coercion, the woman is charged with the task of moral persuasion. The woman brings the children to school and church and is the line supervisor of the child's everyday existence, teaching children right from wrong in the pragmatic daily confrontations with life.

The development of mass transit and communication, the mobility of industrial plants, regional depressions, wars, and the permanent inflationary spiral in the post-World War era have all contributed to the decline of the nuclear family. Concomitant with these changes is the new status of the woman in the labor force. Unlike previous periods of industrial expansion, where the role of women was circumscribed within clerical and light factory occupations, the configuration of American capitalist economy placed women at the center of the expansion. In the postwar period, rising labor productivity and the growing concentration of capital were two of the major results of the acceleration of capital investment and the spread of U.S. hegemony to the entire capitalist world. During the years 1947–65, the manufacturing labor force grew by only thirteen percent, although the labor force as a whole increased by nearly fifty percent. The entrance of women into the retail and wholesale industries, into the vastly expanded clerical work force, which grew by forty-three percent, and, most important, into the employment explosion in the public sector, radically altered their status and the stability of the nuclear family.

Most adult women hold full-time or part-time jobs. Their income is essential for their own support and that of their family. Although women are still responsible for maintaining the home, their role as wage earner is equally important. The rapid increase of the divorce rate means that many women have become sole or primary supporters of their children. Few working class families can survive in the inflationary economy without the income of the working woman.

The challenge to the efficacy of the family and especially its hierarchical mode of organization derives chiefly from the objective changes which have been forced on the family structure by the demographic and economic changes in capitalist economy. Working women, confronted by the reality of their everyday situation, refuse to remain subordinate to men. The revolt of women extends beyond the organizations which articulate the rebellion. In the first place, the cycle of marriage and divorce and the proliferation of common law marriages represent the refusal of women to accept their historical role in capitalist culture. In the second place, the phenomenon of women as heads of household has had a profound impact on the consciousness of children, who can no longer rationalize the myth of the bourgeois family with their own situation. Respect for authority is weakened by the changing role of women. Even though women often reproduce the command patterns of the bourgeois family, the preoccupation with work and the more democratic role they have begun to play within the family mean that the ability of the family structure to deal effectively with its traditional socialization role is limited.

The loosening of family ties is observed especially when both parents are employed. It is not uncommon for a father to be employed on two or more jobs and for a mother to be fully employed as well, and for young children to perform most of their essential life functions themselves. Children are being thrown upon their own resources in typical working class families to a greater degree than at any time in history. Attempts of absent parents to enforce discipline break down under the sheer weight of work responsibility.

Another development which has changed the traditional role of the family is the emergence of youth society, a phenomenon partly attributable to the absent parents. Children are as likely to be socialized by peer groups as they are by parents. These peer groups are not immune to the norms and value systems of the dominant culture. Approved values are learned through organs of mass communication as much as they are in school or in family life. The television culture has become a real influence on youth consciousness. Internally, peer groups often observe rules of conduct which are patterned after canons of bourgeois morality. But youth have great difficulty emulating authoritarian power relations from the larger society. If the development of consciousness is not a passive process; if the consumption of information from mass media or school is not sufficient to *determine* behavior, but can only influence it, social practice is the central way in which consciousness is formed. The youth gang or group may not have thrown out leaders and hierarchy, but the law of the peer group, of the hippie culture, which represents a significant break with family and institutional authority, is arrived at in a more democratic manner than any institution of capitalist society. In a sense, the peer group and the youth culture become an alternate institution to the family and the school.

The loosening of family ties has been recognized by the ruling class for some time, and has resulted in the expansion of the school's role in transmitting approved social values. But the education system itself has been plunged into crisis. Materially, its dysfunction is rooted in the fiscal crisis of the state, that is, in the chronic incapacity of the public sector to finance the elementary public services. In turn, the shortage of funds reflects the enlargement of corporate prerogatives over public functions and resources and their consequent diversion to private hands. Thus at the same time as the education system has been endowed with this enlarged responsibility, it has lost the ability to perform the task. This contradiction is based not only on the economic crisis, but on the general crisis of confidence in the legitimacy of public bureaucracies. In part this crisis originates in the schools' failure to successfully transmit knowledge and technique, especially to Black and Brown children. But beyond the decline in the quality of education measured by traditional standards, another more pervasive crisis is growing—the opposition by the students themselves to the norms and values of contemporary capitalist society.

Students in secondary and higher educational institutions have begun to doubt the efficacy of the objects of education. The jobs offered as payoff for completion of school no longer seem worthwhile in comparison to the length of school time required. In contemporary America good jobs have been intimately linked with educational achievement. The decline of interest in jobs as a valid life ambition is a measure of the estrangement of large sectors of young people from capitalist culture.

But student disaffection goes beyond vocational alienation. It is not merely a question of making jobs more at-
tractive by offering higher pay. A generation reared not on
scarcity but on the culture of consumption cannot be socialized into work with a promise of more and better
gadgets. College students offered nothing but a chance to
serve corporations and the state when they do not accept
the underlying values and norms of bourgeois society will
work only if material necessity forces them to.

The proletarianization of students is expressed in the
mass character of higher education. The proliferation of
degrees granted by colleges and universities has transformed college education from an experience reserved for
managerial and petty-bourgeois professional strata into a
prerequisite for technical labor. The Bachelor's and Master's degrees are now widely diffused among the labor
force and have lost their special connotations.

In the '60s it was students who first challenged the
legitimacy of the state and its ideological apparatuses.
The recognition that the university, long regarded as an
academic market-place, was in fact a knowledge factory
subordinate to the research needs of the corporate war machine, was both the cause and the consequence of student
demands for power to change the university into a parti-
san of its own stated values. It was not that students
attacked the universities and colleges because they felt be-
trayed by the revelation that schools served the imperialist
interests of the state and its corporate masters. Students
first demanded power to control their own lives in school,
to make their educational experience relevant to the contemporary world. The boredom and monotony of the
classroom in the midst of social turbulence on the one
hand, and the perception by students that the work for
which they were being prepared was instrumental for
consumption of waste or production for destruction rather
than the advancement of human needs on the other, were
at the bottom of the student revolt. Students of the 1950s
could not accept the fate of their parents or their quiescent predecessors.

As all educational institutions, universities and colleges serve a twofold function. The first function is to produce skilled labor for manufacturing, government, and service industries. During periods of economic growth, higher education plays an important part in the development of the forces of production. The importance of machinery for modern industry has placed knowledge itself at the center of the productive forces. From the universities private corporations derive practical applications of scientific research as well as cadres for their own plants and laboratories. Moreover, colleges produce teachers, health workers, and others engaged in the provision of social overheads. It is no accident that those engaged in scientific, technical, and medical studies have been the most ambivalent about the worth of their education. Some of these students have joined in the protests but, in the main, scientists and engineers have been least involved in contesting the quality and objects of higher education. To the extent that the economy has made provisions for their employment in *productive* work and the content of science itself remains unquestioned, radicalism has not sunk deep roots among this stratum of students.

Academic unemployment has further eroded the legitimacy of higher education. The public and service sectors have failed to expand fast enough to absorb the tremendous growth of credentialed workers leaving the academy. Concurrently, the production sector is faced with stagnating output on the one hand, and higher output per worker on the other. Layoffs among engineers and scientists have begun to occur in private corporations, and schools and health institutions have cut back in hiring because of fiscal crises.

The requirement demanded by many employers for higher education as a prerequisite for administrative and technical jobs is not rooted in the level of development of the productive forces, particularly modern machinery. Operation of these machines is much less complex than formerly. Automation has destroyed traditional skills, even at the level of operation. Employers demand higher qualifications precisely because increased productivity has created vast labor surpluses as the general level of literacy has advanced. Much of the stratification of the labor force and the relatively minute division of labor in industry are not primarily caused by the new technologies, but by the requirements of corporate and government hierarchies to disguise the community of interest among all workers and to serve their own economic interest. The point is that automation and other modern forms of mechanization require fewer skills than the older industrial processes, except for a few highly trained employees. Yet, institutions demand higher educational qualifications than ever before.

The second function of education is to socialize students into work in general and the hierarchical form of alienated labor in particular. During the era of economic scarcity the work ethic was deeply ingrained into social consciousness, and material necessity has remained a powerful instrument of social integration, despite the appearance of material plenty in society at large. But the contradiction between the technical capacity of the U.S. production system to end scarcity and the persistent need to work at boring, meaningless jobs substantially erodes work discipline. The ideological imperative that liberation can only come through self-sacrifice and hard work has lost its legitimacy. However, the coercive aspect of alienated work still remains the most powerful drive to enforce the system of industrial discipline since technical innovation has been stifled and people must work in order to eat.

Of course Blacks, Puerto Ricans and impoverished whites experience the deterioration of education at a much earlier age. Many Blacks are barred from participation in skilled labor by the school system. The tracking system, according to which students are classified at the very beginning of their school life by intelligence tests based on discriminatory cultural criteria, acts as a demoralizing influence on students and parents alike. The rise of Black militancy in the early '60s was reflected in the demands of Black parents and students for community control over the hiring of teachers, administration of schools, and curriculum. The quest for Black control over public institutions providing services to Black communities was a rejection of the authority of municipal government over crucial institutions in the Black, Puerto Rican and Mexican-American areas.

At first, the struggle to impose forms of popular power over the schools appeared merely to rearrange or "reform" the power structure. But the impulse went much deeper. The struggle for popular control arises side by side with the attempt to create new institutions which go outside the prevailing system. Young people do not simply reproduce the family—they consider the value of communal living, a new way to organize their personal lives outside the old nuclear family. Parents and students try to create their own schools without substantial public support or, if they choose to develop new educational practice within the public sector, they refuse to accept the old structure of authority and simply make themselves new masters over the old institution.

The disintegration of the primary institutions has affected trade unions, which, once viewed as workers' instruments for the defense and extension of class interests, now play a new role at the work place. In part, they have been charged with tasks which primary institutions such as the family and the school have failed to perform. The labor union has been converted, in part, into an ideological apparatus of the state, an institution performing primary socialization functions by collaborating with employers to codify rewards for loyal performance of labor. The union contract not only represents the outcome of industrial struggle; it also helps to reinforce bourgeois ideological and cultural hegemony: it embodies a value system.

The role of unions as bargaining agents for workers is an integral part of the administrative structure of the modern corporation and represents an auxiliary method by which the state establishes control over wages and working conditions. One of the key mechanisms of trade union-government collaboration is the mediation and arbitration procedures of most union contracts, which remove the settlement of disputes from the bargaining table or the picket line to the courts. Arbitration is a quasi-judicial procedure—the arbitrator is usually a private individual or agency rather than an official of the state courts. But the principle of a neutral party making final and binding decisions in labor disputes is parallel to the role played by courts in the judicial system. The fact that we do not have labor courts in the United States is ideologically efficient for corporate capitalism, since it avoids placing the onus for antilabor decisions on the state itself.

In most labor agreements the right to strike is restricted so that strikes can be called only at the expiration of the contract or for a limited number of issues during the life of the agreement. And in the majority of instances strikes can be called during the term of a contract only after the union has exhausted a rather prolonged series of grievance procedures. But no contract formally recognizes the "right" to strike at any time, for any reason. Under the Taft-Hartley Law unions are accountable for abrogation of the "no strike" provision of the labor agreement by any of its members. Thus it is in the union's interest to quell wildcat strikes and to maintain fundamental work discipline.

The role of the union as policeman reflects itself in day-to-day issues. Lateness and absenteeism are usually the mutual concerns of management and the union. It is not uncommon for union stewards and other officials to administer warnings to workers who do not come to work on time, fail to meet production standards, or are insubordinate. Union officials often view themselves as intermediaries between the rank and file, whom they regard as undisciplined and ignorant of broader issues, and the management. In many industries, particularly those in which the strength of the union is greater than the individual employer's, such as garment and construction, the union itself takes responsibility for many important industry decisions. Unions use union welfare funds to help tottering employers and union lobbying power to support industry's concern with imports or government contracts for military expenditures and construction. More fundamentally, where the union controls the supply of labor in industries, such as construction and shipping, its power over the individual worker as well as within the industry itself gives it the appearance of an independent force. Actually, many union officials boast that they are responsible for the economic health of the industry as well as the welfare of the members, although politically they are forced to enter into the management of industry for the ostensible purpose of safeguarding their members' interests.

During the '50s, liberal union officials' complicity in corporate capitalism's drive for maximum profits in the midst of economic stagnation caused an outbreak of wildcat strikes in the auto and steel industries and long strikes in other sectors of the economy. The trade union reaction was swift and sure. It deplored the anarchic strike movements and agreed with employers that militants should be fired and that the injunctive procedures of the Taft-Hartley Law should be applied. At the same time unions and employers took steps to meet the demands of the workers. The no-strike provision of the auto workers' contract was modified to permit strikes over production standards under certain conditions. The steelworkers' union bureaucracy reaffirmed its determination to enforce the provision of the basic steel agreement which prohibited technological change without union consultation.

The wildcat strikes were smashed, but the challenge to the unions did not abate. Workers attempted to capture control over their own working conditions through mushrooming rank-and-file movements to replace the old leadership. Beginning in the late '50s and early '60s, there was a parade of electoral challenges to the leaders of many key industrial unions. Although most of the pretenders to the thrones were middle-rank leaders, they rode to power on the strength of membership discontent. Such contests took place in the steelworkers', rubber workers', textile workers', oil and chemical workers', teachers', state, county and municipal workers', the electrical workers' and in many locals of the auto workers' union, where each collective bargaining defeat was followed by the defeat of a raft of local union incumbents. Another manifestation of the emergence of rank-and-file discontent in the '60s was the rise of the teamsters' unions as a major challenger to traditional union jurisdictions. The apparent militancy of this "outlawed" union meshed neatly with rank-and-file disgust with the softness of the middle-aged CIO labor statesmen. The merger of the AFL and the CIO had prevented workers from seeking alternative representation when their unions engaged in company union practices. The expulsion of the teamsters from the House of Labor in 1957 provided disgruntled workers with a powerful alternative to the old labor unions.

But by the late '60s the initial enthusiasm of the workers for competitive unionism and internal union reform had ebbed. After 1967 real wages declined each year and, after a period of economic growth due to the Vietnam War, the economy began to slow down. The first effects of the slowdown were reflected in rising layoffs and the elimination of overtime, which took the gloss from pay envelopes. Meanwhile prices kept rising.

The last two years of the '60s and the opening of the '70s were marked by a reawakening of rank-and-file militancy, which took different forms in different sectors. Among public workers and workers in voluntary institutions such as hospitals, there was a wave of union organizing and strike movements, led by teachers. The impact of public employee organizing was peculiar because every strike of this group of workers is, perforce, a strike against the state. In many places the pent-up frustrations of these workers, who had borne the worst effects of the inflation and the fiscal crisis of the public sector, caused widespread disrespect for laws prohibiting strikes by public employees and court injunctions aimed at enforcing these laws. In many cities, particularly on the Eastern seaboard, the leaders riding the crest of the wave of militancy became important political figures and were absorbed by municipal governments as warm allies and important sources of political power. Although the fiscal crisis afflicting all public organs prevents a secure alliance of the workers with government authority, the unions do represent the newly discovered power of the membership. Chances of upheaval against the leadership, until the state shows its inability and unwillingness to come through on workers' demands, seem remote for the near future.

But the picture is far from uniform. The 1970 wildcat strike of postal workers took place over the heads of union leadership and became a national strike without central coordination and direction. Even more dramatic was the extraordinary wildcat strike by 100,000 teamsters in the Middle West and the West Coast in rejection of a contract negotiated by their national leaders. The vaunted authority of the union over the membership, its reputation for militancy and toughness at the bargaining table, its myth of invincibility, collapsed beneath the insurgent rank and file which for the first time acted independently of the bureaucracy.

The new form of the labor revolt is not found in rank-and-file protests against specific union leaders. It is expressed in the disbelief in the legitimacy of the unions as well as their leaders to "represent the workers" and the growing disrespect for the old, legally sanctioned bargaining mechanisms. Less dramatic, but equally significant, has been the phenomenal rise of members' contract rejections against the wishes of the bureaucracy. In the older unions, having attempted internal reform of the leadership structure, the members are experimenting with new forms of class struggle. They are not likely to abandon the unions, because in many cases the union has become the chief dispenser of social benefits. But the impulse to dual forms of struggle—shop committees, wildcat strikes, stewards' movements—may become important in the future. New instruments of workers' struggle would have to reject the institutionalization of the class contract represented by the legally sanctioned labor agreement administered by trade union bureaucracies. Workers would have to consciously reject limitations on their freedom to take direct action to meet their elementary needs at the work place. Although many wildcat strikes are implicitly caused by issues which go beyond wage demands, these remain hidden beneath the economic struggles.

Labor unions are not likely to become formally committed to the ideas of workers' control over working conditions, investment decisions, and the objects of labor. On the contrary, they will remain "benefits" oriented, fighting incessantly to improve the economic position of their own membership in relation to other sections of the work force rather than relative to the employers. They will bitterly oppose workers' efforts to take direct action beyond the scope of the union agreement and to make agreements with the boss on the informal basis of power relations rather than within the limitations imposed by a legally sanctioned contract. Trade unions are likely to remain both a deterrent to the workers' initiative and a "third party" force at the work place, objectively serving corporate interests both ideologically and in the daily life of the shop, and diminishing as an instrument of workers' struggle, to be employed only selectively by them.

Anti-union consciousness is confused by the inability of workers to organize on an independent basis. Trade unionism still appears a progressive force to the mass of working poor, such as farm and hospital workers, who labor under conditions of severe degradation. At first unionization seems to be deliverance from bondage. But after the initial upsurge has been spent, most of these unions fall back into patterns of class collaboration and repression, and defend the union contract with all the coercive powers at their command. At the point when grinding poverty has been overcome and the unions have settled into their conservative groove, their bureaucratic character becomes clear to workers.

We are now in the midst of a massive reevaluation by organized industrial workers of the viability of the unions. As already indicated, it is an action critique rather than

an ideological criticism. In the end, the spontaneous revolt
will have to develop its own demands and forms of
struggle. It is still too early to predict their precise configuration in the United States. The European experience suggests that workers' councils and committees or autonomous creations of workers at the point of production will
not replace the unions immediately, but will exist side by
side with them for some time.

The crisis of values in America has affected religious
institutions also. The church has always played a political
and economic role in addition to its ideological function.
Separation of church and state was always more formal
than actual. The importance of religious teaching during
the rise of capitalism cannot be underestimated. Religion
legitimated private property, the alienation of labor, and
industrial progress. As long as the church represented
eternal values reinterpreted in the context of capitalist social relations, its status as a universal institution was secure. But the development of capitalism itself deprived
the church of its functional legitimacy. The bourgeois revolution stripped the church of its property and its power
as the official religion and relegated it to the role of guardian of ideological treasures, and then the industrial revolution required a system of free public education under
secular authority. Having become a subsidiary political
and economic influence, the church's ideological role was
diminished because it was relegated to the spiritual realm
and denied material functions to provide social legitimacy. The erosion of religious authority corresponds to
the decline of its functions in contemporary capitalism.

However, it would be a mistake to discount religious influences entirely. The church remains an important social
institution in America. Churches, especially the Catholic
Church, have a growing role in economic and social life.
Their ownership of property, especially real estate, makes
them an important capitalist institution participating in
many major decisions affecting sectors of the political
economy. But as a political and economic force the
church is forced to deal with secular issues—often

against the interests of its constituency—and thus, through its exposure as an economic interest, the vaunted neutrality of the church from earthly affairs, regarded as the necessary basis of its moral and juridical authority, has been considerably weakened. To counter its ideological weakness, the church, especially the Catholic Church, has vastly expanded its educational system—parochial education in America has grown enormously in many areas over the past ten years. But the reversion to secular functions has demystified the church. It now must be judged by the canons of civil society.

This trend can be observed in all advanced capitalist countries. An indication of the crisis of religious authority is the massive defections of young priests and ministers from Christian churches, the decline of church attendance and income, and the desperate attempts of religious hierarchies to become more relevant to the secular crises which have contributed to their isolation.

Organized opposition to the church hierarchy is most dramatic in the Catholic Church. Having perceived that the Church has become another corporate institution and has lost its unification on the ideological plane, young priests have demanded that the employees of the company be integrated into secular life on its own terms. They have challenged celibacy, Church litany, and other hallowed customs designed to reinforce the spirituality of the Church, its status as a higher moral force. The resistance of the Church hierarchy to the most radical demands aimed at demystification is attenuated by concessions to radical priests who wish the Church to be relevant to contemporary political and social issues. To a certain extent, these concessions are in the interest of the hierarchy, which is desperately attempting to hold on to its young cadre while at the same time enlarging its own political influence. Priests are being encouraged to run for public office, to participate in popular struggles within health and educational instititions, to fight for more housing. In New York, the Catholic Church emerged as a major force in the school decentralization battle in 1966. Many

Church officials as well as active Catholic laymen were successful candidates for local school board seats in 1970.

It would be an error to assume that the church's active role in the affairs of urban life is entirely venal. It is propelled by complex motives. On the one hand, church involvement in politics reflects its struggle to win legislative approval for public funds for parochial schools since they, too, face a deep fiscal crisis. On the other hand, the hierarchy has been forced to be more permissive with its activist cadre, many of whom are influenced by radical ideologies or humanist philosophies. But the church cannot solve the fundamental conflict between its growing secular role as an integral part of corporate capitalism and its need for moral and juridical legitimacy, which supposedly rests on its status as a neutral arbiter of all earthly affairs. The institutional interests of the church have become incompatible with its ideological functions.

The breakdown of institutions is the breakdown of values, norms, and rules of conduct. Law, a system of rules and regulations, provides the cohesion necessary for the preservation of institutional structures. As a system of morality, a lexicon of rights and responsibilities, it establishes the legitimacy for the exercise of institutional functions. It is the critical ideological apparatus of the state. As a mediation between consciousness and the actual character of social relations, juridical relations are the most crucial for the preservation of class society because they embody simultaneously a system of beliefs and rules of conduct.

If law were only operable in its institutional form, that is, as a branch of the state, its power would be limited to political relations. Since man is not a political animal but a social animal, the concept of law must permeate all social institutions. It is called upon to provide standards of behavior in the factory and all other institutions of daily life. In its juridical form, it provides sanction for entering into certain relations. But as a system of rules and regulations it governs the daily activity of institutional relations, prescribing orderly procedures for the business of production and exchange of commodities and for the functions of all intermediate institutions between the state and civil society.

The phenomenon of divorce, the inability of the schools to transmit knowledge and values, the breakdown of industrial discipline and the decline in church authority pose a grave threat to the life of capitalist society. The challenge of mass movements to institutions such as the school, the family, the trade unions, and the church, which constitute the critical mediations between individuals and the class nature of production relations, rips the reified mask from these man-made institutions and shows the bare face of the ruling class. Without ideologies and apparatuses representing them, there can be no class society, unless its power is maintained by repressive violence. Repression is no longer a last resort; it is transformed into a mode of rule.

The fascism of the 1920s and the 1930s based itself on the attempt of a bourgeoisie to save itself from extinction in the wake of the most massive economic and political crisis in the history of capitalism. The bourgeoisie of Germany and Italy were prepared to surrender their autonomy over all basic decisions to a state which, owing to its capacity to suppress the working class movement and direct economic as well as social life, could unify the bourgeoisie. The German industrialists learned that the old parliamentary conservative and social democratic majorities were no match for inexorable social forces which were beyond the control of private interests or the liberal state.

Fascism was an able representative of capitalist interests because it did not advocate them in a period when capitalism as a system had reached its moral nadir. Instead, the fascists presented themselves as critics of capitalism and upholders of a socialism ensconced in the rhetoric and the ethos of imperialism and racism. The fascists were the most articulate critics of bourgeois values and liberal political and social institutions. Parliamentary democracy was the cruelest hoax ever perpetrated upon the working classes, they argued, because it gave the workers no genuine voice in the conduct of political affairs. Instead, the intellectual and political elites who controlled the political parties manipulated popular demands to advance their own special interests. The parliamentary process was nothing but a series of deals between politicians in search of power.

Private corporate interests did not escape the ideological thrusts of the fascists, who declared competition archaic and untrammeled capitalism a detriment to the national good. Fascism proposed to unify the German nation in its quest for its own historic destiny—the civilizing of the world. National reconstruction would proceed without the constraints imposed by a state legislative and administrative bureaucracy hopelessly entangled in bitter internecine warfare. The Nazis promised an end to strife within the German nation. Harmony between workers and capitalists, between men and women, between man and the state would be established under the hegemony of the party and its leader. The enemy was redefined within the socialist tradition—international bankers who had made Germany poor. But Hitler introduced a profound racist strain into his ideological anticapitalist appeal. The real bankers were also Jews. Existing social relations need not be disturbed except that Jews must be separated from their property and their political influence. Thus did the fascists attempt to coopt the traditional anticapitalist traditions of the socialist movement in order to win a mass base among large sections of the working class who had, during the 1920s, experienced the denouement of bourgeois pretensions of democracy, even its social democratic variety.

But the fascists did not renounce all capitalist institutions. They did not define socialism as expropriation of private property by the working class. Instead, in the traditions of the Second and the Third Internationals, socialism was the direction by the state of all economic and political life. Turning to a deformed version of Hegel's *Rechtsphilosophie*, the state was presumed to be the expression of the reconciliation of conflicting interests within the economic and social spheres. Nazi ideologists did not proclaim the end of conflict, but they did reassert in its authoritarian mask the concept of the state as an instrument of social harmony and stability. Stripped of its mystical form, this is simply an ideology of state capitalism according to which the neutral state is transformed into the command and the leadership state—an activist and organizer of social and economic life.

Fascism in the United States is developing under different circumstances, based on its own needs and history. In the first place, the elements of state capitalism, intrinsic in fascist evolution, already exist within the uncomfortable framework of liberal institutions. It is no longer possible to deny the centrality of the state to capitalist survival. No longer merely a coercive instrument for the protection of private property, or a regulator of relations among the capitalists themselves, the newest function of the state is its direct intervention in the economy, particularly its role as investor. In all advanced capitalist societies this development has taken place to a greater or lesser degree. In the United States state capitalism is characterized not only by the accretion of the planning functions of the state, but by the intervention of the state into all institutional life. Institutions, including production, literally depend on the support of the state for their survival. Corporate power is wielded decisively in all organs of the state which, in turn, have been enlisted as economic institutions.

Second, having coopted liberal institutions for authoritarian ends, there is no reason to believe that parliamentary forms must be destroyed to establish an authoritarian state. In fact, the reverse is true. The corporation, in consequence of its inability to survive without the state, did surrender much of its autonomy to it. In the process the corporation colonized the state and brought it fully into its service, although it left the state with its own prerogatives. To a certain extent the state retains autonomous functions and institutions which operate, at least in part, independ-

ently of direct corporate power lest the vital regulatory
functions of the state be undermined. The destruction of
the autonomy of the state is not in the interest of the corporate bourgeoisie in the long run even though it has been
forced to impress public authority directly in its service.
But the process of absorption of the public by the private
is rather advanced in America. Parliamentary institutions
have been reduced to little more than debating bodies at
worst, veto bodies at best. During the past half-century,
Congress has initiated virtually no major legislation. It
acts occasionally to balance the most centralist actions of
the executive branch, which has, with impunity, kept
Congress only imperfectly informed of its actions. America has no articulate parliamentary opposition nor a mass
left movement capable of checking the organizational and
stabilizing functions of the state.

Third, unlike Germany, where the rise of fascism was a
response to visible economic catastrophe afflicting the
country and the chaos which it produced, American authoritarianism is growing amidst a social crisis which
arises from the long-term crisis of the capitalist system as
a whole. Chiefly, the crisis is a crisis of the superstructure
—the breakdown of institutions and of ideologies. Although these crises are not separate from the underlying
instability of the economy and its reliance on the state for
coherence and for growth, the American crisis has a
different configuration from the world economic crisis
forty years ago.

Liberal institutions, for example, have revealed their
disintegration. Liberals still propose that the end of the
Indochina war will be a first step in reordering national
priorities so that the center cities can be rebuilt, school
and health facilities expanded, and local services broad-
ened. A more advanced group asks for new forms of popular participation in order to guarantee a broad base for
institutional reform. But their program of social reconstruction to fill the void of legitimate authority has come
into conflict with the hierarchies which control social institutions and necessary corporate requirements. Since

the consciousness of men does not, in the last analysis, determine being, the reconstructionist wing of corporate interests has entered its nadir and a more authoritarian wing has gained ascendency. The old liberal values, products of a bygone era, can no longer be successfully reconstructed. The polarization of American society has sharpened. The "law and order" forces now dominant in the government and among a section of the bourgeoisie are building a mass base among sections of workers, intellectuals, and small businessmen who have become disillusioned with the old liberal program. The ideological strength of the Right is its critique of bourgeois liberalism, its attack against the bankrupt welfarism of the Democratic Party, and the inability of the liberal bourgeoisie to solve the underlying economic crisis maturing within American society. Indeed, fascism disguises itself in the cloak of a conservative defense of traditional liberalism. In order to reconstruct the existing social institutions, which have failed in their appointed mission, the authoritarians appear as the other side of the coin: the Right criticizes bourgeois values while defending bourgeois institutions.

It is the authoritarians who defend the family as ideology even as capitalism destroys its material basis, who uphold the hierarchies of education and credentials even as capitalism renders traditional skills obsolete and assigns large numbers of the labor force to the historic dustbin. But instead of a material reconstruction of these institutions, the authoritarians seek to superimpose discipline upon them. They dream of schools which train people but do not educate them; families which prepare youth for steady work but do not transmit the old individualistic and humanistic values; religion which teaches obedience not love; trade unions which act as disciplinary forces for the corporations, not instruments of workers' struggles. Law becomes hypostatized as an end of human conduct. Order is a value instead of the outcome of human endeavor. Fascism in America is the form of law without its content.

Liberals themselves have gone over to·the forces of law and order. No less a bourgeois liberal ideologist than John Kenneth Galbraith can simultaneously defend the old civil libertarian values and attack the fundamental right of workers to struggle for higher wages. The necessity of preserving the capitalist economy makes necessary measures to abrogate workers' ability to strike, and to deny, in practice, the myth of free competition by calling for price controls. No more revealing instance of the bankruptcy of liberalism in America exists than the support rendered by the Democratic majority of the Senate and the House to the new administration's "no-knock" legislation which permits, among other things, law enforcement officers to circumvent constitutional guarantees regarding search and seizure and habeas corpus. Together with growing "left" liberal support for wage freeze measures to counter inflation and thus preserve economic values, these indicate the merger of liberal and more openly authoritarian methods to preserve capitalist institutions. No liberal can deny the need to fight chaos, riots, and other instances of social disorder. The ultimate law of a state is to defend itself against those who would overthrow it. Herein lies the identity of interest among both wings of the capitalist class.

We now arrive at the question of radical strategy to confront the emergence of both the void in the legitimacy of institutions and the authoritarian bid to save them. The burden of the ancestral left strategy to combat fascism was the alliance of the social democratic and communist movements in defense of traditional bourgeois liberties. The Communists reacted to the breakdown of institutions in the 1930s by attempting to preserve them, against the right-wing attempt to reconstitute them on an absolutist basis. Everywhere the attempt failed. For beneath the political alliance of left parties was the presumption that there were on the one hand viable elements in bourgeois institutions worth saving, and "progressive" elements of the bourgeoisie with whom to form alliances on the other. The pact made by the left in France and Germany was that the condition for socialism was the defeat of fascism. Fascism, in turn, could only be overcome on the basis of the existing liberal social relations and institutional arrangements. The Communists argued against the "lefts" who insisted that the only way to defeat fascism was the revolutionary action of the working class itself in behalf of its own socialist demands. According to the popular front proponents, socialist activity would only splinter the antifascist forces and insure the victory of fascism.

History has passed judgment on this strategy in France and Spain. The militant defense of bourgeois legality by the Communists in France in 1936 and their opposition to and suppression of revolutionary movements in Spain was consistent with their policy of making alliances with the bourgeoisie to defeat fascism in Greece in 1945, in France and Italy in 1968, and elsewhere. In each case, the ephemeral character of the bourgeois ally was revealed. The collapse of the liberal bourgeoisie in the prewar popular front period, the inability of the popular front to stem the fascist tide, showed the mythological character of the alliance. In the end, the bourgeoisie went over to the Nazis. But not before the juridical and political institutions showed themselves as trusted instruments of class oppression. In fact, in Spain the Communists became themselves instruments of the capitalist state.

In the United States, the Communists and Socialists loyally followed the policy of alliances with the liberal wing of the capitalist class. Within the workers' movement where there were no mass socialist forces, the alliance took the form of the "center-left" coalition between left wing and pro-New Deal trade unionists which, for a time, dominated the CIO. The left played the role of loyal opposition to the Roosevelt administration, its most friendly and persistent critic. During the late 1930s and the World War II period, the Communist Party and the Socialist Party advocated more government intervention into the economy and social life. In the name of social welfare, it prepared the ground for workers' acceptance of government regulation of labor relations. Objectively, the left strengthened the role of the state in the political economy and facilitated the emergence of nascent authoritarianism. The main allies of the popular front, the liberal corporatists, used the left as a means to save capitalism from its economic crisis. The popular front left contributed to the development of new institutions of capitalist stability—social welfare, a powerful labor bureaucracy, and a reinvigorated state machinery.

Another consideration in a determination of radical strategy is the history of the parties on the left themselves. They would replace the capitalist dictatorship with the proletarian power represented by a centralist party at the helm of a socialist state. But these parties have been without significant influence among the underlying population. One factor contributing to the decline of state socialism has been the periodic repression of political dissent in our country. But repression is not powerful enough to explain away the sect-like character of all state socialist movements. Other working class movements, including state socialist movements, have experienced such hardship and managed to gain support among the oppressed classes and strata. Two key developments in America may be decisive in explaining the failure of American socialism. The first is the ethnic, occupational, and racial diversity of the American working class and the consequent racist and elitist ideologies among the American workers. The second is the authoritarianism of the state socialist program and organizations. Leninist and social democratic movements have operated on the principle of bureaucratic hegemony and hierarchical authority, mirroring the prevailing corporate and state structures which they seek to replace. Workers who face the power of bureaucratic corporations every day are not likely to transfer their allegiance to a new bureaucracy, although they will join movements for social change in order to wring concessions from the prevailing system.

The older, sect-like socialist organizations, including the Communist Party, seem to forget that today's institutions are being challenged for just their authoritarian, elitist, corporatist character. The students know that schools do not exist as centers of free inquiry. They have become instrumental to the forces of domination. The trade unions cannot be reconstructed by the rank and file as if they were voluntary organizations. They are now creatures of law, with specific tasks within corporate hierarchies. The internal challenge to the unions simply results in a reproduction of the old leadership. If the new leaders cannot be integrated into the old framework, they are eliminated, by violence if necessary. The courts have their marching orders. The end of the last of the liberal Supreme Courts was accomplished by force. The resignation of Fortas, the elimination of Goldberg, the retirement of Warren and the selection of conservatives, despite liberal rejections of early choices, were no accidents. They were the results of a concerted effort to remove the last barriers to the new authoritarianism.

Therefore, it is extremely important that we make the distinction between bourgeois institutions and bourgeois values. The proposal to defend bourgeois institutions against the bourgeoisie lacks the same material basis as it did forty years ago. These institutions, backed by a legitimacy derived from laws and by force, are under withering criticism and attack by new generations who can no longer live within them. But the challenge to institutions, significantly, has taken place in the name of some of the traditional values, specifically individual liberty, humanism, and democracy.

The radicals and militants, Black and white, today seek neither to modify nor replace the existing institutions with a new system of domination. They reject the Old Left notion that a transitional state as an organ of class oppression is necessary as a transition to communism. The student, youth, and Black movements are a revolt against domination itself. They represent, in embryo, the impulse to liberation from all hierarchical authority—from the concept of right, that is, from the legitimation of rules of conduct from above.

Further, they will not accept the family, the education

system, the trade unions, and the state as legitimate institutions. They have begun an action critique to demystify
them. The law, which presently represents the repressive
power of the bourgeoisie, is losing its mediating role. The
law *is* against the people.

In essence, radicals must be the defenders of the values
inherent in the unfulfilled promise of the great bourgeois
revolutions. The radical movement may not have established the hegemony of its ideas or culture throughout society or even among its constituents. But we must be the
advocates of direct popular democracy—of the reconstruction of society from below, of popular power over all
institutions, and the creation of institutions to meet human needs—not to serve the interests of profit and domination.

2

Challenging the Law

The Panther 21:
To Judge Murtagh

The most significant document presented in the pretrial hearings of thirteen Black Panthers in New York was a statement the defendants prepared in response to the "indefinite recess" of the proceedings ordered by the presiding judge. The case itself, often referred to as the Panther 21 Conspiracy trial, charged members of a Black political organization, the Black Panther Party, with conspiring to bomb police stations, department stores, railroads, the Bronx Botanical Gardens, and attempting to murder policemen. The district attorney's office had devised a plot so bizarre and complex that it would take both the defense and the prosecution until February 2, 1970, ten months after the mass arrests, to prepare for trial. Of the original twenty-two Panthers indicted, comprising the core of the organization, thirteen were captured and separated into several prisons, unable to consult their lawyers together for many months.

Almost unprecedented in criminal trial history, the pretrial hearings were halted on February 25 by State Supreme Court Judge John M. Murtagh for the reasons he outlines in a prepared statement which follows. The response by the defendants addresses itself not so much to the particular action by the judge in halting the trial, but to the treatment inflicted on Black people under the "Amerikan system of criminal justice" throughout American history.

The district attorney's office conducted the longest trial

*in New York history, spent over two million dollars, and
put sixty-five witnesses on the stand. The three major police undercover agents, who had joined the Panther Party
at its inception, before the majority of the defendants, testified that they had never seen or participated in the attempted murder of policemen, actual bombings, or the
attempted bombings of police stations or public places.
The judge had denied almost every defense motion before
and during the trial including the requests to lower the
prohibitively high 100,000 dollar bail set for most defendants, and had ignored the defendants' letter "To Judge
Murtagh: From the Panther 21"; the hearings resumed on
April 7, 1970. But the jury, composed of five Blacks, one
Puerto Rican, and six whites, stunned the nation on May
13, 1971, when they acquitted all the defendants on all
156 charges. A number of jurors expressed the belief that
the judge was biased throughout the trial. Their unanimous decision, their public criticisms of the judge, prosecutor, and prosecution witnesses, and the ideas in the
Panther 21 letter have reached and challenged the highest
levels of the American judicial system and have begun to
be heard and considered by many millions of people in
American society.—Ed.*

THE COURT: Yesterday the court told counsel—
MR. BLOOM: If I may, your Honor—
THE COURT: You may not.
Yesterday the court told counsel that it has a formula for
firmly maintaining the dignity of this court without in any
way sacrificing the rights of the accused.

I stated that I did not intend to use the formula for a week
or two. This was in order to accomplish the end short of using
the formula.

It is obvious that other measures will not prevail. The continued misconduct of the defendants persuaded me to use the
formula without any further delay.

Frequently a formula is as effective as it is simple. If this
formula proves to be effective as the court believes it will be,
it will in large measure because of its utter simplicity.

The court declares these hearings to be recessed indefinitely.
That, in essence, is the formula.

The trial of the charges before this court was delayed for

some ten months only because the defendants refused to proceed to trial.

Reluctantly and only at the coercion of the court, the defendants professed to agree to proceed to trial on February 2, 1970.

The proceedings commenced at the request of counsel with the pre-trial hearings that are now being conducted.

The hearings are proceeding at a snail's pace and are being repeatedly interrupted by the contemptuous conduct of the defendants.

Although counsel claims to urge their clients to abandon such conduct, the defendants continue to defy the court.

The defendants are unwilling to proceed with the trial of the issues before the court under the American system of criminal justice and under the laws of the State of New York.

The court and the district attorney continue to be ready to grant the defendants a fair trial to which they are entitled, but which they continue to reject.

Under all the circumstances, the court has no alternative but to declare an indefinite recess in the hearings.

At any time counsel—counsel will have respect for the court to which it's entitled.

MR KATZ: I'm sorry.

THE COURT: At any time the defendants may make a motion in writing for a resumption of the hearings.

If the defendants and their counsel are sincere in wishing a speedy and fair trial, the court expects that such a motion will be filed within the next forty-eight hours.

The court will give favorable consideration to the granting of such motion if—but only if—it is supported by an unequivocal assurance that each defendant will give complete respect to the court during the continuance of the hearings and during the course of the trial to follow and an assurance that the defendants are now prepared to participate in a trial conducted under the American system of criminal justice. Such statement is to be signed by each and every one of the defendants.

If the motion is made and supported by such a written statement it will be granted and the hearings will resume promptly.

If it is not made or not so supported the hearings will continue in recess indefinitely.

The defendants are entitled to a fair trial under the American system of criminal justice. Such a trial the court and the district attorney are ready to give them. The only thing preventing the defendants receiving such a trial is their continued refusal to accept such a trial.

The defendants are resorting to contemptuous conduct to

obstruct a fair trial. In view of their conduct to date the defendants must give the court reliable assurance that they are prepared to accept a trial—and a fair trial. The trial will not be resumed until such assurance has been given.

This court is responsible for maintaining proper respect for the administration of criminal justice and preventing any reflection on the image of American justice. That responsibility will be discharged.

Counsel are advised that the hearings are now recessed indefinitely. You are not free to represent to any other court that you are actually engaged before this part of the Supreme Court until such time as an order is entered directing the resumption of the hearings.

Prior to that time you are not engaged before this court, and you will so advise any other court before which you represent any other person.

The district attorney may move any other case on the calendar for trial in this part of the court. I will take a brief recess until such matter is moved.

MR. MCKINNEY: May I make a statement, please?

THE COURT: The court is in recess.

MR. MCKINNEY: I would like it on a point of personal privilege.

THE COURT: You have a right to make a motion before the court. The court is in recess. I will hear anything in writing.

MR. MCKINNEY: I should like to express my objection to the court's refusal to hear counsel, in view of the statements the court has made.

(Hearings recessed)

TO: "Justice" Murtagh

FROM: Defendants

* We the defendants named by the state in the proceedings now pending before "Justice" John M. Murtagh, in Part 38 Supreme Court, County of New York, say:

That the history of this nation has most definitely developed a dual set of social, economical and political realities, as well as dynamics. One white, and the other Black (the Black experience, or ghetto reality), having as their roots one of the most insidious and ruthless systems of human exploitation

---

* This letter was prepared entirely by the defendants in the within action, and transcribed, typed and reproduced with the help of their attorneys, due to their present incarceration.

known to man, the enslavement and murder of over forty million Black people, spread over a period of less than three centuries.

Long ago in this nation certain basic decisions were made about Black people, but *not* consulting them. Even before the Constitution was ever put on paper with its beautiful words and glowing rhetoric of man's equality and philosophical rights, human considerations had long given way before white economic necessity. Black people were to legally be defined and classified as nonhuman, below a horse—but definitely not a man.

Color became a crucial variable, and the foundation of the system of Black slavery. While chattel slavery is no longer upheld by the supreme law of the land, the habit and practice in thought and speech of looking at Black people from chattel plain still persist. After much refinement, sophistication and development, it has remained to become imbedded in the national character, making itself clear in organized society, its institutions, and the attitudes of the dominant white culture to this very day.

For us to state there are two realities (experiences) that exist in this nation, is a statement of fact.

When we speak of American traditions, let us not forget the tradition of injustice inflicted again and again upon those whom tradition has been created to exclude, exploit, dehumanize and murder.

Let us not conveniently forget how the system of "American justice" systematically upheld the bizarre reasoning about Black people in order to retain a system of slave labor. And when this became economically unnecessary, how "the great American system of justice" helped to establish and maintain social degradation and deprivation of all who were not white, and most certainly, those who were Black. To be sure, the entire country had to share in this denial; to justify the inhuman treatment of other human beings, the American had to conceal from himself and others his oppression of Blacks, but again the white dominant society has long had absolute power, especially over Black people—so it was no difficult matter to ignore them, define them, forget them, and if they persisted, pacify or punish them.

The duality of American society today need no longer be reinforced by laws, for it is now and has long been in the minds of men: the Harlems of America, as opposed to those who decide the fate of America's Harlems. This is essentially a historical continuation today, of yesterday—the plantation mentality, system and division, in the cloak of twentieth-century enlightenment.

"Traditional American justice," its very application has created what it claims to remedy, for its eyes are truly covered: it does not see the Black reality, nor does it consider or know of the Black experience, least of all consider it valid.

Black poor people are always subject to, but do not take part in your corrupt grand jury system and process.

We as a people do not exist except as victims, and to this and much more, we say no more. For 351½ years we said this in various ways. But running deep in the American psyche is the fear of the ex-slave. He who for so long has been wronged, will be wronged no more, and in fact will demand, fight and die for his human rights.

But why need we feel this way in the first place? Does not your Constitution guarantee man's freedom, his human dignity against state encroachment? Or does the innate fear of the rebellious slave in the heart of the slave-master continue to this day to negate all those guarantees in the cases of Black people? Does this cultural racist phobia make one forget, and abridge his own constitution, as this court has done to us? Do you not know what we mean when we say "NO MORE"? What has been done to us by your court, the district attorney, is only a reflection of all that has been infused into and permeates this racist society.

Black people have said and felt this for over 100 years. But those of the other reality, the dominant white culture, its institutions, had no ears to truly hear. The wax of centuries of slave master-slave relationship had stopped up their ears, your ears. For if our reality, the Black experience in America, is invalid, then so are the institutions and social structure that contributed to its creation invalid. If you then concede it is valid (which it most definitely is), then it must be of consequence in determining what is "justice" compared to us (Black people).

White citizens have grown up with the identity of an American, and have enjoyed a completely different relationship to the institutions of this nation, with that, the unresolved conflicts of the ex-slaveholder.

Blacks are no longer the economic underpinning of the nation. But we continue to be willing, or unwilling, victims. There is a timeless quality to the unconscious which transforms yesterday into today.

On August 17, 1619, over a year prior to the landing of the pilgrims at Plymouth Rock, a Dutch privateer dropped anchor off Jamestown, Virginia. There she exchanged her cargo of twenty Black men, women and children for provisions. According to the Dutch sailors, these Black people had been baptized, they were "Christians" and therefore could not be enslaved under British laws. As a result of that law, we were legally defined as "indentured" servants.

By 1663, though, the "Christian" conscience had given way to the capitalist desire for maximum profits. By 1663 the Carolinas and New York, and Maryland in 1664, Delaware and Pennsylvania in 1682 perpetrated the most heinous and despicable act conceivable to the human mind, that of denying an entire race of people their freedom by relegating them to an eternal status of "chattel slavery" and this abominable feat was done through the courts, legally, and with the backing of guns—our first experience with "American justice."

But it did not stop there. Although later the "Declaration of Independence" proclaimed that "All men are created equal, that they are endowed by their creator with certain inalienable rights, that among these are Life, Liberty and the Pursuit of Happiness," there was a most interesting *omission*. In the original draft there was a paragraph that Thomas Jefferson intended to include in the list of grievances against King George III. The paragraph read: "He has waged cruel war against human nature itself, violating its most sacred rights of life and liberty in the person of a distant people (African, Black people), who never offended him; captivating and carrying them into slavery in another hemisphere, or to incur miserable death in their transportation thither."

This paragraph was omitted in the final document, and understandably. For not only would it have been a valid and factual indictment against King George, but also one against the "Founding Fathers" themselves.

When the "glorious" and "sacred" Constitution of the United States of America was drawn up in 1787, the "noble," "just" and "freedom-loving" men who had fought a long and bloody war against the tyrannical and oppressive British regime headed by King George, for their freedom, wrote into their constitution laws that further sanctified, legalized and protected that most "peculiar institution" (slavery). Apparently they recognized the absurd and repugnant contradiction, but not sufficiently enough to do anything other than exclude the term "Negro" and "slave" from that document.

The Constitution contained three provisions that dealt specifically with the issue of slavery. The first established the policy that in counting population in order to determine how many representatives a state might send to Congress all free persons and "three-fifths of all other persons" were to be counted (Article I Sec. 2). The second forbade the Congress from making any laws restricting the slave trade until 1808 (Article I Section 9), and the third provided that runaway slaves who had escaped from any state had to be returned by any other state in which they might have sought refuge (Article IV Section 2).

The years passed and our wretched plight progressively worsened, the "laws" of bondage became even more institutionalized, inculcated in the dominant culture. In order to further protect and perpetuate their domination over us, the southern states passed many repressive laws called "slave codes." For us, there was not freedom of assembly. If more than four of five slaves came together without permission from a white person, that gathering in the depraved minds of the slave-masters was construed as a conspiracy. The towns and cities imposed a 9 P.M. curfew on us, there was no freedom of movement, a pass had to be carried by the slave whenever he was out of the presence of his master. And to enforce these ignoble laws there were slave patrols, organized like militias, composed of armed and mounted whites. (This mentality persists to this day. Woe to the Black man who is out very late in a white neighborhood; the police—white—suspect him immediately of being up to some foul deed. Even into the ghetto the white policeman brings this mentality.)

Although slavery had been abolished in certain states, the Black people who lived in those states were subjected to degrading laws which belied their so-called free status, and even worse, they were subject to kidnapping and being sold into slavery. The so-called free Black man was anything but free under the "American system of justice."

Throughout this horrid epoch, a few slaves managed to escape, then more slaves. The slaveholders demanded that the runaway slave laws be enforced. They pleaded to the United States Supreme Court, and that "august" body, the most powerful judiciary body in the land, the ultimate interpreter of the Constitution, answered their plea by upholding the 1793 Fugitive Slave Act in 1842, and again in 1845, and made it more stringent yet in 1850. Now for the runaway slave escaping to the North was not enough, for the Northern cities were overrun with slave-catchers.

In July 1847, Dred Scott, a Black resident of Missouri, brought suit in a Federal Court for his freedom. It read:

"Your petitioner, Dred Scott, a man of color, respectfully represents that sometime in the year of 1835 your petitioner was 'purchased' as a slave by one John Emerson, since deceased, who . . . conveyed your petitioner from the state of Missouri to Fort Snelling (Illinois) a fort then occupied by the troops of the United States and under the jurisdiction of the United States."

In essence Dred Scott was claiming that since he had been transported into territory (Illinois) in which slavery was forbidden by an act of Congress as well as state law, he was now a free man. This case was looked upon as a test to determine just what rights a Black man had in this country. It was the profound hope of many that a just and humane verdict would be rendered.

It took the Dred Scott case ten years to reach the "sacred" halls of the Supreme Court, and when that "prestigious" group of men spoke in March 1857 through the voice of "Chief Justice" Roger Taney, the Court ruled that "people of African descent are not and cannot be citizens of the United States and cannot sue in any court of the United States," and that Black people have "no rights which whites are bound to respect"—a classic example of the "American way of justice."

The Reconstruction Era was a time of great and unparalleled hope. It seemed as though Black people were finally to be accorded equal and humane treatment when the thirteenth, fourteenth, and fifteenth amendments were enacted.

But terror, violence, intimidation and murder still haunted us: the Ku Klux Klan did "their thing."

In 1866, 1871, and 1875 Congress enacted the first significant civil rights laws. They theoretically gave Black people the right to equal housing, accommodations, facilities and access to public transportation and places of public amusement. But as Blacks well know and whites deny, there is a world of difference in America between theory and practice. For although the thirteenth, fourteenth and fifteenth amendments and the civil rights legislation "gave" Black people so-called freedom, the right of citizenship and the right to vote, the enforcement of those laws was an entirely different thing. The extent of enforcement was totally dependent upon the degree to which it was advantageous to the Republican Party and the Northern industrialist.

By 1876 it was decided that Black people had served their purpose and, therefore, even the pretense of Black equality was no longer necessary.

The Supreme Court in 1883 embodied that attitude in law by declaring that the civil rights legislation of 1866, 1871, and 1875 was unconstitutional. In other decisions it displayed its remarkable and ingenious talent for interpreting the law according to the needs and interests of the dominant white ruling class. It nullified the fourteenth and fifteenth amendments by declaring that they were Federal restrictions only on the powers of the states or their agents, not on the powers of individuals within those states. Thus it was still illegal for any states to violate or abridge the rights of Black people; but if on the other hand private citizens or a group of them (such as the Ku Klux Klan) within any state actively prevented Black people from exercising their rights, then the crime came under the jurisdiction of the state in which the crime, or crimes, took place.

The court also ruled that if a state law did not appear on its surface discriminatory against Black people, there the federal courts had no right to investigate. But this was not enough. It was necessary to go even further, and they did.

In 1896 the Supreme Court in *Plessy vs. Ferguson,* 163 U.S. 537, upheld a Louisiana law requiring segregated railroad facilities. As long as equality of accommodations existed, the court held segregation did not constitute discrimination, and Black people were not deprived of equal protection of the law under the fourteenth amendment. American justice!

Segregation automatically meant discrimination. Black people were forced to use in public buildings, freight elevators and toilet facilities reserved for janitors. On trains, all Black people, even those with first-class tickets, were forced to seat themselves in the baggage car. Employment discrimination and wage discrimination, "inferior" schools for Black children. All of these inhuman crimes were made legal by the highest court in the land. Typical American justice, for Black people.

In 1954, only after intense domestic pressure and international unveiling as a nation of hypocrites, the Supreme Court reversed the infamous *Plessy vs. Ferguson* decision and ruled that segregated educational facilities were unconstitutional. But this ruling, like virtually every seemingly just decision for Black people, was almost immediately revealed as a sham, a mere gesture to pacify us and alleviate your embarrassment. For the public schools of the nation are still overwhelmingly segregated and unequal, the result of a century of duality.

In the North, in the South, in the East and in the West, all over the country Black people are accused of crimes, thrown in your jails, dragged through your courts and administered a sour dose of "American justice." We are in jail outside, and in jail inside. Black people and now all poor people have been well educated in the American system of justice.

We know very well what is meant by your statement, "This court is responsible for maintaining proper respect for the administration of criminal justice and preventing any reflection on the image of American justice." Properly translated, it simply means that the farce must go on. The image must remain intact.

It is precisely these contradictions—of maintaining justice as a reality or rhetorically asserting such procedure—that must be resolved. The process of judicial determination by which the legal rights of private parties or the people are vindicated and the guilt or innocence of accused persons is established has a history that is as variable as the color and the class of the individual prosecuted. It is not only doubtful, it is appalling, to say the least.

Accusations of contempt for the "dignity" of and lack of respect for the court indicate to us, the defendants, that a devious attempt by the court prevails to obscure the truth of these proceedings. There is a glaring distinction between theory and practice within the "halls of justice" which is consistent with judicial history as it pertains to Black and poor people. This is why the brief history. What fool cannot see that the "justice" of which you speak has a dual interpretation quite apart from the legal definition and is in keeping with "slave-master" traditions?

In light of historical fact, we must put into the proper perspective, context, and true time continuum the question as to whether justice and United States constitutional rights are effectively afforded unvaryingly to all who stand before the "American system" of justice, that exercises due process.

Just law, in reality, shall not be defamed by its dual application according to racial and social values because of wealth, position and influence. History provides doubt of the "American system" of justice when comparison of class orientation defines the degree of rights, respect and justice the individual shall receive. Political favor for judicial position has not varied even to the present.

With such political relationships existing, have the courts, in practice, escaped from the abuse of authority which is a threat to the development of a free nation of people? Fascism encroaches in just such a manner. Historically the qualitative change in society still reveals a lack of humane interaction with the socially, economically and politically exploited and isolated Black and poor peoples. The preceding chronology substantiates a blatant contempt for Black people and other non-white poor people, not recognizing their human rights and liberties as a matter of law, or morality, and substantiates a total disregard to our social reality, and is an insult to us. We can see the yesterday in today, and the history of our particular case runs upon the same tracks as does our people's long struggle.

This court represents the most ruthless system in the world, caring nothing for the wholesale misery that it brings, while at the same time your papers are full of verbiage of your "nobility," "righteousness," "justice," "fairness," and the "good" that you do.

We are very, very sick and tired of the BIG LIE. We cannot stand passive to the big lie any longer. We cannot accept it any longer.

It is time to state the truth, for Black people, for poor Puerto Rican, Mexican American, Chinese American, Indian and poor white people. The "Amerikkan system of justice" is a hideous sham and a revolting farce.

We must look at the situation objectively. As has been implied in the preceding, we realize that we are not second-class citizens at all. We are a colonized people. (Read your own Commission Reports.) We see that we are still considered chattel. We see how the Fugitive Slave Act has been modified in words, but is still being used, how the Dred Scott decision was never really reversed. That the thirteenth, fourteenth and fifteenth amendments of the Constitution did not liberate us— that in fact, in social reality, they only legalized slavery and expanded the Dred Scott decision to include Indians, Spanish-speaking and poor white people.

We see that things have not gotten better, but only progressively worse, and that includes tyranny. We completely oppose racism and tyranny and will continue to do so. You wish us to act according to a decorum set down by an organization, the "American Bar Association," which is not only racist, but is also not against genocide. (Perhaps they realize the truth, and see that the American ruling class is definitely liable for its treatment of Black people?)

In court you ask us to submit to a code of laws . . . your laws, not our laws (Black and poor people) but *your* laws— your laws because we were never asked (Black people) if we consented to having them as our laws, nor are these laws relevant to our ghetto reality. They are *your* laws, and we find them racist and oppressive. They, these laws, perpetuate our plantation continuation. Right now, in 1970, ninety percent of the inmates of your prisons are non-white. Ninety percent! And we (Black people, etc.) have never had the right to decide if we wanted to be governed by laws which we had no part in making. Yet, the primary concern of the men who drafted the "Declaration of Independence" was the *consent* of the governed by laws which they had a part in forming and which were relevant to them. We are in your prison, but these are not our laws. They are your laws, and in dealing with Black and poor people, you do not even adhere to *your own laws*.

In fact, a leading criminologist, Dr. R. R. Korn of Stanford University, has noted that eighty percent of the people now in prison were put there *illegally* according to *your* own law. (Strange that the overwhelming population is Black and non-white?)

Mr. Murtagh—your record speaks for itself. You are known in the ghetto as a "hanging judge." (How many Black and white poor men did you convict without their even having counsel just in 1969 alone, in your clever slick way?) Frank Hogan and his aides are well known—very well known in the ghetto—known for what they are—racist and unethical. (We have knowledge of cases, since our incarceration, of assistant district attorneys or D.A.'s men posing as legal aides to get conviction.) But in our case you and Mr. Hogan have gotten together and have outdone yourselves in denying us *all*, every one of our "alleged" state, federal and human rights. The record clearly shows this, when not clouded with the mist of racism.

A) Let us clear up one basic misconception. You constantly refer to this case as a "criminal" trial, while all of the time we *know*, you *know*, Frank Hogan knows, the people know, the other prisoners and even the guards know that this is *not* a criminal trial. Everyone knows that this is a political trial, for if we were not members of the Black Panther Party, a lot of things would never have been done to us in the first place.

Why are we not allowed to be with other prisoners? Why are we not allowed to even talk to the other prisoners? Why are we isolated? (Something we might say or do that can open their eyes, perhaps?) Alleged murderers and rapists are not treated in this manner, even "convicted" murderers and rapists are not treated in the manner in which we were treated. Why do you persist in the big lie? It is one of many clear contradictions.

B) On April 2, 1969, hordes of "police" broke down our doors or otherwise forced entry into our homes, and ran amuk. Rampaging and rummaging through our homes, they seized articles from us with wild abandon while having no search warrants. The "police" put us and our families in grave danger, nervously aiming shotguns, rifles and pistols at us and our families—even our children.

We were then kidnapped, as were some of our families. We state "kidnap" because many of us were never shown any arrest warrant, even to this day. This is illegal. This is a blatant contradiction of your own Constitution . . . We said nothing.

C) Upon the arrest of *some* of the defendants and before the appearance of any of the defendants, New York City district attorney Frank Hogan appeared on national radio and national television (channels 2, 4, 5, 7, 9, and 11) in a press conference, during which time he gave out information from an "indictment" against us in an inflammatory and provocative manner, deliberately designed to incite the people against us and to deny us even the semblance of a "fair trial." Mr. Hogan implied a lie—that we had been seized on the way to commit these alleged acts with bombs in our hands—rather than the truth—that we had no bombs and that most of us were taken out of our beds.

Subsequent to that press conference, "unidentified police sources" and "persons close to the investigation" stated falsely to the press that we, as members of the Black Panther Party, were being aided and abetted by foreign governments considered hostile to your government (i.e. Cuba and China)— that we, as Black Panther Party members, were stealing money from federal and/or state agencies and many other false, wild charges designed to heighten the public alarm against us and our Party, rather than diminish it, so as to create an atmosphere conducive to the extermination of the Black Panther Party and justify anything that might be done to us.

This unethical behavior gave, aided, and abetted further prejudicial pre-trial publicity, in direct contradiction to your law as outlined in the Fourteenth Amendment of your Constitution of the United States. Due to this behavior alone, we are positive that we could not get a fair trial anywhere in this country . . . We still said nothing.

D) When our attorneys learned of our arrest, they attempted to see us, as we were being held in your district attorney's office. They were refused permission to do so. At the "arraignment" a similar request by our counsel was again refused by Mr. Charles Marks, who presided thereat. These refusals were in blatant violation of your law as outlined in the Sixth and Fourteenth amendments of your Constitution of the United States . . . We continued to be silent.

E) At this "arraignment" this Mr. Charles Marks, who was presiding, refused to read, explain or give us a copy of this "indictment" against us. This is another violation of your law as outlined in the Sixth and Fourteenth amendments of your Constitution of the United States . . . Yet, we remained silent.

F) Bail (ransom) was set at $100,000, which is ridiculous and tantamount to no bail at all. This is another violation of your own law as outlined in the Eighth and Fourteenth amendments of your Constitution of the United States. We state that this bail is not only contradictory to your own law, but that it is also racist. When white "radical" groups are arrested, their bails do not usually exceed $10,000. When three Yemenites were charged with "conspiracy" to murder your President Nixon, and with the equipment to do such, their bail was $25,000; when Minutemen in New York were arrested and charged with a conspiracy to commit murder, the murder of 155 persons, and were arrested with more than enough bombs and guns to do this, bail was set at $25,000. We had no bombs. Our bail was $100,000 . . . We remained silent.

G) At this arraignment, this Mr. Charles Marks, the same "judge" who is alleged to have signed the "arrest warrants," stated in words or substance that he was accepting all of the allegations in the "indictment" against us to be true. On subsequent hearings during April and May 1969, concerning reduction of ransom (bail), at which this same Mr. Marks still presided, he stated that we were "un-American" and that the law "did not apply to us" (sounds of history?). This does not quite show impartiality . . . Yet, we said nothing.

H) Our counsel have been in front of at least 35 "judges" concerning our bail, and this attitude permeates the "great American system of justice." All motions on this were denied, either without comment or because of the "seriousness" of the "charges," but *never* dealing with the constitutional issues involved, and it is *your* Constitution. All of this seems to underlie "judge" Marks's remarks . . . Yet, we said nothing.

I) We have been treated like animals—in fact, like less than animals. On January 17, 1969, Miss Joan Bird was kidnapped, beaten, and tortured. She was punched and beaten, given the "thumb torture," hung upside down by the ankle from out of a third-story window of a "Police Precinct." On April 2–3, 1969, some of us were beaten as we were being kidnapped. From April 2, 1969, all of us were placed under constant abuse and harassment, which included 24-hour lock-in, complete isolation, no library or recreation, lights kept on in our cells for 24 hours, physical assaults, deprivations of seeing our families, at times denied mattresses, medication, sheets, showers, pillow-cases, towels, soap, toothpaste, and toilet paper.

Our families have suffered abuse in visiting us, and mental anguish. One of us suffered the loss of a child because of this. Some of our families had to go on welfare because of our outrageous incarceration and ransom. We were denied mail, even from our attorneys—denied access to consult all together with our attorneys. We have been subjected to the most onerous and barbaric of jail conditions. The objective of all this was our psychological and physical destruction during our pretrial detention.

As *Newsweek* Magazine even states, ". . . the handling of the suspects between their arrest and their trial was something less than a model of American criminal justice," and "none of it was very becoming to the state." (How well we know.) All this is a blatant violation of your own law as outlined in the Eighth and Fourteenth amendments of your own Federal Constitution . . . Yet, we *still* remained silent.

J) You—Murtagh. You came into the case in May 1969. You were informed of these conditions. You could have righted these blatant violations of your own law, the laws you have "sworn" to uphold. But you did not. You refused to do this . . . and remained silent. You tried to rush us pell-mell to trial, knowing full well that we were not, could not, be prepared . . . We remained silent.

We filed motions that are guaranteed to "citizens" by the Fourteenth Amendment of your Federal Constitution. You denied them all. You denied us the right, as guaranteed in your laws in the Sixth and Fourteenth amendments of your own Constitution, to conduct a *voir dire* of the grand jury in these proceedings, knowing full well that they did not comprise members of our peer group . . . We remained silent.

You denied us a hearing with which to be confronted with the witnesses against us, as is guaranteed by your law in the Sixth Amendment of your Constitution . . . We remained silent.

You denied us a Bill of Particulars, which is guaranteed by your laws in the Sixth and Fourteenth amendments of your Constitution . . . We remained silent.

Two "suspects" were kidnapped under the modification of the Fugitive Slave Act in November 1969. You gave them no bail. (No sense pretending anymore, it seems.) . . . We remained silent.

You denied us every state and federal constitutional right, and remained silent. You substantiated Mr. Marks's "the law does not apply" to us . . . Yet, we remained silent.

K) Lee Berry. Lee Berry is a classical example of how you and your cohorts conduct the "American System of Justice" when dealing with Black people. On April 3, 1969, Lee Berry was a patient in the Veterans' Administration Hospital where he was receiving treatment as an epileptic, subject to Grand Mal seizures, which can be fatal. Lee Berry is not mentioned particularly in the "indictment." Yet, on April 3, 1969, your "police" dragged him out of the hospital. These "police" stood him up before your cohort, "judge" Marks. Lee was "arraigned" without counsel. Bail $100,000. He was thrown into an isolation cell in the Tombs without even a mattress. In July 1969, he was physically attacked without provocation and without warning, while he was in a drugged stupor.

You were aware of his condition—you were quite aware. Numerous motions were in your "Great Court System." It took four months to even get him medication, and only in November when he had become so ill, so progressively worse that it was frightening. He finally got consent to be transferred to Bellevue Hospital. Because of the court's decisions under your "American System of Justice," Lee Berry has had four serious operations within the last two months. Because of the court's

decisions under the great American System of Justice at this
precise moment Lee Berry is lying in the shadow of Death with
a possible fatal case of pneumonia. At the very least, your
Great Court System is guilty of attempted murder, and D.A.
Hogan should be named as a co-defendant. Lee Berry is our
Brother, and what is done to him has been done to us all . . .
and we remained silent.

L) In November 1969, four white persons were arrested for
allegedly "bombing" various sites in New York City. They were
arrested allegedly with "bombs in their possession," but they
were white. For three of them, bail was reduced eighty percent
in two days, because "the presumption of innocence is basic
among both the statutory and constitutional principles affecting bail" . . . if you are white. (The political climate is such
today, even this hardly matters any more if one is dissident.)

Two days after that decision, we were brought in front of
you and given a superseding "indictment." We could be silent
no longer. We had been insulted enough—more than enough.
We had been treated with contempt in an atmosphere of intimidation for too long.

We must reiterate—we are looking at the situation objectively. Objective reality.

At the pre-trial hearings we are confronted with a "judge"
who has admitted, in fact been indicted and arrested for ignoring "police" graft and corruption . . . a "judge" who by
his record shows an unblemished career of "police" favoritism
and all-American racism. In your previous dealings with Black
people, you have shown yourself to be totally unjust, blood-
thirsty, pitiless, and inhuman. We are confronted with a district attorney machine which has shown itself to be vigilant
and unswerving in its racist policies. Ninety percent of the inmates convicted are nonwhite and poor. This machine has
shown itself to be unethical in its techniques and practices—
even in front of our eyes—tactics which include going up to
and whispering to the witnesses on the stand, signalling and
coaching them. We know, as *Look* Magazine stated in June
1969, "how the police corrupt the truth . . . Prosecutors and
judges become their accomplices." To cite a small example:
A man, a Black man, was beaten to death in the Tombs in
front of forty witnesses in May 1969 and the police swore that
he died of a "heart attack." Yes, we *know* what the police will
swear to. All Black people, poor people, know what the police
will swear to. With all this, together with the hostility inculcated in the dominant white culture towards anything Black,
is shown by you and your cohorts very well indeed. Under
these conditions, and considering our stand on American racism, this is not only a challenge to us and Black people, but

the whole people. To relate in terms you can understand, which Racist Woodrow Wilson stated (concerning fascism): "This is a challenge to all mankind; there is one choice we cannot make, we are incapable of making, we will not choose the path of submission . . . we will be, we must be as harsh as the Truth and as uncompromising as Justice—true Justice —is on our side." To that we say, Right On!

You have implied contempt charges. We cannot conceive of how this could be possible. How can we be in contempt of a court that is in contempt of its own laws? How can you be responsible for "maintaining respect and dispensing justice," when you have dispensed with justice, and you do not maintain respect for your own Constitution? How can you expect us to respect your laws, when you do not respect them yourself? Then you have the audacity to demand respect, when you, your whole Great System of Justice is out of order and does not respect us, or our rights.

You have talked about our counsel inciting us. Nothing could be further from the truth. The injustices we have been accorded over the past year incite us, the injustice in these hearings incites us, racism incites us, fascism incites us, in short—when we reflect back over history, its continuation up until today, you and your courts incite us.

But we will not leave it there for you and others, to distort, as some are inclined to do. There will be left no room for your courts and media to distort and misinterpret our actions. We wish for a speedy and FAIR trial, a just trial. But—we must have our alleged constitutional rights. This court is in contempt of our constitutional rights and has been for almost a year. We must have our rights first. The wrongs inflicted must be redressed. Bygones are *not* bygones. Later for that. Three hundred and fifty-one and one-half years are enough. We must clean the slate. We do not believe in your appeals courts (we've had experience with 300 years of appeals generally, and thirty-five judges specifically). So we must begin with a mutual understanding anew. When we have our constitutional guarantees redressed, we will give the court the respect it claims to deserve—precisely the respect it deserves.

In light of all that has been said, in view of the collusion of the federal, state, and city courts, the New York City Department of Correction, the city police, and district attorney's office, we feel that we, as members of the Black Panther Party, cannot receive a fair and impartial trial without certain preconditions conforming to our alleged constitutional rights. So we state the following: we feel that the courts should follow their own federal Constitution, and when they have failed to do so, and continue to ignore their mistakes, but persist dogmatically to add insult to injury, those courts are in contempt of the people. One need not be black to relate to that, but it is often those who never experience such actions on the part of the courts who believe they, the courts, can never be wrong.

So, in keeping with that, and the social reality to which that principle must relate, we further state:

1) That we have a constitutional right to reasonable bail, and that a few of us would, if they were white, be released in their own custody. We demand that right, and the court's consistent denial of that right in effect is in contempt of its own Constitution.

2) We demand a jury of our peers, or people from our own community, as defined by the Constitution.

3) We say that because the grand jury system in New York City systematically excludes poor Black people, it cannot be representative of a cross-section of the community from which we come. So in effect it is unconstitutional, and nothing more than a method of wielding class power and racial suppression and repression. We demand to have a constitutional and legal indictment, or be released, for we are being held illegally, by malicious and racist unethical laws.

4) We demand that the unethical practice of the police and D.A.'s office in their production of evidence, lying, and misrepresentation, be strictly limited by the introduction of an impartial jury of our peers for all pre-trial hearings, to judge all motions and evidence submitted, subsequent to a new constitutional indictment.

Therefore, since you have effectively denied by your ruling of Wednesday, February 25, 1970, our right to a trial, and since this ruling will affect the future of Black and white political prisoners, we have directed our attorneys to do everything in their power to upset this vicious, barbaric, insidious and racist ruling, which runs head-on in contrast with the promise of the Thirteenth and Fourteenth amendments of your U.S. Constitution.

Let this be entered into all records pertaining to our case.

All power to the people!

Lumumba Abdul Shakur
Richard Moore (Analye Dharuba)
Curtis Powell
Michael Tabor (Cetewayo)
Robert Collier
Walter Johnson (Baba Odinga)
Afeni Shakur

John J. Casson (Ali Bey Hassan)
Alex McKiever (Catarra)
Clark Squire
Joan Bird
Lee Roper
William King (Kinshasa)

Soledad Brothers and the Marin County Shootout

On Friday, August 7, 1970, a seventeen-year-old Black youth named Jonathan Jackson entered the Marin County (Calif.) courthouse with a satchel full of guns. He promptly handed the weapons to James McClain, 37, a Black prisoner from San Quentin who was standing trial for allegedly stabbing a guard, and to William Christmas, 37, and Ruchell Magee, 31, fellow prisoners who were there to testify in McClain's defense. The three men then took as hostages the judge, Harold J. Haley, the assistant district attorney, Gary Thomas, and three jurors.

They entered a rented van and began to leave the courthouse area when police guards opened fire. The judge, McClain, Christmas and the Jackson youth were killed. Magee and the assistant district attorney were seriously wounded.

Before he left the courtroom with the hostages, Jackson issued a demand: "Free the Soledad Brothers by 12:30 tomorrow."

George Jackson, one of the three Soledad Brothers, is Jonathan's actual brother. Coincidentally, his story and that of his codefendants, all accused of murdering a prison guard, had just appeared in the August 1970 issue of Ramparts Magazine in Eve Pell's "The Soledad Brothers: How a Prison Picks Its Victims." Included at the end of the article was one of George Jackson's letters from *prison. It was part of a collection of letters published a few months later as* Soledad Brother: The Prison Writings of George Jackson *(New York: Bantam Books, 1970). Reprinted here is the Eve Pell article and an original letter, "George Jackson Speaking—From Dachau, Soledad Prison, California," smuggled out of jail just two days before the Marin County incident. (This letter was published in* The Village Voice, *September 10 and 17, 1970.)*

I have included a third document, the first news analysis of the shoot-out in the local underground press—"We Are the Revolution," published in the August 14–21, 1970 issue of the Berkeley Tribe. *The relationship among the Soledad Brothers, George and Jonathan Jackson, and the Marin County courthouse shoot-out have a historical unity and political significance which illustrates the anguish of those who are forced to live, submit, and die in American prisons by way of the American system of criminal justice.* —*Ed.*

How a Prison Picks Its Victims
by Eve Pell*

Think of California's Monterey County and you'll probably imagine quaint shops in Carmel, gnarled pines hanging wind-swept above one of the most dramatic beaches on the West Coast, or exclusive mountain hideaways for the wealthy. You may remember that Joan Baez has her school for nonviolence in Monterey, that the Esalen Institute offers sessions in sensitivity training, or that hitchhiking hippies are taking over beautiful Big Sur.

Images of the easy life come to mind quickly. But there is another side to the county not mentioned in Chamber of Commerce leaflets and not part of the tourists' beaten

---

* Copyright © 1970 by Eve Pell. First appeared in *Ramparts*, August 1970.

paths. Inland from the resorts lies the Salinas Valley, flat acres of rich farmland whose white owners once employed vigilance committees and strikebreakers to intimidate and occasionally kill migrant workers. This is the part of the county that John Steinbeck saw. South from Salinas is an even uglier reality—Soledad Prison. Here, the violence and brutality that were once part of the chaos of the Depression have been evoked again with the murders of three of the prison's Black inmates.

When Soledad (more properly known as California Training Facility at Soledad) opened in 1946, it was touted as a progressive institution. Perhaps it is, but over the years prisoners have come to know it as the "gladiator school" or the "front line" because of the intensity of the racial hostility which exists between guards and inmates, and among the inmates themselves. Letters detailing the brutality of daily life inside the prison have made their way to inmates' families and attorneys and finally to the attention of legislators in Sacramento. Finally, in June 1970, California State Senator Mervyn Dymally made an inspection of the maximum security part of the prison, accompanied by two staff members and Bay Area attorney Fay Stender. The group wanted to distribute a questionnaire, to be filled out and returned on the spot by prisoners so that no one would be punished for complaining about conditions.

The plan ran afoul of Ray Procunier, Director of the California Department of Corrections, and of the czars of the prison. "If there's any questionnaire," said Procunier, "I'm going to put it in there. If there's anything wrong going on down here, we want to be the first to know about it." Dymally submitted, and after touring the prison's "O" wing, the senator's group reassembled in the warden's office to talk over what they had learned from brief discussions with inmates. They were especially concerned about Black prisoners' complaints about food being contaminated. Urine in their coffee, and similar harassments.

"It's my opinion that the food is not being tampered with," said Procunier. "From a management point of view, we don't want it. There's just a bad set of feelings going around this joint." When Dymally suggested that there must be some basis for the fact that so many letters and complaints had mentioned this, Procunier turned to his prison officials. "Now I want you to tell me the truth," he warned. "Has it ever happened that someone has urinated in anyone's coffee?" When the four men shook their heads from side to side in unison, he turned back, satisfied.

After they had asked a few more questions and received Procunier's arbitrary answers, Dymally's group left Soledad without ever getting to the prison's major problem— the rampant racism that has led to a series of murders of Black inmates and, more recently, to the outrageous framing and prosecution of three others who have become known as the Soledad Brothers.

A Black inmate in Soledad's maximum security section wrote recently about the racial hatred there:

> On——, A.B. and myself were transferred to Soledad Correctional Facility. We were placed in the Max Row section, "O" wing. Immediately entering the sallyport area of this section I could hear inmates shouting and making remarks such as, "Nigger is a scum lowdown dog," etc. I couldn't believe my ears at first because I knew that if I could hear these things the officers beside me could too, and I started wondering what was going on. Then I fixed my eyes on the wing sergeant and I began to see the clear picture of why those inmates didn't care if the officials heard them instigating racial conflict. The sergeant was, and still is, a known prejudiced character towards blacks. I was placed in cell No.——, and since that moment up til now I have had no peace of mind. The white inmates make it a 24-hour job of cursing black inmates just for kicks, and the officials harass us with consistency also.

On "Max Row," prisoners remain in solitary confinement in little cells like iron boxes twenty-three and a half hours a day. Heavy screens, not just bars, shut them in, and they are fed through holes in their respective doors.

Another prisoner wrote from "O" wing about food service there:

The prison officials here stopped serving the meals and deliberately selected the Caucasian and Mexican inmates to serve the meals and they immediately proceeded to poison our meals by filling food to be issued to us with cleanser powder, crushed glass, spit, urine and feces while the officials stood by and laughed.

For many months prior to January 1970, inmates of "O" wing had not been permitted to exercise in groups. The deputy superintendent of Soledad, who has called "O" wing "a prison within a prison," explained that "difficulties between inmates had occurred, and fights—serious fights, assaults, assaults without weapons, assaults with weapons—had occurred when we attempted to permit people to exercise together." Last December, a new exercise yard was built for these inmates. It didn't open on schedule because some work remained unfinished. A Black prisoner wrote, "I did notice that white inmates and officials were awfully cheerful for some reason or another and they continuously didn't forget to remind us of the yard opening soon."

In the second week of January, thirteen inmates were skin-searched—stripped, their clothes examined, their buttocks parted, and searched for concealed weapons. The guards found no weapons and allowed them into the yard. No guards went with them, but Guard O. G. Miller, known to be an expert marksman, was stationed in a tower thirteen feet over the yard, armed with at least one loaded carbine.

Predictably, Black and white inmates began to fight in the yard. Without a warning the guard in the tower fired four shots. Three Blacks—Alvin Miller, Cleveland Edwards, and W. L. Nolen—were fatally wounded, and one white was shot in the groin. At least one of the Blacks remained alive and moving. His friends wanted to get him to the prison hospital as fast as they could.

"I looked at the tower guard," one of them later explained,

and he was aiming the gun toward me and I thought then that he meant to kill me too, so I moved from the wall as he fired and went over to stand over inmate X, all the while looking the guard in the gun tower in the face. He aimed the gun at me again and I just froze and waited for him to fire, but he held his fire. After I saw he was not going to fire I pointed to where inmate X lay, with two other Black inmates bending over him, and started to walk to him very slowly. The inmate I had played handball with suggested that I take inmate X to the hospital so I kneeled so inmate X could be placed on my shoulder, then started to walk toward the door through which we had entered the yard, and the tower guard pointed the gun at me and shook his head. I stopped and begged him for approximately ten minutes to let me take X to the hospital but all he did was shake his head. Then I started forward with tears in my eyes, expecting to be shot down every second. The tower guard told me, "That's far enough." Then another guard gave me permission to bring X off the yard and I was ordered to lay him on the floor in the officer's area and go to my cell.

By the time this drama was completed, the wounded man was dead.

Why were these three Black men shot? W. L. Nolen had been known throughout the prison as a tough man who had maintained his identity and his pride. Cleveland Edwards, in jail for the political crime of assaulting a police officer, had also been a visible Black leader. Alvin Miller had been neither militant nor a leader, but he closely resembled the ranking Black Panther in Soledad, Earl Satcher, who was also in the exercise yard at the time of the shooting. Nolen had known that he was marked for death. He had told his father so during a recent visit. The father had tried to see the warden in order to arrange protection for his son, but the warden had been "too busy" to see him. Miller also had had a premonition of death, perhaps because of the taunting he had received from whites about the opening of the yard. One week before it opened, he wrote a farewell letter to his mother.

In a civil rights suit filed in federal court against prison officials Cletus Fitzharris, Superintendent; William Black, Deputy Superintendent; Clement Swagerty, Associate Warden; and O. G. Miller, Guard, attorney Melvin Belli states that

O. G. Miller maliciously shot and killed W. L. Nolen, Alvin Miller, and Cleveland Edwards, because of his general hatred of persons of African descent and because of his particular hatred of one of the decedents, W. L. Nolen, who had struck O. G. Miller during a previous altercation between the two. . . .

[Miller] knew that the possibility of serious bodily injury or death from the engaging in fisticuffs was minimal and that his shooting at the decedents' vital parts would almost certainly cause their death or serious bodily injury; yet he made the deliberate choice to shoot.

The suit further charges that prison officials "fostered" extreme racial tension in the prison by maintaining rigid segregation of the races; that they knew O. G. Miller to be prejudiced against Blacks; that they did not arrange for prompt treatment of the injured prisoners and so they are responsible for the deaths.

After these killings, the already tense atmosphere at Soledad became explosive. When the Monterey County Grand Jury held hearings at the prison to decide if charges should be filed against O. G. Miller, no Blacks who had been in the yard were permitted to testify, although some whites were. As they were being walked over to appear before the Grand Jury, they were reminded by guards, "Remember, there *was* a warning shot."

Shortly after the prison radio broadcast to the inmates at Soledad that Officer O. G. Miller had been exonerated of the murder of the three Black inmates, a white guard named John V. Mills was found dying in "Y" wing. He had been beaten and thrown from a third-floor tier down into the television room thirty feet below.

Deputy Superintendent William Black stated, "We believe that the death of Officer Mills was reprisal for the death of the three Black inmates." And, as if to balance some score being kept, prison officials proceeded to find three Black suspects who, they said, had killed Mills. The accused were Fleeta Drumgo, 23; John W. Clutchette, 24; and George L. Jackson, 28. Tall and bespectacled, Jackson handles himself well. He is serving a one-year-to-life sentence for robbery and has done ten years. Although the

median sentence for that crime is two-and-a-half years,
the California Adult Authority has yet to set his parole
date. Like the three Black inmates murdered in January,
he is known throughout the prison as a Black who has
held onto his identity, who has refused to lower his eyes
and accept indignities. Jackson was not politically aware
when he entered prison, but during the past ten years he
has read extensively and has understood from his prison
experiences what has happened to Black people in America. Jackson is a writer.

His father has worked hard all his life, often holding
down two jobs so that his family would have enough. He
preached the traditional virtues to his children, as well as
faith in the American way.

George Jackson and his mother are light-skinned. His
younger brother is very light and has reddish hair. When
Jackson was fifteen, he remembers being brought before a
judge after he had piled up the family car. The judge told
him that he could go far if he would behave. "Look at your
little brother," said the judge, "how cute and nice he is.
And your mother is a nice-looking woman. You know that
families like this go farther than the real dark families
and the real black people." Later George said to his
mother, "Somehow I wish he'd have gone on and sent me
to jail rather than say that to me." That was Jackson's first
experience with "justice."

Jackson's route to Soledad is a familiar trail for Blacks.
Poor young Black men from the ghetto in their first brush
with the law are tarred with a record they would never
have if they were middle class or white. Later on they get
into suspicious circumstances and are arrested on heavier
charges. They plead guilty because they can't establish innocence and already have a record; they don't get the light
sentence they were given to expect, and end up in prison
for long stretches.

Perhaps because the prison system forces definite
choices upon Black men, they have to define themselves
very clearly. Jackson got into trouble while he was first at
Soledad because in the television room he would not sit in

the back section unofficially "reserved" for Blacks. A fight broke out and authorities punished Jackson by sending him to San Quentin, where he spent two years isolated in the maximum security section.

Jackson, Drumgo, and Clutchette maintain that they were nowhere near the third tier of "Y" wing when John Mills was killed, and that they are innocent. Clutchette, who was imprisoned for burglary, had already been given a parole date and was to be home on April 28. Drumgo was scheduled to appear before the Adult Authority in April and had an excellent chance of getting a release date.

After the murder of the guard, all the inmates in "Y" wing were locked up and questioned for many days by guards, prison officials and the district attorney. From the beginning a terrible teamwork began to operate against the three who had been selected as victims. No defense attorneys were present at the questioning. Prison officials never notified the families of the suspects that their sons were in trouble. Jackson, for instance, had been in court twice before his mother ever heard of his situation. John Clutchette's mother was told that her son did not need a lawyer and that she need not attend his arraignment. "Your son will advise you by mail," she was told by Lieutenant Leflores of the prison staff. However, she scurried to legislators, the NAACP and other organizations, and was able to find an attorney, Floyd Silliman of Salinas, who would help her son. Clutchette, anxious after days of questioning and solitary confinement, prepared a list of witnesses who could testify to his innocence. He attempted to give this list to his mother, breaking a prison rule which forbids giving written material to anyone but an attorney—at the time, he had no attorney. The list was discovered and taken away from him; the inmates whose names were written were transferred to other prisons. Mrs. Inez Williams, mother of Fleeta Drumgo, heard about the guard's death on the radio and phoned the prison to see whether her son was in any way involved. Prison officials assured her that the investigation was "routine" and that she had no need for worry. "The prison gets the parents' consent for having a tooth pulled, and informs the parents of other things," she said, but she was never told her son was accused of murder.

State officials dealing with this case have been passionate in their desire to keep records secret. The Adult Authority will not let George Jackson's lawyers know how they decided his status. Prison officials won't let the lawyers see all of Jackson's files or look at any of their records about the killing of the three Blacks. The State of California, as both custodian and prosecutor of the three, holds control of the witnesses and the evidence. In the person of Judge Gordon Campbell, Presiding Judge of the Superior Court of Monterey County, it is also sitting in judgment.

A small old man with a shiny bald head, Campbell sits high in his chair overlooking the court, his face often blank and preoccupied. At pretrial hearings in March, April and May, he seemed like a Monterey version of Judge Julius Hoffman. At one hearing, the first to be packed with supporters and friends of the three defendants, he told the spectators that they probably would not like a visit from the bailiff and that they should sit quietly and not act as if they were "at a barbecue table or the local pool hall."

Campbell sometimes did the District Attorney's work for him; sometimes he even consulted him. He denied nearly all the motions made by the defense. In one instance, when the defense had asked to have a copy of the manual for correctional officers at the prison, Campbell said to the D.A., "I presume you object to that." The D.A. nodded. "Motion denied," said Campbell, and the defense could not have the manual.

As soon as better-known Bay Area attorneys entered the case in late February, the judge issued an order forbidding them or the prosecution from making any statements to the press about matters relevant to the case. The attorneys were barred from the prison, unable to see the site of the murder until it had been remodeled, unable to interview witnesses. The prosecution, which had had unlimited access to the prison from the very start, refused to divulge the names of witnesses or their whereabouts until forced to do so by a court order obtained many weeks later.

None of the accused has been convicted of violent crimes or of crimes against persons. Yet they have been chained and shackled whenever they speak with visitors or attorneys; they are chained and shackled even in the courtroom itself. Chains encircle their waists and hang between their legs; cuffs bind their ankles, which are chained together, and their wrists, which are chained to the waist chains. Padlocks swing as they move. In court when friends greet them with raised fists, the three lift up their fists slightly above their waists—as far as their chains allow.

In February, when the earliest court appearances took place, families and friends of the prisoners were not present. The prisoners were driven to the courthouse from prison and were marched in chains across the sidewalk through the main entrance to the courthouse while passersby hooted at them. Since that time the case has received some publicity and has attracted a concerned and sympathetic following. Now the three are driven in a station wagon which has had special screens constructed to fit over the windows so that neither people nor cameras can intrude; they are driven directly into the basement garage of the courthouse and hustled upstairs through corridors where the public cannot go. Thus the men, who spend their other hours in solitary confinement, cannot even glimpse the crowd of their well-wishers.

People are beginning to find out who the Soledad Brothers are, and they're learning a little about what California prisons are like. But bitter winds of repression are blowing once again inside Monterey County, and it is likely that the three men will be on Max Row for a long time to come.

George Jackson Speaking:
From Dachau, Soledad Prison, California*

This message was smuggled out on roll-your-own ciga-
rette paper at great risk to the prison's one sympathetic
guard. Its intent is to make it impossible for you to claim
ignorance later on, after the war, when the world sits
down to judge you, Amerikan society, Anglo-Saxon law.
"We didn't know those things were going on," will not save
you from the condemnation of history and the world's
people.

Behind prison walls, that's where I've been for ten years
now. Seven years at "the end of the world, San Quentin"
(that spot on the social map where one falls over the edge,
into infinity), three years of being shuttled back and forth
between the other concentration centers instituted to confine the most desperate victims of the Amerikan corporate
nightmare; I have spent the last year-and-a-half here in
Soledad. Consequently, the seriously revolutionary groups
and parties developed out of their colonial capitals in my
absence. The Black Panther Party, DRUM, SDS, the Peace
and Freedom Party, the facets of La Raza, the gratifying
and anomalous Weathermen, the Che-Lumumba Collective were all delivered into the bowels of the beast when I
(and my class) could do little more than watch and ap-
plaud. With periscope up and ear to the ground, I watched
with remorse as the revolutionary infant mortality rate
swelled to claim many whom I had known personally or
had come to regard as kindred spirits.

We were not, however, completely disconnected from
the poor people's revolutionary stirrings. I lost nothing
these ten years. There were, as always, the singular examples of revolutionary spirit from the Blacks who under-

---

stood, the survivalists, men who under normal circumstances would have been to our people what Uncle Ho,
Castro, The Bung, and Mao were to theirs—if we would
have protected them—if we start protecting them now.
Men forced into economic crimes, or crimes of passion
against the forces that oppress them, should not be judged
by those who have escaped similar fate merely by chance.
The Eldridge Cleavers, Huey Newtons, Bobby Seales, and
all the others who have resisted, survived, and by their
exemplary sacrifices promoted the survival of our people;
the ones who are never heard from, who live through their
desperate days, years, in and out of these places of wrath
and tears, Joe Cline, George "Big Take" Louis, Bill Christmas, James B. Johnson, Nate Boothe, Clifford Jefferson,
Lacy, and the thousands, the best of our whole kind, the
most desperate and damned, the future of our people—
these brothers are slated for immolation, they're made of
unbendable Black fiber and are standing unsupported,
growing unnaturally against a thing that constricts,
twists, remolds all its related parts to "fit" a dominant
enemy culture whose principal feature is an economics so
cruel, so grinding, so omnipresent and demanding of conformity that its "misfits" are so numerous as to form an
entirely new class, the new class leaders slated for immolation, large round pegs doggedly existing under pressure
from above to "fit" into small square holes. The process
will kill them. The square hole will be a grave.

I love them. I *feel* for them, as the most desperate and
advanced of the new revolutionary breed, as men. I'm
compelled to great feelings of love for these cats who refuse to kowtow, an unrestrained love, an inundation of
my damndest for these comrades who refuse defeat, who
stand at the center of Hades and spit at the flames. We
must support them.

Prisons, concentration camps, and similar places of
exile and detention are often the starting and, almost
equally often, the finishing point of the revolutionary
mind. No other experience, no other social phenomenon,
can equal the traumatic effect of imprisonment, the total

loss of all liberty. Any further downward movement takes
one out of this existence. Very few men forced into economic crimes by so impersonal a society as this one actually feel guilty enough to remain inside one of the walled
prisons two days. Were it not for the gun towers, the only
occupants would be the rats (four- and two-leg varieties).
Because a small body of men cannot govern a larger body
without either the consent of the larger body or force,
making the larger body submit, the prisoner has an opportunity to see his society and some of its products at its
worst. All pretenses and disguises are abandoned; the
guard is there to hold you, there is no need for him to fake
the idea that he is a public servant. He is there to kill you
if you touch the wall or resist his heavy hand too strongly.
Reducing men to dormancy and trembling is his trade.
There is no other method to successfully hold a man inside an Amerikan prison. A bad contact with just one of
these guards can literally kill you; his weapon may be the
pen or the rifle.

This is where "misfits" learn their proper role in society,
they are taught how to "fit"; in simple, graphic terms, they
are shocked into an understanding of "what it's all about."
The unrestrained brutality, the strict regimentation, all
under the title of rehabilitation for return to society, the
whole thing is a very strong comment on the real nature
of the society in which one is expected to "fit," on the men
who control that society, direct its thinking, strangle its
movement with an interlocking dictatorship that makes
its presence felt at every level of that society's existence.
Here capitalist and fascist man give full range to their ex-
cesses.

There is great significance attached to the sentiment
that to deprive another of his freedom can also mean a
concomitant loss for the man who is depriving. The obvious loss suffered by the guard is the time spent watching
the victim—but within the atrocious Amerikan prison
systems the whole intent is to trap, hold, and isolate its
victims. It shouldn't be hard to imagine what side-effects
this sort of activity will have on the mind of the guard.

Most of the men attracted to concentration camp work do not, to begin with, have a great deal of tenderness left in them. The preconceived notions regarding prison rationale in general are enough to dissuade any really healthy person from ever voluntarily signing on as a guard. Consider what types are usually drawn to gunslinger jobs. Any man who enters this work with his feelings, his sensibilities, intact must lose them or lose his job. Most prefer to keep the wage. We have then all of the ingredients of an extremely explosive exchange. The relations, on all levels, between keeper and kept will be defensive and antagonistic.

One senses immediately the reasons that underlie a defensive, reactive attitude on the part of the man who is trapped, but the reasons for a similar attitude on the part of the guard calls for a little more elaboration. Since the guard controls the gate and may call on the organized violence of his and other government forces, up to the U.S. Airborne Army, it may seem odd for him to feel insecure. This is the case, however—and I speak here as objectively as is possible, I never underestimate the intelligence of the people. It is a matter of *fact* that the guard is *less* psychologically secure than the man he has trapped. He is more defensive, reactive, *hostile*, than his victim. Although he controls the greater violence, he still feels that he can never relax. He knows he is one of forty men whose function is to suppress thousands, and although he can bring into play a superior arm, any prisoner among the thousands streaming past him on normal errands could be armed with a crude but lethal knife, club, or zipgun with silencer. Add to all of this the mechanics of control: aren't the forty who control the thousands the most hated of men? How else can they maintain internal control of the prison except through fear and terror tactics?

In these California prisons the usual setup is for several riflemen to take positions in towers or on catwalks over the heads of the entrapped and the rest of the guards. The catwalks are attached to the inside and outside walls of the connected cellblocks in San Quentin. Gun cover over the general population of Soledad comes from outside a centrally located "window gun post" in each of the wings. The guards are generally rotated so that every one of them enjoys the opportunity to man a tower or catwalk. But the days and months that a guard has to spend on the ground are what destroy anything at all that was good, healthy, or social about him before. Fear begets fear. And we come out with two groups of schizoids, one guarding the other. The spiral extends outward and up.

The guards who think for the others do not come into close contact with the prisoner but their responses are governed by some of the same fears that are driving the lowliest of turnkeys. These older and sometimes intelligent guards are actually the initial source of the organized violence, the planned terror. Their wage depends on control "without incident." When Sacramento is forced to wield its axe to satisfy political demands for stronger control (less killing and escape), the cuts will be aimed at the captains and wardens. The people who appoint them and the people who read newspapers don't like to hear of stirrings and discontent from behind the walls. It implies a lack of control over the men, that the system has turned against itself when the victims of the nightmare have been made to seem, and in some cases are, a threat to its continued existence.

For the intelligent inmate, the strongest deterrent to getting involved in any sort of violence at all is the observation that a serious injury will almost certainly result in death. The hospital facilities of one of these towns are very similar to what one would expect in any depressed or ghetto section of the country. Just always a little worse. We get an aspirin for a hole in the back. They put me to work in the hospital some years ago in San Quentin. I accepted the assignment only because it was in relatively clean surroundings. I would have plenty of time to follow my own pursuits and, being communistic by nature, I hoped to be able to change—any change would be an improvement—some of the conditions that were so damaging to the overall health of the inmate population, and in particular the Black population. The racist traditions of this "land of the free and home of the hunter" always seem to work to send a disproportionate percentage of Blacks in search of medical treatment. I set up my own clandestine medical clinic. Pain killers and suture, both sanitary, were my principal services, but any other item that I could liberate from the state was also available, from cough syrup to eye wash, and sometimes even food. The difference between my clinic and the state's was that mine remained available at all times in the cleanest possible setting. Also everything was available in the desired amounts. Of course there was no charge for any of this. The medicines that contained narcotics were the most expensive items. When I couldn't liberate enough of these I had to buy them with funds taken from our "people's mutual." The keepers objected and I eventually ended up working the graveyard shift in the psych ward. Power will never endure any challenge without an automatic reactionary response. A comrade took over the clinic.

The fear tactic reaches its finest development in the procedures governing the granting of paroles and discharges. In California courts a sentence of "what the law prescribes" means an "indeterminate" stay in the state's prisons. "Indeterminate" loosely translates "inconclusive, indefinite."

For what worked out to be a second-degree robbery I received a sentence of from one year to life. In other words, I may do life for the same economic offense that I would do one year. All the other sentences for various types and degrees of offenses are in general the same: three-to-life, five-to-live, ten-to-life, on up. "Lesser" sentences can also be drawn: six months to five years, six months to ten years, six months to fourteen years. The "to-life" sentences are technically considered life terms. A state law, especially designed to affect men doing life or "to-life" terms, can be found under section 4500 of the State Penal Code. It provides "that every person serving a life sentence who assaults another with a deadly weapon or by means likely to produce great bodily injury is pun-

ishable by death. If the person assaulted is another inmate, the punishment may be death or life without possibility of parole for nine years, consecutive to the present
term." I didn't change a word; it reads that way from the
Code Book. The language of "4500" is well known to all
lifers. It's the very first statute described in the little rule
book we are given upon our arrival. It's the first "rundown"
we receive from a comrade.

The obvious imbalances of this law are written right
into its face. Assault directed at another inmate "could"
mean death for the attacker, assault directed at a guard is
"certain" death for the attacker. But several other compli-
cations, ambiguities, and hidden fear-control devices
spring from this statute that affects the great majority of
the state's prison class (most of us are lifers!). Its first
and deepest psychological effect is to cause a transference
of hostility inward. I've seen the "keeper" slap a man at the
food serving line, take his trays and send him back to his
cell without dinner. The man that was slapped may have
been old enough to be the keeper's father. The urge to
strike out at the "keeper" will almost always be repressed.
In fact, most of the spontaneous fistfights between inmates occur immediately following an encounter between
one of the participants of the fight and a "keeper." I've
seen brothers that I would have never suspected to be
cowards, brothers and others of our class confined for rob-
beries, gun battles, and murder, I've seen them grovelling,
accepting the boot. "4500" and the indeterminate sentence
make the hardest man think ten times before defending
himself.

On the surface "4500" can be justified as a deterrent to
violence in general. In reality, it deters only the prisoner,
and as it works out in fact, it deters only the violence that
is aimed at the guard. No court system could possibly
handle all the fights that occur between prisoners, since
these fights are actively encouraged by the guards on the
safety-valve and divide-and-conquer principles. It flies in
the face of "equal protection" by making the death penalty
mandatory for a crime that is often dismissed with a light

county jail sentence and makes the question of a jury "penalty hearing" redundant since death is mandatory. This statute, aimed at one class only, when taken into context with the indeterminate sentence, works to destroy the "first and last freedom," the most basic right, the right to live.

The character of prison existence over these last ten years has changed so radically in flavor that the sense of fascist political reaction can no longer be hidden by the language of Establishment criminologists. The first changes, relatively small ones, came about just prior to the riot stage of the present Amerikan revolution, and as a result of Malcolm X's Muslim-style nationalism. A sizeable percentage of the Black prison population (about forty percent of the whole) went Muslim mainly to give some meaning to their persecution. Islam was the thing. At its upper levels were some seriously concerned brothers, down through the ranks were the objects of their concern, young brothers usually fresh from the outside prison, green, extremely retarded in survival technique and the intellectual or psychological stability required of life at the barricades.

The Muslims offered a small measure of group protection from the more flagrant abuses of the pig and against the customary racist attacks leveled at Blacks from the dozens of white and Mexican extortionists or right-oriented political cliques. These brothers encouraged their following to avoid the pig by respecting his exacting commandments right down to the "yes, sir" bit. The hostile convict groups were counterpoised by means of an extremely diplomatic bluff. The whole of their ideology was predicated upon prayer and nonviolent supplication. The keepers reacted with pick handles, tear gas, infiltration, special lockaway confinement, and new laws that of course created new crimes, which in turn meant longer prison terms for some—the always expected overreaction. Power's defense reflex reacted blindly to any and all fancied or real challenge. A few of these brothers at the upper levels suffered, but taken all together, the effect upon the

grass roots was in keeping with the general development
of a revolutionary cadre.

I did not join the Muslims because in principle I'm absolutely opposed to prayer. My philosophical persuasion
was, is, and always will be materialism, dialectical materialism; my economics, proletarian socialism; my understanding of problem-solving in general, workers'-people's
war on all that presently exists. After laboring through
Marx, Engels, Lenin, Mao, Nkrumah and the others I was
irreconcilably repelled by the gossamer slush talk, abraca-
dabra, the sheer distortion of, or absence of, historical
reality in the Muslim approach. I existed on the fringes of
their group with my much smaller, selective, highly disciplined, hopefully clandestine group. Our aim was to protect and to channel the rage into revolutionary "thinking,"
to superimpose upon the criminal mentality, the Muslim
mentality, and the barren mentality, the explosive doctrines of "Mao-think," people's government, self-determination.

It was at this point, after the first whisper of anti-
Establishment, that the concatenation of horrors began in
earnest. In '63 comrade Cleaver was instrumental in organizing a "physical criticism" of the kennel-like living
conditions inside San Quentin's adjustment center. The
following day another group of us outside the adjustment
center "physically criticized" the killing of one brother
Booker, the fatality of the preceding day's efforts. Huey
Newton and Bobby Seale were introducing people's revolutionary culture into the Black colony in the wake of
the riot stage. Just across the bay (I was then in San
Quentin), the terrible Black cat, product of the people's
indignation, was beginning an act that would soon transform the Black colony into a free fire zone of the occupy-
ing army and glut the prisons with a different form of
economic criminal, the "political" economic offender. The
myth of Amerikan acceptance of opposition party politics
was once more demonstrated, a final demonstration. The
Establishment's hypocritical tolerance of a Black Panther
Party, a Che-Lumumba collective, a DRUM has made the

nation's undertakers rich and concentrated so many thousands into these places of confinement, excruciation, wrath, terror, tears that we can no longer believe. We have lost the faith, all faith. Redemption to us means *death!* Ours, or the death of fascism.

We have no choice; our change is a natural, inherent response to the fact that they are now literally killing us. And no longer simply as example, but in a determined effort to be rid of us; to halt antithesis. Amerika does not seem to be unwilling to admit the existence of the fascist mentality. But we're under attack by a determined enemy who feels that he is right, who feels threatened, challenged by our existence. They have settled on us as "the problem" with Amerikan society. Intellectual arguments that destroy the logic of violence can never overcome our atavistic urge to survive; millions of years of conditioned reflex cannot be explained away, or even washed away in so short a time. It's too late to reform, the need is too immediate, and we have lost faith. We *will not* walk meekly to the "showers."

Because Amerika's thought control program allows for no political prisoners, the men and women who criticized the system in the language of those that call for redistribution of wealth and power, are crowded into these concentration centers in the name of the established law. Blacks have been returned to prison for "parole violations" when their only offense was perhaps selling a Black Panther newspaper or being seen at the headquarters. There are first offenders here whose only crime was being in the same city block in which a shoot-out took place. Black Panther Party members are sent to prison with one clear intention: to silence them. Since the political soldier must teach, the process has affected every Black man in prison, and further, just being seen with a Black Panther Party member will be cause enough to share in his impending ordeal.

The political presence and its concomitant reactionary violence and repression have affected our mailing privileges, our visiting privileges, access to court officials, reading material, all contact with the outside. Usually, I should say, the right to communicate is not openly abridged—our mail is simply lost or returned to sender by mistake, but usually lost. All incoming mail will be delayed if not thrown away. Visitors of unpopular inmates will be turned away or made to wait hours longer than necessary—discouraging without denying the contact. Queries regarding all this are invited, then it will be carefully explained to the would-be visitor that a comrade's behavior is so erratic or violent that special precautions were required to move him. And to some extent it will be true. We're being isolated so that the killings will go unnoticed.

All over the country the weakest of our class are being hired by local and federal governmental agencies to speak at ghetto gatherings, over the media and even in other prisons, in an effort to hide what is happening in the walled maximum security prisons. Feeble-minded, broken inmates are being used to assure the people that all is well behind the wall, that we're "all" alive and well, being educated, properly fed, reasonably disciplined, civilized, processed with velvet touches. They *are* attempting to cloak their murder strategy.

The real weight of this fresh wave of terror is falling with greater emphasis upon a certain type of Black, the ones who have not lost the cat instincts, the brothers who have stepped out of their places, with talk of people's government, decentralization of privileges, a kinship with other revolutionary cultures like Cuba, Vietnam, or China. We're being locked away from the general prison population, our food is being poisoned, medical treatment is being denied (or so delayed that every serious illness means death), "setups" based on racial antipathy encouraged, even promoted, by most of the "keepers." Most of the "setups" take place under the gun. It goes like this: a convict working with the police comes in low, swinging a knife. You block and flow into a counterattack, he leaps away, falling to the ground. The keeper, whose job it is to stop fights, shoots you through the heart. Simple, justified homicide, an officer performing his duty. Weapons don't have to be involved. Another inmate could merely swing his arm at you and get out of the way—you're dead.

It has happened just like that. Three Blacks were killed with four shots by a Soledad guard January 13, 1970. The guard was supposedly stopping a fight between one white inmate and a Black Panther Party member, who had been told by a high-ranking guard the week before that he didn't have long to live! Good people, the best of our kind, they're being locked away into special units, cellblocks, wings, segregated from the general prison population and warehoused—or simply killed.

How logical it is to break up a fist fight by killing a cat! Justify it with words if you can. You've got to convince us who are doing the dying that it is justified. Sell everyone else in the world, persuade the whole damn planet, but it's *me* that you really are burdened to brainwash. I'll never see the logic behind my own murder. We're not going for it! These are the last *words*.

The National Lawyers Guild is helping us now, and has helped in legal matters surrounding our survival for thirty years. As a result, they are poor, harassed, never far from being prosecuted by the same interlocking dictatorship that persecuted us. The collusion between prison officials, D.A.'s office, judge, grand jury, city council in places like Salinas (for Soledad), San Rafael (for San Quentin), Sacramento (for Folsom) and all the Salinases around the country—the collusion between these men who work, play and fight together, belong to the same clubs, to the same schools, fought in the same political corners for years, works to rob us of almost all redress. Our lawyers have been treated like enemy agents.

It's very clear, upon reflection, what function law serves within any culture. It protects the culture's ideology. Under capitalism it protects property, the men who own it and guard it. An entity, however, never needs protection until it comes under determined attack, which, I am sure, brings into question the validity of those ideals or policies that are being attacked. So these are the last words of the last days for what could work out to be a huge section of

the Amerikan population and its property. We're under attack. The next move is ours. The only way you who have
read this far can help me is—learn how to *make us know*
where you're at.

Power to the People,
George

"We Are the Revolution"

Berkeley Tribe*

August 14–21, 1970

San Rafael, Calif.—It has taken a seventeen-year-old warrior with guns to bring justice into an American courtroom at last. Jonathan Jackson, warrior for his people, put
repression on trial with his opening remarks to the court:
"This is it, gentlemen. I've got an automatic weapon, every-
body freeze." And before this frozen scene, as frozen as any
historic tableau, James McClain placed his hand on his
gun and offered his testimony: "Take these handcuffs off
me, I've been in San Quentin for years and I want to be a
free man, so help me God." And then: "We are the revolution, free the Soledad Brothers by 12:30 tomorrow."

And so began a new stage of combat against repression.
These were the first prisoners of war to attempt liberating
themselves and others with guns in hand, consciously de-
ciding that death in struggle is better than life in solitary.
That they fell minutes later killed by maniacs who would
rather unleash a slaughter than allow their system to be
defied makes little difference. They strode beyond the
world as we knew it, Huey says, beyond the experience of
Watts, Detroit, beyond even the most romantic fantasies
of young whites. In death they redefined life. Where they
fell we begin.

The reactionaries are covering the truth in this event
quicker than they covered the corpses. The warden calls

---

* Reprinted by permission of *The Berkeley Tribe*.

these men hoodlums and criminals. In the words of the yellow press, their lives were "a sisyphus of human violence, seemingly ordained to conclude an incident of fatal violence." McClain, after all, had a prior record of assaulting a policeman. Jonathan Jackson, the "good student" with no criminal record, is passed off as a case of extreme family loyalty. Even opinions in "enlightened" radical circles have been slow to grasp the positive significance of this event. Many people unconsciously echo the theory, put forward by a University of California researcher just this week, that young blacks are psychologically bent on suicidal confrontation. Writers like Julius Lester mourn that Panther-style rhetoric fires the fuel of anger to self-destructive extremes. Some ask, why should they be so desperate and irrational when the release of Huey Newton has just proven that the system can be budged? Even if the desperation is understandable, why do they adopt such an insane plan?

First, what about their escape plot—was it so irrational? Suppose they had driven to the San Francisco airport, demanded a flight to Cuba or Algeria and taken their hostages with them promising their safe return when the plane landed and the Soledad Brothers were freed.

Impossible? Not in the context of recent skyjackings and kidnappings.

In fact the only apparent reason they were killed was because individual guards did not follow their superior's orders to avoid a shoot-out. If the police could control themselves a bit more, if they had followed the desires of the now-dead judge, we might have witnessed the successful jailbreak-kidnap-skyjack-prisoner exchange.

Second, whatever the exact plans were, in fact any such escape plot is quite rational when compared to the possibilities of an unknown prisoner "escaping" through the legal system. The prisoners live under the arbitrary and sadistic rule of the Adult Authorities—a body which is virtually beyond pressure. The case of the Soledad Brothers only shows the surface of oppression to the public. Quite frankly, it has gathered a margin of interest because

George Jackson just happens to be a brilliant writer, not because the people know there is a real movement to shatter the prison system. Even this notorious trial has little to do with the three brothers' possible liberation. They are in prison for as long as the Adult Authority plans to keep them. The trial is only about sentencing them to death in addition to everything else.

As for Huey's release, few people should be fooled into a new confidence in the legal system. Huey was released because of enormous public pressure and because the authorities feared an outbreak of Latin American-type kidnappings here.

Third, it is insulting to consider these men as "cons" with "nothing to lose." This cannot explain the role of Jonathan Jackson, the young man with the open future, the good grades. Certainly he was not cornered and driven to violence in the ordinary fashion. Jonathan Jackson thought the entire plan through while he was enjoying his life. Nor can the "desperate men" theory explain the words and deeds of the other two. Both must have known that the risk of death was more immediate than escape from prison. Common self-interest cannot explain their willingness to die. Nor does it explain their testimony in court, "We are the revolutionaries."

Why did they want photos taken if not to communicate their message in example to others? Why did they swear to God their desire for freedom? Their act was not taken because they had nothing to lose but because they had everything to win. They believed in justice, they had a vision, they felt solidarity with other people. They were willing to sacrifice their lives as a contribution to a better world rather than waste their lives in acceptance of the status quo.

So we have seen the arrival of people who somehow live beyond death, who know, as Huey said upon release, "You never get out of life alive." Eldridge calls us "Kamikaze madmen who step on the stage of history when the good and responsible people have failed." When people are prisoners of war they will act like warriors.

Why do we think it normal for men to die senselessly in Vietnam but abnormal to die for real values here in America? Why do we accept slave revolts when they appear in history books but reject them when they happen before our eyes?

In whatever way we act we should be grateful to these men for being pioneers who set a standard for what is possible. Let them be called "adventurers" if necessary. It is the adventurer, after all, who charts and masters the unknown. The confrontation with the state is only suicidal for the state. If the rulers do not free our prisoners of war and cease their universal aggression, if they do not make peaceful changes possible, then it is tragically clear that all of America will be taken hostage in the vast jailbreak ahead.

The Rutgers Report: The White Law School and the Black Liberation Struggle

Background

In the blighted inner city of Newark, New Jersey, stands the neat glass and cement buildings of Rutgers, The State University. The university is tidily embedded in the filth-strewn streets of the Black community. Its well-paved and lighted tree-lined streets clearly define the finite nature of the class and racial privilege extended to the transient school population. The ornamental vegetation and smooth paving stop abruptly at the limits of the campus; no extra inch of renewal has been extended beyond the campus buildings.

Around the perimeter of this tidy rectangle huddle the ramshackle, dilapidated frames and the cracking brick structures which represent the available housing for the poor Blacks and Puerto Ricans of Newark. Abandoned businesses, blown-out windows, desolate stretches of rubble serve as constant reminders to the poor and oppressed of the systematic, institutionalized neglect of their vital needs.

The presence of the university in these surroundings

has acted as a goad to community outrage more than once in recent years. The Black uprising in the summer of 1967 was in part triggered by university acquisition of property and the razing of homes which displaced and dispossessed thousands of poor families. Community resentment at the turn of the decade continued; on some school property a medical school and hospital facilities had been planned, yet delayed for years. Far too much university and city-owned land still lies fallow and empty, a tribute to bureaucratic decision-making which has been consistently and wantonly contemptuous of the rights of the Black, Brown and white poor.

Newark's population in 1970 is about 400,000, at least sixty percent of whom are Black and Puerto Rican; more than fifty-eight percent of the households have incomes of less than $7,000; more than twelve percent have incomes under $3,000. The election of the city's first Black mayor gave the people hope, but it has not made a change in economic and property relationships. The smell of oppression hangs over the city, foul and pestilential; the decay and corruption result from the misuse of political, economic and social power under lily-white administrations.

Rutgers University has attempted to respond to the realities of the city by devising pacification programs. Students from the environing community are invited to prepare themselves for entrance into the university by "upgrading" their academic skills and processing their attitudes in the model designed by a bourgeois white administration for bourgeois white students.

Rutgers Law School decided to deal with the outrageous lack of Black representation in the state's legal profession (fewer than sixty in a bar of 8,000 as of 1969). The school made a commitment to graduate one hundred minority group students in five years beginning in the fall of 1969, because of the faculty and administration's implicit faith in the efficacy of the law as a remedy. If a Black lawyer could but develop minority "professional representation," this could "provide substantial benefits in terms of

overcoming the ghetto resident's alienation from the institutions of government by implicating [sic] him in its
processes." * Then the law and legal processes could serve
the ghetto residents as equitably as their middle and upper
class white countrymen. A Black lawyer then could "redress legitimate grievances through orderly channels" † as
his response to the implicit mandates of the Newark
scene.

We have a word for all that in the streets of Newark.

Much of this volume is devoted to an analysis of the
role of the law and lawyers as primary instruments in the
protection of those who own property and in the perpetuation of social, political, and economic institutions which
guarantee continuation of the racism and white economic
power of the propertied classes. The essentially racist
character of the law and its capacity to be manipulated to
serve the interests of white racism are ably documented
elsewhere in this collection.

As Black law students in a previously all-white law
school, we recognized the immediate necessity to confront
class and racist biases in the Rutgers Law School practices. Through an effort to define our own roles in the
Black liberation struggle, a struggle which reflects conflicting visions and various levels of development, one element in the total educational process became clear: the
class and racist nature of the law school curriculum. The
curriculum and related aspects of the law school showed
that we were being used in a liberal hoax which only
promised change: to be Black lawyers with white minds.
We were invited (by carrot-and-stick motivation) to join
the conservative, conformist, elite society which is the
legal community.

Carrot: "Join us in the ruling power group. You, too,
can placidly advance justice within the framework of ex-

---

* *Report of the National Advisory Commission on Civil Disorders.*
New York: E. P. Dutton & Co., Inc., 1968, p. 152.
† "Request for Financial Assistance to Support the Training of
Black and other Minority Group Lawyers," Rutgers Law School,
1968, p. 1.

isting jurisprudence. There is no need for radical change
—the law is power enough."

Stick: "If you agitate too violently or you flout legal
conventions too conspicuously we sadly fear you will never
pass the bar association's character and fitness committee."

As the Association of Black Law Students shared, discussed, struggled and developed ideologically, we knew
that we would not accept the traditional roles assigned to
Blacks in the legal community. We knew that its design
did not speak to the needs of oppressed people. We knew
that we must struggle for pervasive change.

As we defined the role of the Black revolutionary lawyer, a totally restructured curriculum became a prelimi-
nary necessity. Lawyers can play an important role in
support of revolutionary change. They can keep fighters
out of jail and in the streets to continue the struggle. Liberation lawyers can use the courts as a forum to publicize
the inequities and contradictions inherent in the American judicial system.

Black lawyers must privately study and publicly define
the law in human and ideological terms which expose its
essentially oppressive nature.

Black lawyers must be highly skilled in order to provide
basic day-to-day legal services for the community, while
they wage broad attacks on the system.

Black lawyers can bring strategic skills to community
planning, while they fight for people's control of local institutions.

To prepare us for these kinds of roles, we proposed a
curriculum which posited the need to provide an alternative to the traditional legal preparation, and to train us to
become "People's Lawyers" * on behalf of the oppressed
and the emerging forces for change.

We know that our original indictment of November 4,
1969 struck responsive chords in those faculty members

---

* Kinoy, Arthur, "The Present Crisis in American Legal Education,"
Vol. 24, *Rutgers Law Review* (Fall 1970), p. 1.

who have struggled for change and those white students who are no longer content with racial and class superiority as a substitute for social justice. They supported our lead.

The unified struggles of a Tripartite Commission composed of three Black law students, three members of the students' bar association (one of whom was Black), and three faculty members, resulted in changes in the law school which were long overdue educationally, socially and politically. Our own struggles as Black students illustrated the role that we must be prepared to accept as leaders without fear of retribution and with full knowledge that each step forward is but a short step on the long road of struggle ahead.

Lennox Hinds, Chairman
Association of Black Law Students

Indictment of the Rutgers Law School Community
by the Association of Black Law Students
November 4, 1969

I. If, as we believe, the foundation of the judicial system is the law school, then there ought to be a direct connection between the concepts that are taught in these schools and the art that is practiced in the courts. And if the relationship can be established in those areas of the law which deal with the interests of white society, but not in those areas of the law which deal with the interests of Black people, then there is a continuing violation of the due process taking place within the law school to the detriment of all Black people.

II. Furthermore, assuming that there may be a rational relationship between all of the law that is taught and that which is applied, and yet those areas which deal with white interests are emphasized to the virtual exclusion of Black interests, then, within the law school itself, there is a continuing violation of due process to the detriment of Black people.

III. And finally, if it can be established that the equities are actually balanced in the two above areas—which we don't believe for one moment—but because of the form of the law school teaching process it becomes intrinsic to the nature of the judicial system that the interests of Black people are not as fully protected as the interests of white society, then the form of the law school stands as a violation of due process and equal protection under the laws as required by the rhetoric of the wartime amendments.

As Black law students here in this university, we do not believe that an argument could be raised to rebut any of the three above outlined violations of due process. We believe the law school is directly responsible for the fact that the judicial process is effective in protecting the interests of the white society and totally ineffective—perhaps intentionally—in protecting the interests of Black people.

Recent events in the courts where the interests and rights of Black people are at stake have made it patently clear to us as Black students that we can no longer study the rhetoric of due process in the very seat of the major obstacle of applied due process for Black people. But we have a right to be here, and therefore we recognize a duty to take those measures necessary to acquire equal protection under the law for Black people at the foundation of the legal system.

The present form of the law school teaching process is inadequate, not only from the standpoint of the curriculum, but also from the standpoint of technique. Consider the basic curriculum in the light of the most significant white and Black interests without considering arguable courses sustaining co-interests. On the one hand, we as Black students who hopefully will litigate the problems of the ghetto in the courts face:

Contracts
Commercial Law I & II
Business Association I & II
Trusts and Wills
Future Interest
Insurance
Tax

while on the other hand, it is interesting to note that there are only two courses taught in Criminal Law: Criminal Law and The Administration of the Criminal Law; and no seminars. We are also offered the debatable benefits of certain seminars such as Problems of the Urban Poor, Small Business Problems of the Urban Poor, and International Race Relations.

We conclude that a mere cursory examination of the curriculum forces one to realize that the private interests of white society are far more thoroughly protected by the curriculum than the private interests of Black people. It should also be noted, at this point, that even a more narrow disparity between curriculum interest protection cannot easily be brushed aside; for the negative effect of this disparity on equal protection under the law for Blacks is compounded when one takes into account that in most of these areas, the interests of Blacks and whites are adverse! White people are protecting acquired and vested property rights within a system of legal nepotism that forecloses most Blacks from entry. Black people are subject to the repressive tactics of those who would shout "law and order" to protect white interests from the envisioned threat of Black emancipation. The curriculum at this law school is a violation of a Black person's rights to equal protection under the law.

We must now consider both the presentation and application of legal concepts as taught within the law school. A disciplined reasoning process is developed; esoteric theoretical considerations of hypothetical fact patterns are explored; and strictly legal arguments are conceptualized, all the better to equip the law student to deal with the subject matter of the curriculum and its application in the courts, particularly at the level of appellate review. From the vantage point of sociological conclusions, it is apparent that white society benefits to the detriment of Blacks. More white litigants reach the appellate level for consideration of their legal dilemmas than do Black litigants. The law at the trial level goes virtually untaught and the true legal issues are rarely argued at the trial court level; this technique is not relevant to the protection of legal rights for Black people—but is for whites. Therefore, the teaching techniques utilized at this law school are a violation of a Black person's rights to equal protection under the law.

Recognizing that the law school provides the genesis of all legal theories, and that without them we would be confronted with an entirely different system, then as the school is fulfilling a duty owed to the legal system by advancing these legal theories, it ought to recognize a duty to see that the legal theories are put into practice on a practical basis; if not that, at least brought before the courts in the manner that they were intended. To make ourselves more clear, it should suffice to say that one who creates a dangerous instrumentality in our society ought to be made to control it. If it can be shown that the legal theories, when construed by the courts, operate to the detriment of Black people's interests on behalf of whites, then the law school is negligent to the point of culpability and should be held accountable for its failure to act. The absence of control in this area constitutes a violation of Black persons' rights to equal protection under the law.

As Black law students, and as a party to these violations of the rights of Black people, we make the following proposal:

I. Close the law school, and seriously consider the grave constitutional questions that are raised herein, demonstrating good faith dealing with our mutual interests and outrage at current events taking place in the court room.

II. Be prepared to accept the ensuing outline that describes how we feel that this law school can function:

    A. Construct a curriculum for the first year which consists of those courses basic to an understanding of the underlying premises of the law and how the law operates.

        1. These courses could consist of:
Constitutional Law
Criminal Law
Contracts
Remedies
Briefwriting, etc.

        2. These conventional courses could be taught in the conventional Rutgers manner by a small group of instructors who would share the full responsibility for insuring that at the end of two semesters each student would be "a Lawyer," as opposed to a counsellor.

        3. Each student should know how the library works and it should be the responsibility of first-year instructors to insure that this is accomplished.

    B. In both the second and third years the students should not only expand their legal perspectives in terms of theory but they should also become cognizant of the pragmatics of the judicial system in general, and the trial court in particular.

        1. *Each* course should be a "clinic" in which each professor of law secures and maintains a docket of cases that he himself is in the process of litigating.

        2. Each student must be made to play an active role in at least

one of the cases on the course
docket.

3. By the judicious selection of
cases, in the hands of competent counsel, the problems of
stare decisis—establishing a
good historical record for assess-
ing balanced equitable rights for
parties litigating for white interests in business matters, but
not for Black interests in such
areas as landlord-tenant relationships, consumer credit pur-
chasing, welfare, and the criminal law—could be ameliorated.

4. Every faculty member must be
accountable to the law school.

We further demand that the law school offer courses which
are relevant to Black students; that these courses be taught
by Black instructors, which are selected by the Black students
in this law school.

We as Black students feel so strongly about the inequitable
role that the law school plays in its present form, relevant to
securely protecting the rights of white society while behaving
somewhat oblivious to the rights of Blacks, that we seriously
question our role in this process. We cannot be a party to rhetorical rights for Blacks and protected rights for whites. If the
school cannot be temporarily closed to halt these gross injustices, we cannot be further participants in this horrendous acting out of equal justice while Black people continue to suffer
from the outcome—we must, therefore, then resign—resign
on the day that the rhetoric of Black rights faces the prag-
matics of judicial authority, and the law school refuses to consider for adoption a policy designed to convert rhetoric into reality. Yet we have a legal vested interest in the law school
which we intend to protect.

We will bring an affirmative action in the Federal District
Court, asking for injunctive relief—to enjoin the continuation
of the law school in its present form; for a declaratory judgment that we as a class have a vested interest in both the real
property of the law school and its administrative utility to the
extent that it must be made available for our use. We will then
establish for ourselves a viable approach to the legitimate legal
needs for Black people. Our claim is obviously based upon the
rhetoric of the Thirteenth and Fourteenth Amendments.
Clearly if they are in any way real as opposed to rhetorical

we will win—and that says something; however, if they are
rhetorical, that says something else! Not only to us as Black
students, who would ask that our rights be protected, but to
every Black man and woman in the nation!

*On November 5, 1969, Rutgers Law School, Newark Campus,
closed for one day during which time the entire student body,
the faculty, and the administration considered the demands of
ABLS. A Tripartite Commission was established [see Back-
ground]. The ensuing months led to the following Strategy for
Change.—Ed.*

*Strategy for Change by the Tripartite Commission
of the Rutgers Law School
May 6, 1970*

These proposals are being submitted to the entire law
school community as a basis for discussion, critical thinking, and action towards implementation. But now, the
time has come to place the essence of the proposals before
the law school community.

We have had many discussions, both among ourselves,
members of the student body and the faculty and legal
educators from other sections of the country. We do not
propose to reproduce in depth the controversies and dialogues we have engaged in, but it is clear that a duty is
imposed upon all of us to insure that all of the legitimate
legal needs of society, to which a practitioner of the law
must minister, must be examined under close scrutiny by
those institutions that would train lawyers. It is not clear
that the traditional form of the law school accomplishes
this fact. The Commission was convened to examine, pass
upon the validity of, and make appropriate recommendations to cope with those legal problems articulated in the
allegations and demands of the Association of Black Law
Students in their petition of November 4, 1969, and, in
addition, to reexamine the effectiveness of the relationship between a legal education and all segments of society. It is our belief that the proposals contained herein
disclose that we have accepted this mandate, and, if im-

plemented, would permit the university and the law school
to respond to their obligation in this matter in a concrete
and substantive fashion.

THE ROLE OF THE LAW SCHOOL

At the very least, fundamental questions about the role
of the law school must be acknowledged and answered.
We recognize that the primary role of the law school is to
provide a legal education—an education for each student
devoted to one purpose: the provision of a sound, well-
rounded program conducive to inquiry, learning and
training which is responsive to the legal needs of all members of society. Such a program of legal education, based
upon a coherent view of the nature of our present society
and the role which law can play in optimal future change,
may then produce a "new breed of lawyers" characterized
by their compassion, competence, and commitment to the
cause of equal justice and positive social change. Thus,
social reform, as such, is not the primary role of the law
school. But, it is clear that when the law school acts to
fulfill that which *is* its primary role, social change may
well be enhanced and strengthened.

And so, by coming squarely to grips with its fundamental task, the law school, by making this kind of legal education available to all who choose it, contributes to society,
through the men and women of the profession, the human
tools necessary to secure and protect the rights of all.

In order to meet the imposed requirements of the
sought-after role of the law school and with due recognition of legitimate legal needs permeating society as a
whole, the law school must assume a somewhat different
posture.

If the form of the law school, by means of its curriculum and teaching techniques, is to be altered in order to
more adquately service all of the compelling legal interests of our segmental society, certain underlying assumptions are accepted as follows:

(1) That "to train lawyers who can meet the chal-

lenges and obligations cast upon the profession by contemporary society," [1] will require more than methods change or materials change alone—the very substance of legal education must be expanded.

(2) That a pervasive, *institutionalized* response which affects the orientation and premises of the law school is required.

(3) That temporary federal grants for "experimental demonstration projects" either die or are disciplined by the cutoff or curtailment of funds.

(4) That impromptu, noninterrelated courses offered in any given semester by individual faculty members, consistent with their singular objectives, cannot be viewed as even an attempt to deal legitimately with the legal demands of contemporary society.

(5) That the presence of a law school in an urban center creates distinct opportunities and responsibilities for the development of a unique law school curriculum approach.

Therefore, we propose that Rutgers Law School create a law school curriculum which addresses itself to the two realities of American society today: by providing a legal education for those who would practice law on behalf of the traditional interests of society and those who would become ". . . a new breed of lawyers with deep roots in the honored past of our profession, who [we] would characterize as people's lawyers." [2]

THE FIRST-YEAR CURRICULUM

We propose that the present courses in Contracts, Legislation, Property, Torts, Constitutional Law, Criminal Law, and Remedies be continued.

We propose that a required course in legal representation of the poor and the interaction of the legal system and Black people be added to the first-year curriculum. As a required course, it will result in exposure to the wealth of opportunities available to a practitioner in this much neglected area. It would expand the basis upon which each student can choose his ultimate area of concentration.

We propose that legal writing, in the form of legal problem-solving, be taught as an integrated facet in small sections of the regular substantive courses; in short, that
every first-year student have the opportunity of participating in at least one small section of a regular course in
which legal writing and problem-solving become a primary teaching tool of the instructor.

Furthermore, we strongly urge that a revision of casebook materials in each of the standard first-year courses
be undertaken to include substantially more case materials which relate to contemporary urban problems.

THE SECOND- AND THIRD-YEAR CURRICULUM

Students should be wholly free to choose from a selection of courses, clinics and seminars to shape, in their
own discretion, one of three possible directions to their
studies: (1) A continuation of general legal studies as
presently offered. (2) A concentration in urban legal
studies. (3) An eclectic direction, majoring in a specific
area, e.g., criminal law, and including selections from
both the arena of general legal studies and the new field of
urban legal studies, available as options to the participating student.

Our recommendations for methodological and substantive innovations are concentrated upon the proposed new
urban law program. We believe that many of the proposals advanced here have applicability to sorely needed
changes in *every* aspect of the curriculum, but we will
concentrate here upon the development of an urban law
program and leave it to those who specialize in traditional
legal practice to work out these details in other areas.

Because of the pervasive effect of poverty, racism and
injustice throughout all of American society, there are un-
explored and unutilized areas of traditional subject matter
courses offered in the law school which must be developed
and probed. Therefore, the content of such an urban law
program must, of necessity, cut across the subject matter

ranges of the traditional study of law. We do not believe that the problems of the poor and the Afro-Americans can be dealt with within the confines of a narrow subject area. This would deny the all-encompassing societal effect of class and race in contemporary America.

Accordingly:

I. We propose that a program of clinical educational studies be developed which touches upon every critical aspect of the legal needs of the poor and the Black communities.

The inner city is particularly rich in legal ramifications. With the change in the role of government, both national and local, has come a profound, though insufficiently noted, change in the legal relationships between the poor and the environment in which they find themselves. Increasingly, the significant contacts of the poor man with the law are with various administrative agencies, city, state, or federal. We recognize that the inner-city resident is forced by the circumstances of his life into frequent contact with impersonal public agencies created by legislative action, such as housing authorities, welfare departments, educational programs, health and safety agencies *inter alia*, over which he has little control.

In addition, he is affected by the policies and practices of public agencies charged with the responsibility for upholding the law, such as the police and the courts. As tenants, complainants, defendants, suspects, welfare recipients, public housing residents, receivers of unemployment insurance benefits, taxpayers, litigants in workmen's compensation cases, and holders of installment-buying contracts, the youths and adults of the inner city constantly interact with the legal establishment. Urban law students, by their carefully designed participation in legal clinics, will be exposed day by day to the infinite array of legal problems which proliferate in the city—they will gain experience and knowledge in the "so-called 'legal' problem of the poor [which] is often an unidentified strand in a complex of social, economic, psychological, and psychiatric problems." [3]

The involvement of law students and faculty can provide legally appropriate directions for institutional change through legislation and litigation. Also, the concentration of data for research purposes will provide a specific focus for individual attorneys and community groups interested in expanding the concepts of social justice through the law.

We note the existence of important clinical experimentation already underway in the law school, namely, the clinical program in Administrative Law and the clinical program in Constitutional Law. We feel that these programs demonstrate the vitality of a clinical approach which is rooted in the law school and fully conducted by members of the law faculty. Accordingly, we propose an immediate and full-scale expansion of clinical programs in the urban law area open to second- and third-year students. These clinics should, in essence, function as "law offices" within the heart of the law school, in which students are taught in the course of reality experiences by members of the faculty the deep interrelationship of theory and practice. Such clinics should be organized in such fields as housing,[4] economic problems,[5] criminal practice and precedents,[6] domestic problems,[7] welfare,[8] community health,[9] education,[10] environmental problems,[11] political and civil liberties,[12] women's rights,[13] as well as many other potential subject matter clinics touching on central problems of the urban communities.

These clinics within the law school, taught by members of the faculty in the spirit of Jerome Frank's "lawyer-teachers," would utilize the reality of ongoing problems as fundamental pedagogic tools. They would be directly involved in every form of legal activity including litigation, administrative activity, legislative activity and community planning and would become, in the deepest sense, "living classrooms." Students would receive substantial credits for the clinical work and be permitted to take at least two full semesters of clinical activity during the last two years of law school.

II. We propose that a Legal Clinic be created in the city

of Newark under the sponsorship of Rutgers Law School which will include in its planning and operation representatives of the community as well as the faculty and students of the law school, legal services representatives, and private practitioners who wish to participate.

Such a clinic would have as its guidelines

(a) providing and identifying legal problems for the Newark poverty community;

(b) providing a pedagogically desirable synthesis of theory and practice for Rutgers law students;

(c) providing a means to bring together those lawyers practicing within the central areas of Newark with those students who desire to develop a greater understanding of the problems faced by urban lawyers.

III. We propose that joint degree-granting curricula be developed with the Departments of Political Science, History, Sociology, Economics, and Urban Studies to prepare both scholars and legal practitioners for a merging of law as a discipline with its social and political implications in the interest of societal change.

The development of a joint degree-granting curriculum will institutionalize the clearly established connections between the implementation of the law and the nonlegal environments in which it operates.

Clearly, scholars in law as well as social work, sociology, political science and economics have established beyond question that race, class, income, and mores affect significantly the ways in which justice is administered.[14]

Our particular emphasis is on creating a J.D. (Doctor of Jurisprudence) who, at the same time he has deepened his legal tools, has immersed himself significantly in an allied field which will deepen his specific skill level as a people's advocate.

The acquisition of the skills and substance of a Master's degree in Sociology, Social Work, Political Science, Economics, jointly with the J.D. will provide an opportunity for students to synthesize these disciplines in a structured way. It must be noted that courses in criminology and criminal justice are typically taught in Departments of Sociology, the effects and content of welfare legislation are generally found in schools of social work, and courses in legal history and constitutional law are provided in political science programs.

Those who perceive the solutions to the economic oppression of the inner city as caused (in sum or part) by the lack of knowledge of the manipulation of available economic strategies on behalf of the poor should be able to select a Master's in Economics with emphasis on public finance, economic development, or urban economics.

Typical fields for combined study in political science could be comparative law and comparative politics; American politics and constitutional law; government regulation and public administration.

Based on the experience at Stanford University, it can be anticipated that a joint degree program leading to a J.D. and Master's in one of the above disciplines should require four years of carefully designed study.

Although we are particularly concerned with the development of attorneys whose social insights and skill levels are enhanced by formalized exposure to the social sciences, many of the courses in the law school should be opened to students in other disciplines. Thus, students of architecture could well be interested in courses in land use; environmental law has relevance to many subject areas. Many courses, both those existing and those proposed, are germane to the study of a number of disciplines.

Many departments in the university, among them the Graduate School of Social Work, the Graduate School of Education, and the Departments of Political Science, Sociology and Urban Affairs have engaged in research which can clarify the nonlegal environments in which the law functions, as well as provide directions for the needed legislation.

IV. We propose that the law school establish a Research Institute that is interdisciplinary in its approach and which will undertake ongoing investigations into the needs, present and anticipated, the problems and proposed solutions of these crises of the urban community, of which the law school forms an integral part.

The Urban Research Institute should be based in the law school so that the functional connections between data and appropriate action can be translated into recommendations for legislation. Research projects developed by graduate students in a variety of fields under the supervision of the appropriate faculty should be focused on specific urban issues which require scholarly scrutiny to identify goals, consequences, and needs: the implications of the tenant-landlord law or the rate of local taxation may lead to the abandonment of inner-city housing by landlords. What are the directions that legislation and housing structures should take to alleviate housing problems? The entire area of welfare law and its demographic and social implications is in need of exhaustive research.

What have been the real effects of educational laws and policies? The organization and practice of the law itself could well stand the rigorous scrutiny of sociologists skilled in social research techniques. The list of possible research topics is as broad as the social, political and economic problems which afflict the inner city.

It is therefore proposed that the potential of an interdisciplinary faculty and student body with research skills, social commitment and a legalistic base can add the following dimensions to legal education and the law:

(1) The development and assessment of supportive research on the social, political, and economic implications of laws and legislation.

(2) The synthesis of the provision of social and economic analysis for the drafting of new legislation.

(3) The translation of the urban legal needs defined by the urban legal clinic into concrete predictions of the legal problems likely to arise in the inner city, and the remedies which might be appropriate for successfully meeting those needs.

(4) The evaluation of legal resources and manpower

required to provide adequate *broad* legal services in the urban community.

(5) The provision of a central repository for cognate materials which would clarify the nonlegal environment of the law which might include literature, statistical data, teaching and learning materials.

(6) The extension to lawyers of the opportunity to learn the skills of social science research and the corollary opportunity for members of the social science professions to learn the potential of the law for social reform.

V. We propose that the law school undertake the responsibility to assure the training of both paraprofessionals who can work with lawyers and subprofessionals who can work independently in quasi-legal tasks in the community for the purpose of freeing lawyers from work which can be done by others, providing an essential opportunity for the urban legal clinic to reach out into the Newark community and to expand the legal and semilegal services available to the community.

IMPLEMENTATION

We propose the *immediate* implementation of these proposals. As soon as they are agreed upon in principle by the faculty and the student body, task forces should be set up to discuss, explore and solve the many practical problems involved in instituting these proposals. These task forces, composed of students, faculty members and, where necessary, representatives of the community, are not for the purpose of further debate and contemplation, but must be mandated to put into operation the various phases of the program committed to their responsibility.

The accomplishment of these objectives will require an enormous commitment of energy, resources and creative ability on the part of the entire law school community. Without such a commitment, neither this law school, nor any other law school, can reach the goal perhaps only now within its grasp—that of achieving a real and viable compatibility between the ideal role of the law school as the foundation of a legal system and the realistic and legitimate legal needs of all society.

On May 6, 1970, the entire law school community voted on and approved the above "Strategy for Change as outlined by the Tripartite Commission." An Implementation Task Force was immediately organized and began its difficult work during the succeeding summer months to restructure the Rutgers Law School—Ed.

Notes

1. Northeastern University *School of Law Bulletin,* Boston, Mass., 1970, p. 7.
2. "I would suggest that the law schools must capture, if they are to overcome the deadly symptoms of the fundamental malaise that inflicts us all, the excitement of the new challenge of making law serve the needs of people in struggle, as well as continuing to fulfill the needs of corporations and business. I do not argue for an abandonment of the latter role; I argue simply that, at a minimum, the law schools must no longer be, in essence, one-sided representatives of the dominant power group in society . . . [but must become institutions] for the training of people's lawyers." Kinoy, *loc. cit.*
3. Douglas, Justice William O., dissenting in *Hackin v Arizona,* 389 U.S. 143 (1967).
4. Such a clinic would concern itself with such questions as landlord-tenant problems, evictions, housing code enforcement, discriminatory rental and sales policies, zoning laws, urban renewal, relocation, and public housing, for example.
5. Such a clinic would concern itself with such questions as credit buying, interest rates, consumer frauds, defense of debt claims, bankruptcy, garnishments, real estate financing practice of banks, repossession, foreclosures, and default judgments.
6. Such a clinic would concern itself with such questions as availability of counsel, bail inequities, abuse of discretionary powers of the police, jury representation and selection, rights of prisoners, police harassment of the Black communities, disparate sentencing, and other problems.
7. Such a clinic would concern itself with such questions as divorce, separation, custody, support payments, child care, and other problems.

8. Such a clinic would concern itself with such questions as eligibility for public assistance benefits, invasion of privacy, residency requirements, mandatory job training, and other problems.

9. Such a clinic would concern itself with such problems as Medicaid, inadequate hospital facilities, and other health problems of a legal nature.

10. Such a clinic would concern itself with such problems as segregation in education *de facto* and *de jure,* community control of education, inequity of public spending for education in ghetto and poverty communities, rights of students and faculty, and other problems.

11. Such a clinic would concern itself with environmental problems which particularly affect the urban community.

12. Such a clinic would be an expansion of the present constitutional law clinic and include such urban problems as gerrymandering, hiring policies, political disenfranchisement, political persecution of minority parties, and other problems.

13. Such a clinic would concern itself with the many problems of discrimination against women, abortion laws, discrimination in employment and in the professions, including the legal profession, and other problems.

14. Attorneys who have written extensively on the broad social questions which affect legal rights include Charles Reich, Edward Sparer and Jerome Carlin. Reference is directed to the previously submitted extensive bibliographies which include scholars from all the fields mentioned above.

The Radical Lawyer Under Attack

by Gerald B. Lefcourt*

Oppressed peoples, and the young especially, are demanding their own kind of lawyers. These lawyers have been asked to take on a variety of new issues and play a special role in support of their clients. Welfare rights, students' rights, draft counseling and draft resistance, military organizing, rent strikes, all kinds of demonstrations, Black liberation, women's liberation, community control, integration and separatism, wildcat labor strikes, poor housing, ecological concerns, illegal imperialist wars, poverty, flag desecration, school injunctions, and consumer legislation are just some of the issues which traditional lawyers and elected officials have neglected, and to which the new breed of lawyers has been asked to respond.

The existence of radical lawyers who identify with the needs and aspirations of people whose interests and human rights have traditionally been unrepresented challenges the legal process and those who administer it. It is not really the tactics of the lawyers which bother traditionalists; it is the issues they support and the clients they defend. It is not any disdain they might exhibit toward the courts and oppressive laws which anger those in power; it is their sustained advocacy of the principles of liberation which their clients demand. For their efforts, these law-

---

yers have become the target of increasing repression, leveled against them by the government, the Establishment bar associations, prominent individual attorneys, and the courts themselves.

The initial indication that lawyers had begun to change their attitudes toward the courts and the judicial system was the first lawyers' demonstration in the history of the United States, which was held in New York at the Federal Courthouse on Foley Square, April 30, 1969. It was the day before Law Day which is annually dedicated by the President of the United States to the reaffirmation of "Amerikan" justice. The demonstration was aimed at countering the platitudes about this "reaffirmation" of the concept of justice. The lawyers wanted to express their belief that justice, in reality, is limited to a few in this country, and that they were, as lawyers, prepared to go into the streets and say so publicly for the first time. The demonstration raised a series of demands aimed at basic inequalities in the legal system. Although about five hundred lawyers and law students attended the rally and march near the courts, the event received little publicity and no direct response from court officials or elected representatives. It is not surprising, however, that this further example of the widespread distrust among oppressed people toward the administration of justice in the courts, did little to change the judicial system to reflect the concern of the people. Therefore, it is important that the demands of that day, aimed at the basic inequalities in the legal system, once again be presented:

Ad Hoc Committee of Lawyers for Justice
Demands of April 30, 1969

1. *End Preventive Detention and Excessive Bail*

If a man is denied his liberty pending trial solely because he is poor, freedom in our country is an exercise for the affluent. Yet the large majority of those now in jail awaiting trial are there because they don't have enough property to pledge for their freedom. New and far reaching bail reforms are necessary to prevent such pre-trial detentions resulting solely from poverty.

If this inhuman practice of caging the poor were not enough, preventive detention is now to be made available as another weapon against the freedom of man. The unrestrained power to deny a man his liberty pending trial would be granted through preventive detention. Suspicion often based upon skin color would be enough to imprison a man.

Nevertheless, in defiance of the Eighth Amendment to the U.S. Constitution, excessive bail exists and preventive detention is about to be baptized. We condemn both, and demand their abolition.

2. *Jury Trials Where the Punishment Is One Day or More* *

No longer can defendants in criminal prosecutions receive a fair trial without the protection of a jury of their peers.

As the Supreme Court recently proclaimed in *Duncan v Louisiana*, "those who wrote our Constitution knew from history and experience that it was necessary to protect against unfounded criminal charges brought to eliminate enemies and against judges too responsive to the voice of higher authority." Basic liberties require the check of a jury of citizens who do not have the burden of thousands of trials a year to distort their impulses and visions. Indeed we contend that the mandate of the Bill of Rights requires jury trials for all cases that may result in loss of freedom. To allow a jury trial in a controversy over $500 in civil court and to deny the same to a man whose liberty is at stake is an admission of the priorities of this country which we cannot countenance.

3. *Grand and Petit Juries that Are Representative*

The basic liberty of a jury of one's peers is a meaningless right if the jury is not in fact representative of the community. Grand juries which were designed to check the power of government by presentment of an indictment in all serious cases cannot perform that function as intended because the composition of grand juries is not representative of the community. The systematic exclusion from grand jury service of the nonwhite, the poor and the young creates jurors that represent a class of citizens that cannot relate to other groups. The same inequities existing in grand juries are true for petit

---

* New York City was one of the few places in the country that did not allow jury trials in cases where punishment could be as much as one year. This denial was based on the "convenience" of the courts which are so overcrowded that administrators feared chaos with jury trials in every case.

The Supreme Court has since granted juries for so-called "serious crimes" in which the penalty is over six months' imprisonment.

juries. The overwhelming majority of criminal cases emanate from the ranks of the very groups that are excluded from jury service and this exclusion we condemn.

4. *Penal Reform*

Our prisons are a barbaric remnant of a low stage of civilization. Their justification is society's vengeance. In the face of rampant recidivism, especially amongst juveniles, attempts at rehabilitation are seldom properly made, and then poorly funded. Detention centers are pens for animals where repeaters and first offenders are lumped together and the presumption of guilt pervades everything.

We call for changes to permit more individual creativity and greater use of work release programs. We also call for a vast expenditure of funds to increase the quality and breadth of correctional services. We finally demand a change in concept, so that those who administer our prisons may recognize that prison should not destroy, but should help a man to be a man.

5. *Victimless Crimes*

Crimes of abortion, homosexuality, vagrancy, gambling, prostitution and possession of narcotics should be abolished. The existence of such "crimes" is an unwarranted societal invasion into areas best left to individual decisions. In the area of narcotics, we call for quality governmental treatment of persons addicted including drug maintenance on a voluntary basis.

6. *Judicial Competence*

The mere fact that a man has the financial ability to buy his way into a judgeship, through contributions to a political party, does not mean that he is competent to be a judge. We call for the end to judgeships that come from political deals which produce judges responsible to higher authority. These men are usually racist and expose an immediate dislike for those people they must judge. Their supposed "impartiality" results in the complete dehumanization of defendants and lawyers who appear before them, due to their inability to properly use the immense power bestowed upon them and this we condemn.

7. *Adequate Legal Services Controlled by the Poor*

Equal justice demands that the poor obtain at least the same legal representation as the rich. The absence of such assistance has encouraged fraud and injustice upon the poor.

The current provision of an insignificant number of lawyers has afforded little more than a salve for the conscience of the state. It often means an impossibility of professional performance by those lawyers who participate and represent sometimes over 1,000 clients a year. In addition, the services available are controlled and directed by those representing exactly the interests antithetical to those of the poor.

If criminal justice is to be more than plea-bargaining, if landlords and tenants are to be equal before the law, if possession of life is to be considered as important in this country as possession of property, then the poor must have enough lawyers, good lawyers, and lawyers truly chosen and controlled by the poor.

8. Civilian Control of Police

More and more in the United States today, the police force is the institution of government used to oppress and degrade the poor, the dissenter, and particularly the Black community. The brutality and horrendous treatment of citizens by police is not just the result of some untrained, unfit or brutal officers, but is rather the result of the functions assigned to the police as an institution. We call for a restructuring of the police that would provide services, not sadism, for the community. We call for community control of all police personnel, expenditures and law enforcement priorities. Only in this way can the function of police be changed.

9. End the Activities of the Character Committees which Deny Attorneys Political Freedom

Once lawyers stray from the orthodox political framework of this nation, and participate actively in the quest for change of a grossly unjust society, the full power of the established bar is brought to bear through the vehicle of the Character and Fitness Committees.

We deplore the activities of these policing committees, composed in the main of the most reactionary members of the bar. Their illegitimate use of the power to deny admission to and to remove from the legal profession those they deem "politically undesirable" violates the rights guaranteed to all citizens by the First Amendment. The Supreme Court held it unconstitutional to threaten with disbarment those attorneys who exercise their constitutional rights. In this spirit we call for an end of the Character and Fitness Committees, and an end to the oppression of those attorneys who advocate unpopular causes.

10. *End Legal Exploitation of the Poor*

Teachers strike and the poor get arrested. Living costs rise
and legislatures cut welfare. Evictions occur in days and re-
pairs never do. Sellers act unconscionably and the poor still
pay more. Examples abound of the duality of our system,
where power is rewarded and justice is denied to the powerless poor. If rich and poor alike are to respect the law, then it
must be changed to grant fairness to the oppressed of our
country, however unpopular their views, however empty their
pockets.

Despite the failure of the mass media to publicize these
demands, word of mouth spread the enthusiasm of the
demonstration around the country. Within the year that
followed, many lawyers took to the streets around a variety of issues. On the West Coast, lawyers burned their cer-
tificates of admission to the federal courts to protest injustices in the courts, and in Chicago, lawyers demonstrated
in support of four brother attorneys (including this
writer) arbitrarily held in contempt of court by the presiding judge in the Chicago Eight Conspiracy case. In each of
the eight cities, lawyers and law students protested the validity of the "political" attacks by the government in that
court, especially since the defendants in Chicago were
leaders of a growing movement for radical change.

Soon after the demonstrations in New York and Chicago, government lawyers in the Civil Rights Division of
the Department of Justice protested the Nixon administration's racist policies of deliberate slowdown in the
Southern integration movement. A brief strike by Legal
Aid Society lawyers in New York City in the spring of
1970, the first of its kind, demanded a restructuring of the
courts so that indigent defendants would not be punished
for the inadequacies of the court system. (The lawyers'
rebellion was much less dramatic than their clients' takeover of detention facilities a few months later. In the list
of grievances, the prisoners in the Tombs stated that "the
Legal Aid Society aids and abets the incursions and
abuses of our rights in the courtroom . . . under the
present system of the courts that we cannot receive any

justice. . . .") After the first nationwide, spontaneous strike by students, who angrily protested the government's invasion of Cambodia and its killing of students at Kent State University, barristers characterizing themselves in a *New York Times* advertisement as "establishment lawyers" marched on Washington to lobby against the government's expanded role in the Indochina war. On Law Day 1971, over two thousand lawyers amassed again in New York, protesting the war and others also demanding changes in the legal system.

The idea of lawyers going into the streets was unthinkable prior to that first act at the Federal Courthouse in April of 1969. It is not that the demonstration tactic was so effective (although it does sometimes have impact), but that it was symbolic of a departure from the traditional role of the lawyer. It crystallized the growing feeling that change is sorely needed and that more radical actions are necessary. No longer can the thinking creative lawyer accept the status quo; but he or she must fight openly on the side of radical change and take on the forces of reaction whenever and wherever.

The alliance between the lawyer and his client is now political as well as professional; legal skill is offered in support of the activities, goals, and aspirations of dissidents, even where these goals embrace revolutionary ideologies. The alliance is indispensable in order to protect and further the rights of political activists and to help air the views they represent. Movement clients now seek lawyers who will respond to their problems with undivided loyalty and commitment. Thus, Movement lawyers have started a process of challenge and protest that counters the "officer of the court" consciousness and affirms their role as political beings struggling against illegitimate rulers and fighting for the rights and aspirations of oppressed people.

The struggle carried on in and out of the courts of America by lawyers dedicated to the principle of representing their clients' views as well as defending their liberty, has led to vicious political attacks against the

Movement lawyers. The most controversial attack was the incredible sentencing of William Kunstler and Leonard Weinglass in the Chicago Eight Conspiracy case to four years and two years in jail. These contempt sentences were imposed without giving the accused lawyers an opportunity to answer the charges, without a jury to determine guilt or innocence, without even a trial by an impartial judge. Judge Julius Hoffman acted as complainant, judge, jury, and prosecutor. In effect, he sentenced the two for attempting to represent their clients in a vigorous and meaningful way. The vengeance and ferocity of those sentences signaled the beginning of a new attempt to repress the sympathetic counsel of Movement criminal defendants.

From my point of view, the road chosen by the lawyers and their clients in the case was one of education, not premeditated disruption. Throughout the prosecution, before, during, and after, the defendants and their lawyers swept the country with speeches and rallies in a massive attempt to educate the young as to what was at stake and what the case was all about. In truth, the trial had nothing to do with the law, nor with what happened in the streets at the Democratic Convention in August of 1968. It was clear from the evidence presented, from the treatment the case was given by the government, as well as the media coverage of the events, that the defendants were on trial because of who they were, what they advocated politically, what they wore, how they looked, and the challenge they posed to government policy.

Although the defendants faced maximum five-year sentences after conviction, the long-range effects of their efforts were to convince masses of people that the government had become insanely repressive and out of touch with the country's youth. The government lost more than it gained and the defendants perhaps proved more by the trial than they did by coming to the Democratic Convention originally. The immorality of the government's prosecution was exposed so that the government lost more credibility in the process and enlisted greater support for the views and goals of the movements for change that the defendants represented.

In the courtroom, the lawyers helped to project the issues that should have been on trial—racism, capitalism, war, poverty, and repression. In a five-and-a-half-month fight, they consistently withstood the onslaught of the government and turned every attack into an illuminating exposure of the immorality and impropriety of government policies.

The attacks against the lawyers and defendants by the mass media and bar associations, of conservatives and liberals alike, simply could not or would not distinguish between the destructive level to which government policies had gone and the attempts to expose those policies. The criticisms of disruptive defendants and their "unruly lawyers" did not get to the heart of the problem at that trial—the law and the legal system had become overt instruments of repression. This fact could not be tolerated passively.

Another example of the kind of trial, on a much smaller scale, which has unleashed attacks against the lawyers was that of the Buffalo Nine. In this trial, four of nine leaders were on trial for assaulting FBI agents. The case grew out of the arrest of two draft resisters who had taken sanctuary in a church after a raid by FBI agents, during which they beat supporters and arrested their leaders, charging the victimized with assault. Although the charge was assault, the Buffalo Nine was still a political prosecution; the governmental goal was to jail four Buffalo leaders of four different Movement groups. The lawyers and their clients chose to pursue a strategy which showed that the trial was an attempt to "nip in the bud" a local antiwar and antiracist movement. The zeal of the government was clear from the use of every FBI agent in the Buffalo area as a witness to testify at the trial. As the persecution proceeded, more and more support developed for those on trial, and the closing arguments by the lawyers best illustrated what the community became aware of during the trial: that the government owned the building, indicted the defendants, paid the salary of the judge, paid the salary of every witness that testified for the government, while it was the U.S. government and its policies which the defendants opposed.

The result of the trial was a hung jury (no decision reached), but more important, the trial solidified and expanded the growing Movement in Buffalo. The trial became an issue that later caused the shutdown of the University of Buffalo and led to a coalition of students and striking Black construction workers on the campus.

The experience of both of these cases indicates the reasons the new lawyers are being attacked. Not only have young lawyers begun to respond to the call for "social justice," but they have become effective. Realizing that the skills of an attorney are a valuable asset to a movement in struggle, the political lawyer attempts to apply these tools to that struggle. The application of creative legal talents to the needs of many groups engaged in protracted struggle has added a new dimension to the spectrum of opposition to government policies. The lawyers are a cross section of the country and their practices have stolen most of the law students from the elite law schools which had always served the giant corporate rulers.

The response by the legal establishment, therefore, has been bitter and sharp. The American Bar Association recommended a series of new ways to discipline lawyers which smacks of political persecution. Such a highly paid Establishment lawyer as Louis Nizer authored a one-sided, inaccurate, scathing attack against lawyers involved in controversial political trials. Nizer's piece, printed by the eager editors of the Sunday *New York Times Magazine* in the spring of 1970, was part of a series of articles and speeches by Establishment lawyers portraying Movement lawyers as people who deliberately try to destroy "justice."

Recently, the American College of Trial Lawyers published a report widely interpreted as the answer to the question of how to control the "unruly lawyer." Of course, they never considered whether in fact the trials of the Chicago Eight and the New York Panther 21, implicitly the motivation for the report, presented examples of the "unruly lawyers." Nowhere in the record of either case does there appear evidence that those lawyers were attempting to "disrupt the judicial process." Close identification with the client's views as well as a vigorous attempt to air the real issues underlying both prosecutions are their crimes.

The Trial Lawyers' report made several recommendations of sanctions to be utilized against the lawyer, including jail or fine, removal of the lawyer from the case, suspension of the lawyer's right to practice, and referral to the bar association for disbarment or other disciplinary action. The threat and challenge are clear, so much so that the president of New York's Metropolitan Trial Lawyers Association was forced to say,

> In a democratic society an independent bar is just as important as an independent judiciary. The public will not long be properly represented if the bar becomes subservient and pusillanimous. . . . Judges will become overbearing and many lawyers intimidated. . . . [In] countries where dictatorships began or exist, one of the first steps was the silencing of independent lawyers. . . .

What, however, was clearly ignored by the attack against Movement lawyers was an understanding of who they are and why our society has fostered their births. People's lawyers do not go into the courtroom to try to prevent or disrupt the process. They represent a plea for truth and an end to subterfuge, political retribution, and camouflaged legal destruction. Those lawyers know only too well that everything Hitler accomplished was absolutely legal under German law.

Joining the assault on the principled defenders of change within the legal movement have been substantial numbers of judges. Pursuant to policies reportedly developed at judicial conferences across the country, some judges jail lawyers at the slightest opportunity when they vigorously advocate the views or rights of their Left-leaning clients. Many lawyers now face attacks designed

to force them away from the defense of the Movement and
to the defense of themselves. A few of those facing disbarment, censure, or discipline are Kenneth Cockrel, a Black
Detroit lawyer charged with publicly denouncing a judge
as racist; Philip Hirschkop, a noted Washington, D.C. attorney connected with the American Civil Liberties Union
and accused of contemptuous conduct in the trial of antiwar activists arrested for destroying Dow Chemical files;
Willard Meyers, a young Movement lawyer in Buffalo attacked for a speech he made at an antiwar rally; and To-
bias Simon, a prominent Florida Civil Liberties lawyer
disciplined for "publicly impugning the Notions of the
Court" in criticizing an injunction against striking teachers.

The reasons for these attacks are important to discuss
to enable a well-reasoned response and an increased understanding of the institutions involved. What is important about the attacks on the Movement lawyer is that the
legal institutions are turning on themselves and casting off
their own principles. In the past, the "Amerikan" bar has
been critical of lawyers who have refused to bear the burden of social consciousness. A former Chief Justice of the
U. S. Supreme Court condemned most lawyers as "obse-
quious servant(s) of business . . . tainted with the
morals and manners of the market place in [their] most
antisocial manifestations," and called for lawyers to become devoted to social justice. Now that a legal movement
has developed, aligning itself with the poor and the racially and politically oppressed, even lip service is no
longer paid to these principles.

In one sense, the attacks clearly reflect the legal profession's support for the insidious policies of the Nixon-
Agnew-Mitchell junta. In another sense, they completely
lack an understanding of the polarized legal community.
Why the brightest law students in the country upon graduation seek roles which make these traditionalists their
enemies, fazes them not. Why the most popular speakers
appearing at every law school in the nation are those who
denounce the American Bar Association for its rubber

stamp approval of the policies of government which have brought this country to the brink of mass domestic violence, seems not to concern them. Racism, war, and poverty are none of their business, and the overt repression of movements for social change by the executive, the legislative, or the judicial branches of government is swept quietly under the rug. In effect, the attackers criticize radical lawyers for showing in court that a particular criminal case was motivated not because of crime but because of politics.

It must be made clear that when lawyers are attacked during the course of their representation of clients, the attack is motivated by a desire to repress the clients and the Movement they represent. The lawyer is the protector and defender of that client and the attack against the lawyer becomes the symbolic destruction of the client. The government, fearing meaningful change, increases repression of Movement groups by attacking the lawyers in an effort to hinder and even eliminate a potential threat to its foreign and domestic policies. When radical lawyers intercede their bodies and minds in an effort to prevent the government assault from succeeding, then they, too, must be intimidated or eliminated. The lawyers are under attack not because they alone pose any threat, but because they lend the kind of support which causes the rulers to pay dearly in effectiveness and credibility when they make these assaults.

The entire process of Movement struggle and government repression, heightened first by the attacks against political defendants and then their lawyers, has been the experience of every country that has achieved radical social change. This process is also symptomatic of decay— decay in a system that must be changed but stubbornly resists change. The rulers attempt to destroy the lawyers who fight for the activists, the unpopular, the poor, and the politically or racially oppressed, and show that they are determined to halt dissent and resistance itself. They will end by embroiling themselves in the mass violence that should be avoided. It could be avoided by the encouragement of a people's movement which will struggle for the transformation of an aged and lunatic economic and political system into one that honestly seeks justice for all the people, not just a few.

Open Resistance: In Defense of the Movement

*by William M. Kunstler**

In his most recent book, *Points of Rebellion,* United States Supreme Court Justice William O. Douglas labels "today's Establishment . . . the new George III." In so doing, he prophesies that, should it continue to adhere to the British monarch's oppressive tactics, "the redress, honored in tradition, is also revolution." While he acknowledges that violence has no constitutional sanction, he recognizes that, "where grievances pile high and most of the elective spokesmen represent the Establishment, violence may be the only effective response." [1]

Assuming Justice Douglas' belief in a basic "right of revolution" to be true—and I, for one, for what it's worth, wholeheartedly share it—then what is the role of the progressive American lawyer at a time somewhere between the ballot and the barricades? Created and licensed by the very system that seeks to destroy, isolate, or immobilize many of his clients, operating under its substantive and procedural rules, indeed serving as an "officer" of its tribunals, he is, at the same time, painfully aware that he is himself perpetuating one of its cruelest illusions—that justice is truly evenhanded. At one plateau or another, he must, if he has any sensibilities at all, wonder whether he can continue to live with a paradox that daily confronts and confounds him.

For the practitioner who sees the law as the natural and even the only way to solve the majority of mankind's pressing problems, there may be little or no inner turmoil. What the institution fails to correct or alleviate at one stage of its development, it most certainly will at another. And if he occasionally feels a vague sense of malaise at its inability to answer most of the questions addressed to it, he can, with only minor effort, assuage his uneasiness with the soothing rationale that perfection, while a wholly valid ideal, is attainable only where the angels dwell.

But for those who regard the law as nothing more—or less—than one of many useful environmental tools, it becomes intolerable when that law openly differentiates between large segments of society on economic, political, social, or other equally untenable grounds. Then they must begin to ask hard questions and seek even harder answers. Is it merely a question of more efficient judicial administration or selection? Can things be set right by a better system of legal aid for indigent defendants or by pumping more social consciousness into law school curricula? Does salvation lie with the reform of bail procedures or by making civil libertarians out of patrolmen and politicians?

On the other hand, there is the disquieting thought that the legal subsystem itself is nothing more than the new tyrant's most reliable weapon to ward off any seemingly potent threat to the continuation of yesterday into tomorrow. If the injunction and the conviction can achieve the same results as the rope and the sword, judges are, after all, far more comfortable companions than executioners. And in the last analysis, due process of law is exactly what the high and mighty say it is.

If this be the case—and, I submit, there is convincing evidence that it is—then the role of those lawyers who can no longer remain their society's most complacent eunuchs must pass from passive or active acceptance to open resistance. Even an officer of the court cannot be precluded from resorting to any approach for the "redress of grievances" available to his fellow citizens. If he firmly believes that the Black and the poor, the activists and the militants, the students and the radicals who are being crushed by laws that, on their face or as applied, violate every tenet of equality and fair play, then how can he pretend to his clients or himself that his only legitimate function is to play out the string?

In an editorial in February 1970, *The New York Times* called the refusal of Judge Julius J. Hoffman to permit former Attorney General Ramsey Clark to testify before the jury in the conspiracy trial of the Chicago Eight "the ultimate outrage in a trial that has become the shame of American Justice." (The initial outrage, of course, was the charges against the defendants: crossing state lines to incite a riot, and conspiracy to do so, all of which stemmed from the demonstrations surrounding the National Democratic Convention in August 1968.) At the same time, the newspaper sharply criticized the defendants and their attorneys for "their defiance and clowning," which, it stated, "had turned the proceedings into a mixture of chaos and cabaret." Yet, what are honest and sensitive people— whether they be lawyers or laymen—supposed to do when confronted with an "ultimate outrage" except to register, in their own way, their reaction to what is going on before their shocked eyes?

For example, when Judge Hoffman ruled on February 2, 1970, that Ralph D. Abernathy, a crucial witness for the defense, would not be permitted to take the stand because he was sixteen minutes late in arriving at the courtroom, he ordered the attorneys and the defendants not to mention Reverend Abernathy's name in front of the jury. I informed him that I intended to violate his order, and I subsequently did so. My reason, as stated in the official transcript, was phrased as a question: "What is an honest man to do when Your Honor has done what he has done?"

Three days later, after the revocation of David Dellinger's bail, my colleague Leonard I. Weinglass attempted to make an argument on his behalf. When the Court refused to listen to him, Mr. Weinglass explained, "You are keeping a man in custody and you are not permitting a lawyer to make an argument for his freedom." After the judge had ordered him to sit down, Weinglass persisted in crying out, "You have no authority for taking that man's freedom away, and . . . not let me make a legal argument in his behalf." Although the episode was to cost Mr. Weinglass one month of his total punishment for contempt, silence in the face of such judicial autocracy would have been unthinkable.

But such conduct does not come easy. For lawyers, inculcated for centuries with a virtually blind respect for the law and its administrators, it is indeed a difficult thing to express open contempt for either. In fact, from almost the beginning of their legal educations, they are taught that, while judges may be incompetent, corrupt or worse, it is the institution rather than the individual which merits veneration. Otherwise, they are warned, the public will lose confidence in the law itself, thereby endangering the very existence of organized society.

Almost two hundred years ago, in addressing the Virginia Convention, Patrick Henry, a relatively new lawyer, asked, "Is life so dear or peace so sweet as to be purchased at the price of chains and slavery?" His spiritual descendants might well ask a similar question today. "Is law so dear and order so sweet as to be purchased at the price of our brothers' chains and slavery?" If the answer is no, then, like Henry, must we not thunder some appropriate equivalent of his "Forbid it, Almighty God!"?

The central problem, however, is that the radical lawyer is in an utterly impossible position. On one hand, he is bound by the strictures of an institution, which has, after all, become an indispensable Establishment bulwark. On the other, he has an equally pressing obligation to defend clients who may want to destroy or drastically overhaul that very Establishment. Ethically and psychologically, he cannot fulfill both duties at one and the same time.

The anomaly becomes even more striking when the lawyer shares the general political philosophy of his clients. For example, if he, too, believes that the courts are, in many instances, the instruments of an oppressive system determined to preserve itself at all costs, then he may find himself constitutionally unable to accept rules which he believes further that purpose. Yet, these same rules will govern the conduct of trials which may subject his clients to stringent criminal penalties, thereby destroying or minimizing their ability to effect meaningful social change.

Moreover, these difficulties are considerably aggravated if he is convinced, as I am, that the Anglo-American legal system is, in theory at least, a generally satisfactory institution. It contains all of the ingredients necessary to insure the equitable and egalitarian resolution of conflicts among citizens and between citizens and the state. Centuries of progressive, often abrasive evolution have created a rather remarkable structure, wholly capable of delivering due process to all seekers.

The trouble, however, is that, in order to achieve the equal justice it proclaims as its essential goal, it depends wholly on the reasonable approximation of practice to preachment. If jurors were really selected from one's peers, if judges were truly impartial, if prosecutors always sought truth rather than convictions, if the poor and the benighted had access to the same legal talent available to the darlings of the system, then perhaps even lawyers could accept all the lofty pronouncements at face value. But the sad fact of the matter is that one hour in any police court in the United States should convince all but the blind and the deaf that none of these is the rule.

Unfortunately, it is not enough to point out that, no matter how unjust the system may be at the trial level, there are always the higher courts to undo the damage. The judges on those lofty tribunals come, in large measure, from the same milieu as their colleagues below, and react in much the same fashion to significant threats to the social order which created and maintains them. Furthermore, even assuming courts which can rise above their own instincts of self-preservation, the gradualism of the appellate process often runs counter to the immediacy of human needs at the very moment they most cry out for recognition and fulfillment.

In a rather perceptive, if overly simplistic, analysis of American justice, Jerry C. Rubin, one of the defendants in the Chicago Conspiracy trial, recently wrote:

> Justice in America is a supermarket. Pigs arrest us for expensive crimes—and let us off pleading guilty to cheap ones. Fucking deals. The judge is a poker player and the cards are other people's lives. It's blackmail. If we demand our constitutional rights—a jury trial—we pay even more heavily when found guilty.
>
> The courtroom is a negotiating session between State and criminal on how much the criminal must pay for having been arrested. Ninety-five percent of the people busted make deals to get lesser punishments. The poor stand helpless in the face of the state's power. The rich get rich man's justice; the poor get poor man's justice. *As Lenny Bruce said, "In the halls of justice, the only justice is in the halls."* [2]

If only the profession—judges, lawyers and administrators—could admit publicly the essential truth of his observations, perhaps we could begin to return to the original premise that justice, not class expediency, is the only criterion worth acknowledging.

However, while a few attorneys are radicalized by what they see done in the name of justice, most ignore or quickly forget it. After all, there is little profit and less inspiration in human misery, and it is downright uncomfortable to view at close range the tragic malfunctioning of a system widely heralded as near-perfect. Pausing only long enough to make a mental note to increase next year's donation to the Legal Aid Society, the average lawyer turns back to the corporate merger, the lucrative matrimonial, the promising personal injury action or the big-money land contract on which he is currently working, scarcely conscious that, in so doing, he is eschewing the shining promises of his own profession.

The irony of this dichotomy has not been lost upon law

students across the country who are becoming increasingly mystified and bitter about the ever-widening gulf between the dream and the reality. Young men and women who, a decade ago, would have been camping anxiously in the anterooms of the large firms, which insure the smooth and profitable functioning of the American economic system, are now finding their way into neighborhood or communal law offices. Governmental legal programs, originally designed as a sop to liberal reformists or a method of controlling restive segments of the population, are being converted by many of these youthful pioneers into effective system-challenging devices.

As one young Black Detroit attorney recently put it, the progressive lawyer is rapidly becoming a double agent. True, he is, by dint of environmental benefits accumulated over the centuries at the expense of the lives and liberties of less fortunate men, a part of the Establishment which created and nurtures him. But, in his heart of hearts, he is devoted to the service of those who have much to gain and little to lose by the drastic alteration or even destruction of the status quo.

It is certainly not coincidental that Lenin, Gandhi, and Castro were lawyers. Those most acutely aware of the failure of social institutions are often the first to articulate the need for their fundamental change. But it is equally true that such apostasy is achieved only by the subjugation of the deepest instinctual urges to follow those elementary rules of survival which have almost always guaranteed safe passage to their adherents.

It is not easy to turn away from the comforts and luxuries we were taught to expect from our favored status as members of the bar. It is infinitely disquieting to become so controversial that often even friends and relatives have to resort to varied degrees of apologia in order to explain away your sins. There is no joy in being labeled everything from an eccentric to a slavish employee of Castro, Kosygin, or Mao.

And yet the Movement lawyer, like so many of his clients, has access to replacement values that make his defection not a sacrifice but a salvation. To sense that one is reaching for dimly viewed stars, that dedication and inspiration are not confined to madmen and martyrs, that fingers brushing over a cheek may have more meaning than all the poems and profundities ever uttered, that there is true magic in clasped hands, shining eyes, and pounding hearts, that a life of love is infinitely more meaningful than one of acquisition, is to understand, albeit vaguely, the transcendental nature of man. The moment one can build enough personal faith in the reality of such a life, then will the clutch of clay at last begin to loosen and the heavens seem closer than ever before.

Perhaps all this is an overly romanticized view of what is, after all, an ancient concept of the dedicated life. But, just as Cervantes saw the essential nobility of even his broken-down and outmoded knight, the superficialities of our current civilization cannot disguise the utter need of all men to look beyond their own chimneys. The fault of romanticism is not that it lacks all validity, but that we are somehow ashamed or afraid of being caught up in it. The tragic result is that we leave the skies to the astronomers who promptly reduce them to dust and gases.

In the last analysis, each man must live the life his own sensibilities dictate. But it is sad, even tragically so, to see so many once shining hopes sullied over with the crass blandness of self-interest, to witness at near hand the death of dreams that, in the beginning, were as compelling as existence itself, and to understand that, at one stage or another, every truth is a lie, and every lie a truth. Yet it may still be possible, in the convenient microcosm of the courtroom, occasionally to bring off the most righteous of triumphs.

These victories, however, are only attainable if we are able to develop a new breed of lawyers, men and women who recognize the law's destructive quotient and are not afraid to expose and, whenever possible, counter it. Such attorneys, who are able to put client before self and social progress before dollar signs, may well find that the people's service has infinitely more to offer in human terms than that of the system. Len Weinglass put it perhaps best when, just prior to his sentencing for contempt, he told Judge Hoffman, "I welcome the opportunity of whatever the Court does which will enable me to once again rejoin the defendants and Bill Kunstler, wherever they are, in what has been for me the warmest and richest association of my life."

But the lawyer cannot, even with the best or most grandiose of intentions, be society's savior. The most that can be hoped from him is that he will exert whatever professional skills he possesses in reasonable harmony with the political objectives of his clients. Nothing less than this union will meet the inexorable needs of social movements which cannot either understand or tolerate dispassionate middlemen.

We live, as men have always lived, in perilous times. If, as Holmes insisted, the law is the result of experience rather than logic, then we lawyers must sense the sweep of wind and wave and act accordingly. The generations behind us cry, as perhaps they always have cried, for total commitment. Honorable men, lawyers or otherwise, can offer no less.

Notes

1. William O. Douglas, *Points of Rebellion*. New York: Vintage Books, p. 95.
2. Jerry Rubin, *Do It!*. New York: Simon and Schuster, 1970, pp. 159–160.

The Role of the Radical Lawyer and Teacher of Law

*by Arthur Kinoy**

I have recently been referred to by the Establishment press as a *"radical* professor of law." This has occasioned sharp inquiries from both my academic colleagues on the one hand and my friends in the people's movements on the other, as to whether I am comfortable with the characterization. At the heart of each inquiry is an unspoken challenge. As a "radical" teacher of "law," am I not caught in an impossible dilemma? Am I not torn by what appears to be an irreconcilable conflict between the objectives of a radical commitment to a society founded on the common good—in which the exploitation of man by man and woman by man is forever eliminated, a society in which war and poverty and racism are dim memories of a barbaric past—and the harsh realities of a profession in which I function as teacher and lawyer—a profession which is an integral part of a mechanism which is used by the dominant class groups in society to maintain ruling class power, property, and class rule? [1]

My colleagues in academia press me least. To some of

* Copyright © 1970 by Arthur Kinoy. First appeared in The National Lawyer's *Guild Practitioner,* 1970.

them, unhappily, an adjustment to the gap between ideals and the reality of the legal system has become a way of life. But to my colleagues in struggle, and particularly to those who have newly come to the battle, the questions are often more pressing. Is it not a total contradiction to be a "radical" teacher of law, a "radical" lawyer—a contradiction which can only be resolved by exculpatory proclamations that "law is illegal" or hortatory pronunciamentos that the "only struggle is in the streets?"

To these earnest and deeply troubled lawyers I have but one reply. Yes, the "radical" teacher of law, the "radical" lawyer, lives, functions, struggles, in the midst of contradictions; his or her life is itself a contradiction. But this should be no shock, no surprise. Every radical who has honestly attempted to study society, as one great student of society once remarked, not for the purpose of understanding it but for the purpose of changing it, knows that "there is nothing that does not contain contradiction; without contradiction there would be no world." [2]

It should not so disturb us to discover that the role of a radical teacher of law, or a radical lawyer, plays itself out within the framework of a vast contradiction—is itself a contradiction. One of the most honored teachers of all contemporary radicals, Fredrick Engels, wrote over a hundred years ago that

> life consists just precisely in this—that a living thing is at each moment itself and yet something else. Life is therefore also a contradiction which is present in things and processes themselves, and which constantly asserts and solves itself; and as soon as the contradiction ceases, life too comes to an end, and death steps in. [3]

Let me be very blunt. The role of the radical in the law is the same as the role of the radical in any arena of life. It is to study in depth and in precision the *particularity* of the contradictions he or she operates within, in order to understand how best to participate in the resolution of these contradictions in a forward motion; in a manner which assists in the resolution of the principal contradic-

tions of society in the direction of the emergence of a new
society free from the oppression, the brutality, the frustra-
tion, and despair of the old. Such a study requires first of
all an examination of the contradictions within the institutions in which we operate as lawyers and teachers as
they exist *today,* not yesterday or fifty years ago. It requires an examination of the *particularity* of the contradictions in these institutions in this country at this moment. We cannot be content with analyses which rest
upon examination of the particularity of legal institutions
or ideologies of, for example, Czarist Russia, or industrial
Britain in the nineteenth century, or imperialist-exploited
countries of Latin America in the twentieth century. As a
well-known teacher of the science of the laws of motion of
society once wrote:

> Processes change, old processes and old contradictions dis-
> appear, new processes and new contradictions emerge, and
> the methods of resolving contradictions differ accordingly.
> In Russia the contradictions resolved by the February Revo-
> lution and the October Revolution, respectively, as well as
> the methods used to resolve them were basically different.
> The use of different methods to resolve different contradic-
> tions is a principle which Marxist-Leninists must strictly
> observe. The dogmatists do not observe this principle. They
> do not understand the difference between the various revo-
> lutionary situations, and consequently do not understand
> that different methods should be used to resolve different
> contradictions; instead they uniformly adopt a formula
> which they fancy to be unalterable, and inflexibly apply it
> everywhere. This can only bring setbacks to the revolution
> or make a great mess of what originally could have been
> done well.[4]

Unless our examination of the institutions within
which we operate proceeds upon the basis of a "concrete
analysis of concrete conditions" [5] as they exist *today,* in
this country, at *this* moment in our history, we will continue to be subject to a rash of analyses about the role of
radical lawyers which are essentially one-sided and based
upon sweeping generalizations about the oppressive na-

ture of the legal superstructure which radicals, Marxist and non-Marxist alike, have written about and polemicized against for many years. A number of radicals have recently clearly recognized the truth which has been apparent for many years to most Blacks in this country as well as to large numbers of working people—that the instrumentalities of justice provide justice only for the rich and powerful. This has encouraged useful and helpful probing into the class nature of the system of justice. But this exposure cannot by itself substitute for a fully rounded definition of the role of a radical lawyer or teacher of law at this precise moment in our history. Blacks, Browns, and working people, the oppressed sections of society, who daily live with the clubs of the police and the callousness of the courts, rarely need lessons in the "demystification" of the institutions of justice. Their crying need is quite different: what course of conduct will result in a favorable resolution of the fundamental contradictions of the society they live in, a resolution which will once and for all eliminate the oppressive role of present institutions of "justice," and class rule itself?

Let us turn then to the task at hand: the analysis of the *particularities* of the contradictions we live with today as radical lawyers or teachers of law. The reader will have to bear with me because such an analysis, to be of any use, to say nothing of avoiding making "a great mess of what originally could have been done well," must be based, not upon radical-sounding one-sided rhetoric, or fire and brimstone generalities from another day and another age, but upon what that master of socialist methodology called "the most essential thing in Marxism, the living soul of Marxism, the concrete analysis of concrete conditions." [6]

We live today at one of the most historic turning points in American history. The nation is at the edge of events which may shape the destinies of millions for years to come, and we radical lawyers are caught in the very center of the interplay of contradictions which are conditioning this course of developments.

On the one hand the dominant section of the American

ruling circles, represented by the Nixon-Agnew-Mitchell-Pentagon clique, is moving rapidly and openly in the direction of experimentation with sweeping repressive measures of a legal and extralegal character. These measures range from the nationally directed plan to uproot and destroy the cutting edge of Black militancy, the Black Panther Party, through the device of massive frame-up trials, the contrived prosecutions against the national white leadership of the antiwar movement and the expanding youth culture revolt, to the hundreds of local prosecutions in every section of the country of the Black and white opposition leaders. The wholesale utilization of "legal" forms of repression of political opposition has now been coupled with extralegal measures of murder, assassination, and the active encouragement of open vigilantism of a mass character. This all has an ominous and familiar ring.

We are in a transition period in which the dominant sections of the ruling powers are edging toward a substitution of the present form of rule by the capitalist class—the form of rule classically known as bourgeois democracy—by another form of rule—the open terrorist dictatorship classically known as fascism. It is simply not helpful to evade this question, to avoid the word "fascism" because it evokes emotional connotations of horror and nightmare emanating from an earlier era. We Americans are masters at running from political reality when that reality is distasteful and shocking to our image of ourselves. For a hundred years the word "slavery" was erased from any considered analysis of the reason for the continuing oppression of Black people. Only the recent powerful upsurges of the Blacks themselves have forced the word "slavery" back into the contemporary political and juridical lexicon. Nor is the practice of fascism an alien method imported from abroad and antithetical to our cultural patterns. The Southern slave masters utilized the form of "open terrorist dictatorship" after the destruction of the Reconstruction governments, and clung to the essence of its form of rule until shaken by the first waves of Black upsurge in the sixties. Americans invented genocide on the Trail of Tears of the Cherokee Nation a hundred years before Buchenwald. In words which today invoke a prophetic chill, an astute Southern politician said thirty years ago that when fascism came to the United States it would come "wrapped in the American flag."

It is desperately critical for all Americans to consider carefully the dynamics of the contradictions which shape the contours of this transition period in which the ruling class is *edging* towards a qualitative change in form of rule. But it is especially important for radical lawyers and teachers of law to grapple with these questions since the particularities of the contradictions dominant in this period of transition shape our role and our responsibilities.

It is essential, I think, to recognize that the ruling class turns to fascism, to an open terrorist dictatorship, abandoning its classic form of class domination, bourgeois democracy, out of *fear* and not out of strength. Faced with a growing radicalization of large sections of the people, an ever increasing inability to solve the immediate and pressing problems of the people, which in turn leads to further radicalization, the response of the rulers has been to turn increasingly to intermediate forms of repression which pave the way, unless checked, to the ultimate transition to the open terrorist dictatorship. An astute and experienced student of the transition period from the rule of bourgeois democracy to the rule by open terrorist dictatorship, Georgi Dimitrov, the Bulgarian Communist who won the admiration of millions throughout the world in 1934 because of his courageous stance before the Nazi tribunal during the historic Reichstag Fire Trial, warned that "the accession to power of fascism must not be conceived of in so simplified and smooth a form, as though some committee or other of finance-capital decided on a certain date to set up a fascist dictatorship." [7] This is not to say that the coup d'etat blow is utterly impossible in the current American scene. The events following the Cambodian invasion have evoked too many parallels to that once fictionally regarded motion picture *Seven Days in May* to dismiss the

military coup d'etat as an American impossibility relegated to the Late Late Show. But the dynamics of the present situation point in a direction less dramatic, but equally
dangerous: the increasing utilization of legal and extralegal measures which repress the leadership of the revolutionary forces and which curtail and limit even the most
elementary democratic liberties of the large masses of
people who are thrown by events into an increased radicalization. Thus the ultimate fascist danger and the
sweeping intermediate repressive steps which pave the
way to the change in form of state rule must be viewed as
one side of the basic contradiction, the other side of which
is the unprecedented and extraordinary growing radicalization of vast numbers of Americans who are experiencing the inability of the rulers to solve any of the immediate problems of this society.

These two phenomena are occurring simultaneously
and are reacting upon each other. The rulers are unable to
solve the problem of extricating themselves from an unpopular and disastrous colonial war, so they seek to avoid
the nightmare of both military defeat and increased economic crisis at home by turning to the "solution" of extending and enlarging the war. This in turn sets into motion the most extraordinary reaction among millions of
people reaching up into conflicts and splits in the highest
circles of government. A crisis in government begins to
develop in which the very *forms* of bourgeois parliamen-
tarism are under attack by the ruling powers. For a moment, but an important moment, the structure through
which the ruling class has maintained its power for the
entire history of the country, the very form of representative government, an "independent" legislature, becomes
itself an obstacle to the dominant governing circles and
the object of its attacks. In the same sense the present
Mitchell-instigated prosecution of the Black Panther
Party, the antiwar leadership, the youth culture leadership, and the dozens, if not hundreds of political trials to
come, contain the seeds of the potential ultimate thrust of
the rulers—the abandonment of all bourgeois democratic

forms as a method of rule and the substitution of the open terrorist dictatorship. This is a characteristic of the present period which must be understood and studied particularly by the radical lawyer.

For years, the ruling class has governed through the utilization of the forms of political democracy, principal among them the formal constitutional protections of political and individual liberties contained in the Bill of Rights. The many political prosecutions already held, now in progress, and yet to come are shaped by this newly emerging contradiction. Although utilizing the *form* of a judicial proceeding and supposedly bound by the old rules of law, they cannot achieve their objective of mass repression and terrorization without in fact undermining and abandoning, one after another, the most elementary bourgeois democratic rights. The right of citizens to bail, the right under the First Amendment to organize an opposition political party, the right to privacy against government wiretapping under the Fourth Amendment, the right to an independent jury of one's peers under the Sixth Amendment, the very right to a fair trial by an impartial judge under the Fifth Amendment—these rights, and many more, formerly called, if you will, the "trappings of bourgeois justice," the so-called "rights of man," were grafted onto the Constitution of the propertied classes in an earlier revolutionary era to obtain the support of the masses of people for the struggle against feudalism or foreign imperial control. Now, in a new era, these forms become dangerous to the ruling class, an obstacle to their plans, and must be undermined, ignored, and ultimately totally abandoned by them. The ruling class begins to turn upon its own ideas, its own forms, its own institutions.

In every institution the contradiction begins to break loose. It is a moment of splits, of indecision—the old ideas and the old forms retain some strength and some support even in high circles. The impact of the new contradictions affects every institution in the judicial system from the trial courts to the Supreme Court itself, as indeed it affects every institution in political life. As the major contradictions intensify—the growing dissatisfaction and increasing radicalization of millions on the one hand and the increased legal and extralegal repressive measures moving in the ultimate direction of open terrorist dictatorship on the other—the internal stresses within the judicial system intensify as the pressures mount to eliminate or ignore the oldest and most elementary substantive and procedural forms of fairness and individual liberties. As in the parliamentary arena, we are approaching a crisis of government within the judicial arena as well.

What is the role and responsibility of the radical lawyer or teacher of law at such a moment in our history? Earlier in this article I said that the role of the radical in the law is essentially the same as the role of the radical in any arena of life: to utilize his or her skills to participate in the resolution of these contradictions in a forward motion. The responsibility upon us all at this moment is awesome. The stakes are high; for those of us in this country who call ourselves radical, never higher. There is a new renaissance of Black struggle in the heartland of the South on a level of militancy and unity which leads one white Mississippi newspaper to say recently "the deepest, most fundamental crisis since 1860 stares us in the face." [8] This time the upsurge in the South is coupled with the perspective of Black struggles of every form in the Northern urban areas, which will shake the country to its very core. These struggles are merging in time, if not in form, with the unprecedented motion of millions in opposition to the insanity of our military adventures, spearheaded by a youth movement which has already shaken the highest circles with fear. They will be accompanied by the inevitable development of the broadest economic battles of working people seeking to remove from their shoulders the burdens of growing unemployment and an economic crisis which now no one can ignore. There lies ahead a perspective of rapid radicalization of millions which could lead to a realization of the goal which must not be merely a paper slogan but our constant central strategy—the concept of power to the people.

On the other hand it is not written in stone that the other pole of the major contradiction may not temporarily prevail: that the dominant sections of the ruling class may succeed in substituting the open terrorist dictatorship as the form of rule. And it is at this point that we must be brutally honest with ourselves. On the one hand the open terrorist dictatorship would mean the probable deaths of thousands, if not hundreds of thousands, of the finest sons and daughters of the American people, both Black and white, to say nothing of the possible destruction of the entire world in a nuclear holocaust. On the other hand, in a country in which even remnants of democratic liberties survive, the people, despite the heaviest repressive measures, still have the possibility of organizing and fighting openly for their needs and perspectives.

It seems almost pathetic that one should have to spend any time at all arguing that a victory, even temporarily, for fascism in this country would be a disaster not only for the millions here but for the people of the entire world. Unfortunately there are a few among the Left who are captivated, as were their analogues in Germany in the fateful last days of the Weimar Republic, by the wishful illusion that open terrorist dictatorship would move people more speedily to radicalization and militant struggle. That illusion should have been shattered in the concentration camps of Belsen and Dachau, on the battlefields of World War II and in the ashes of Hiroshima. More fundamentally, such an illusion runs counter to what Lenin once called "the fundamental law of all great revolutions": that the masses of people must learn through their own political experience in struggle.[9] It is precisely for these reasons that radicals and radical lawyers must fight skillfully and tenaciously for every scrap of democratic liberties. This is particularly true at a moment when masses are in motion and are groping for solutions to fundamental problems. At such a moment the ability of radical leadership to exercise that leadership openly and legally is crucial. This is exactly why the ruling class turns at such a moment *against* its own concepts of bourgeois democracy and seeks to isolate and destroy the radical leadership, so that the crucial element of theoretical and political leadership required if the motion of the masses is to be transformed into the highest level of radicalization—the taking and democratization of power —will be temporarily eliminated, or seriously restricted.

It is within this context that the role of the radical lawyer or teacher of law begins to emerge more clearly. It is to utilize to the utmost all of his or her skills and energies to assist in a *forward, successful* resolution of the major interacting poles of the central contradictions of the day. On the one hand, the radical lawyer must assist in the increasing and exploding radicalization of masses of people learning from their own political experience. On the other hand, all of the lawyer's skills and energies must be utilized to resist in every way the efforts of the dominant sections of the ruling class to solve their crisis, even if temporarily, by substituting the open terrorist dictatorship for the present forms of bourgeois democracy, both within the parliamentary and judicial systems. I suggest that these two aspects of the role of the radical lawyer are not isolated, are interrelated and interact each upon the other. That such a role may often place the radical attorney in what seems to be a contradictory position, a changing position, is inevitable. That his or her position may not necessarily at all times be the same as a radical defendant in a political trial is also true. But as we have remarked before, contradictions are not in and of themselves reflections of weakness. Quite to the contrary, they are reflections of life, and if understood and mastered, they are the key to forward motion.

Let us consider first the special features of the role and responsibilities of the radical lawyer or teacher of law in participating in the resistance to the efforts of the rulers to edge towards an abandonment of the forms of bourgeois democracy. It is *precisely* because of the lawyer's classic role in the *maintenance* of the system of bourgeois democracy as a form of class domination that a radical lawyer who understands the dynamics of the period is peculiarly able at this moment to assist in the essential struggles, both in the judicial and legislative arenas, against those transitional reactionary moves and measures which directly facilitate the substitution of the open terrorist dictatorship as the form of class rule.

History is filled with the ironies of reversal of role—conflict often results in the negation of certain characteristics and the creation of their opposite. Under the system of bourgeois democracy the lawyer more than often plays out the role of guaranteeing the existence of the facade which masks the oppression lurking beneath the superstructure of "rights and liberties." The lawyer becomes identified with these "frills," these "rights," these "liberties," the term depending upon the analysis of function in the system. The lawyer's particular role in the system is to make it look good, to provide at least the appearance of justice, as one Supreme Court opinion so candidly once put it.[10] But it is this very role assigned to the lawyer which enables the lawyer to be particularly effective at the present moment in a struggle to safeguard and to preserve these forms as the ruling class moves, out of fear and desperation, to abandon them and destroy them. But this requires flexibility, skill, and above all, understanding on the part of the radical lawyer. He or she must find every opportunity to expose, within the framework of the judicial arena itself, the extraordinary fact that the rulers and their servants in the judicial system, be they prosecutors or judges, are turning upon their *own* system, are abandoning their *own* stated rules, designed once in a bygone day to embody the then revolutionary principles of fairness, equality, justice, and liberty. When the radical lawyer aggressively struggles for the right of citizens to bail, or against the concept of preventative detention with its overtones of Dachau or Buchenwald, or against the undermining of the Fourth Amendment guarantee against wiretapping, or against forced and coerced confessions, or for the promised right of a fair jury of one's peers, he or she is not engaging just in an important struggle for the rights and even liberty of the particular political defendant on trial. More importantly, the lawyer is participating in a political struggle of the greatest significance: the struggle to preserve and protect the most elementary democratic liberties and safeguards not only for his or her clients then on trial, but for all the people.

Such a struggle, if it is waged aggressively, if it is not perfunctory or routine, if it is related to and becomes a part of the experience of thousands beyond the immediate confines of the courtroom, teaches a profound lesson. It exposes who is really in "contempt of court," who is really "undermining the principles of a system of justice." It is not the radical lawyers who are meeting their responsibilities to the people by fighting insistently and courageously for the preservation of those elementary rights and liberties which are supposed to protect *all* the people, but rather it is the judges and the prosecutors who, in obedience to the needs of their frightened masters in power (it was Jefferson who wrote of Federalist judges too obedient to the rich and wealthy), are undermining, ignoring and destroying the liberties of the people.

It is in this context that I say to my radical colleagues at the bar, whose courage and skill I admire, that their frequently expressed formulation of their central role and objective as being that of "delegitimizing" the institutions of the law is at once too narrow and too one-sided. In its one-sidedness it obscures, and even hinders, the fulfillment of the more complex, more critical role, which a study of the *particularity* of the present contradictions places before us. The struggle to preserve the elementary forms of procedural guarantees, designed originally to protect individual liberty and the right to a fair trial, is *not* a struggle to "delegitimize" or "demystify" these forms. The struggle is to *defend* these forms, to *protect* them; if you will, to *legitimize* them against the efforts of the rulers to *delegitimize* them. There is no contradiction between such an approach and the necessary exposure of prosecutors and judges who, at the government's bidding, brush aside and trample on elementary rights. Such an approach is not only in the interest of effectively protecting and defending one's political clients, a not unimportant consideration, but also permits the radical lawyer to emerge as the champion of the people's liberties which the ruling class is abandoning. It provides a focus for the organizing of massive support among the broadest sections of the people, to whom the protection of the "right" of American citizens to liberty and justice remains an important question. It permits the development of alliances, even if temporary, with forces who for their own reasons are not yet prepared to abandon these elementary democratic forms; alliances which are essential if masses of people led by radicals are to frustrate the designs of the rulers and move forward to higher objectives. But most important of all, it permits the raising of the central political questions: Who is conspiring against the liberties of the people? Who is undermining and subverting the people's heritage of freedom? And the answer to these— that it is the ruling class itself which is moving toward the destruction of the most elementary liberties of the people, is critical to a further radicalization of the people.

True, it is not always simple to wage this struggle with dignity and power, so that this central question repeatedly emerges. I commend to my radical colleagues at the bar the often-mentioned and little-studied proceedings in a Cuban courtroom in Santiago in 1953, one year after the Batista coup d'etat which eliminated the presidential election scheduled for June 1. A twenty-seven-year-old Havana lawyer, Fidel Castro, stood trial with 122 codefendants for an attack upon the Moncada military barracks. This was a trial taking place *after* the Batista coup d'etat, under conditions of terror.

"All the approaches to the courthouse were blocked by armored cars. Lining both sides of the road from Boniato prison to the courthouse, a distance of six miles, were 1,000 soldiers with automatic weapons at the ready." [11] The proceedings of this trial are wonderfully instructive on many counts which go beyond the present scope of this paper and ought to be carefully studied by radicals, whose knowledge of the trial is unhappily only too often confined

to a recollection that it was the occasion of the now famous utterance "History will absolve me." For example,
Castro's response to the prosecutor's question as to why he
had not used "civil means" to accomplish his purpose was
a brilliant summary of the point of view that revolutionary military measures are correct and will receive the support of the people only when the people are convinced by
their own experience that all other channels of struggle
are closed and futile. Castro's response to the prosecutor's
question was,

> Simply because there is no freedom in Cuba, because since
> the 10th of March [the coup d'etat] nobody can talk. I al-
> ready said that efforts were made but the government, al-
> ways intransigent, did not want to give ground. I accused
> Batista before the tribunals of justice, but the courts did
> not resolve the case, as we expected.[12]

Castro's reference to his "accusation" of Batista refers
to a rather astounding action he undertook *as a lawyer*
two weeks after the Batista coup d'etat. He appeared before the Urgency Court in Havana and submitted a written complaint charging that Batista and his "accomplices"
had violated six articles of the Code of Social Defense for
which the punishment prescribed was 108 years in
prison. He demanded that the judges do their duty, writing in his brief:

> Logic tells me that if there exist courts in Cuba Batista
> should be punished, and if Batista is not punished and
> continues as master of the State, President, Prime Minister,
> Senator, Major General, civil and military chief, executive
> power and legislative power, owner of lives and farms, then
> there do not exist courts, they have been suppressed. Ter-
> rible reality?
> If that is so, say so as soon as possible, hang up your robe,
> resign your post.[13]

To those who today sometimes fail to consider the *particularity* of every situation and instead engage in sweeping generalizations that *any* affirmative utilization of existing legal procedures is "illusion-creating" and not a

"radical" form of struggle, I commend to their attention this extraordinary petition filed by Fidel Castro two weeks *after* the Batista coup d'etat.

During the Moncada Barracks trial a year later, after the first unsuccessful military assault on the open terrorist dictatorship of Batista, Castro returned again and again to this theme: it was the regime and its servants in the judiciary who were undermining the integrity of the Cuban judicial system—not the rebels. He asked for, and was granted, permission to sit with counsel for the defense as a lawyer. He was so effective as a lawyer in demolishing the prosecution's witnesses and in establishing evidence proving the Batista officers guilty of torturing and murdering the captured rebel prisoners that he was excluded from the courtroom on the pretext that he was "sick and needs absolute rest." The next day Dr. Melba Hernandez, one of the two women who had participated in the attack on Moncada, interrupted the proceedings when the chief judge announced that the trial would proceed without the presence of the "sick" prisoner-lawyer. She walked to the bench saying, "Mr. President, Fidel Castro is not sick. Mr. President, here I bring a letter from Dr. Fidel Castro, written in his own hand and addressed to this respectable and honorable court." The paper, hidden in her hair, was then read by the judges. The full text of it is well worthy of study by radicals both from the point of view of style and content. But what is most revealing is the constant emphasis upon the concept that if the "honor" and "integrity" of the Cuban system of justice was being undermined, it was being undermined by the surrender of the court itself to the demands of the fascist regime. Thus after exposing the falseness of the pretext of illness and condemning the brutal conditions under which he and his fellow prisoners were restrained, Castro concludes his petition to the Court in these words:

> I request the Court to proceed to order immediately my examination by a distinguished and competent doctor such as the President of the Medical Association of Santiago de Cuba. I propose also that a member of that Court, especially

appointed, accompany the political prisoners on the trips
that they make from this prison to the Palace of Justice and
vice versa. That the details of this brief be communicated
to the Local and National Bar Associations, to the Supreme
Court of Justice, and to as many legal institutions as that
Court esteems should know these facts.

The importance and the category of the trial that is being
held imposes exceptional obligations.

If it is carried out under the conditions which I have de-
nounced, it will not be more than a ridiculous and immoral
farce with the full repudiation of the nation.

All of Cuba has its eyes focused on this trial. I hope that
this Court will worthily defend the rights of its hierarchy
and its honor which is at the same time, in these moments,
the honor of the entire judicial power before the History of
Cuba.

The action of the Court up to now and the prestige of its
magistrates accredit it as one of the most honorable of the
Republic which is why I expand these considerations with
blind faith in its virile action.

For my part, if for my life I have to cede an iota of my
right or of my honor, I prefer to lose it a thousand times:
"A just principle from the depth of a cave can do more than
an army." [14]

The petition caused consternation in the courtroom.
The regime retaliated immediately and, despite the certifi-
cation of court-appointed physicians as to Fidel's perfect
health, the army refused to permit the judges to order his
return to the courtroom. Finally, on October 16, he was
brought in secret before the Court. Only the three judges,
the two prosecutors, six reporters (prohibited by the censorship from reporting the proceeding), and an armed
guard of one hundred soldiers were present in a room in
the Civil Hospital. Here, Castro, lawyer and political defendant, spoke at great length in his final defense. It was a
learned, dignified, and brilliantly courageous statement. It
teaches much on questions which go far beyond the immediate scope of this paper. In it, Castro the lawyer and
Castro the radical synthesized the contradiction between
the role of the lawyer in defending the *legitimacy* of the

procedural and substantive forms of political liberty be-
trayed by the dictatorship, and the role of the radical who
utilizes every avenue to advance the radicalization of the
masses of the people.

His opening analysis takes the political offensive and
attacks the regime for undermining and destroying the institutions of justice. The entire text must be read to grasp
its full power—the audacity, the courage, the dignity with
which he uses the occasion of his summation to proclaim
boldly the full program of the July 26 Movement, accepting the responsibility which he enunciates in these words:
"The revolutionaries must proclaim their ideas courageously, define their principles and express their intentions so that no one is deceived, neither friend nor foe."
His central objective as a radical, therefore, is to use the
courtroom—yes, even the courtroom of the fascist dictatorship—as a forum from which to defend, proclaim and
teach the ideas, the principles, the programs which will
liberate the people. But central to the ideas and principles
which he seeks to announce, over the head of the regime
which is attempting to silence him and the movement he
leads, is that it is the Batista regime which is destroying
the institutions of Cuban law and justice, that it is the
Batista regime which is destroying the Constitution of
1940 and it is the regime which has shown "contempt" for
the law.

> . . . an unheard-of situation had arisen, Honorable Mag-
> istrates. Here was a regime afraid to bring an accused be-
> fore the courts; a regime of blood and terror which shrank
> in fear at the moral conviction of a defenseless man—un-
> armed, slandered and isolated. Thus, having deprived me
> of all else, they finally deprived me of the trial in which
> I was the principal accused.
>
> Bear in mind that this was during a period of suspension
> of rights of the individual and while there was in full force
> the Law of Public Order as well as censorship of radio and
> press. What dreadful crimes this regime must have com-
> mitted, to so fear the voice of one accused man! . . . .
>
> As a result of so many obscure and illegal machinations,

due to the *will* of those who govern and the *weakness* of those who judge, I find myself here in this little room of the Civil Hospital—to which I have been brought to be tried in secret; so that my voice may be stifled and so that no one may learn of the things I am going to say. Why, then, de we need that imposing Palace of Justice which the Honorable Magistrates would without doubt find rather more comfortable? I must warn you! It is unwise to administer justice, surrounded by sentinels with bayonets fixed; the citizens might suppose that our justice is sick . . . and that it is captive.[15]

In the same spirit, after proving in one of the most erudite and eloquent arguments ever heard in any court of law, that the right of insurrection against a tyrant is a "fundamental tenet of political liberty," [16] Castro concludes his summation by returning to the question of who is in fact destroying the law.

Honorable Magistrates, I am that humble citizen who one day came in vain to punish the power-hungry men who had violated the law and had torn our institutions to shreds. Now that it is I who am accused, for attempting to overthrow this *illegal* regime and to *restore the legitimate constitution,* I am held for seventy-six days and am denied the right to speak to anyone, even to my son; guarded by two heavy machine guns, I am led through the city. I am transferred to this hospital to be tried secretly with the greatest severity; and the prosecutor with the Code in his hand, solemnly demands that I be sentenced to twenty-six years in prison.

You will answer that on the former occasion the court failed to act because force prevented them from doing so. Well then—confess: this time force will oblige you to condemn me. The first time you were unable to punish the guilty! now you will be compelled to punish the innocent. The maiden of justice twice raped by force! [17]

It is difficult to embellish with one's own conclusions this extraordinary example of a lawyer and radical leader who under the most adverse conditions combined both the denunciation of the destruction of the elementary forms of justice and liberty by the open terrorist dictatorship and the promulgation in the courtroom of a political program designed to achieve the ultimate goal of the radicalization of masses of people—the overthrow of a tyrannical regime. Only a few comments are appropriate in the light of the previous discussion.

Castro's conduct, both as a lawyer and political defendant, was at all times aggressive, dignified and calculated to inspire respect and admiration among the people. He took deeply seriously the proceedings, not because they held in balance his personal liberty or life but because, as he put it, they held in balance the liberties and future of the Cuban people. But perhaps most important of all he never fell into the trap of losing sight of the real enemies: the regime, the ruling circles, the army. He did not single out primarily the judges sitting in the courtroom, or the "forms" or "trappings" of the judicial system itself. Quite to the contrary, his imagery was always the reverse—"our justice is captive" [of the regime], "the maiden of justice twice raped by force." He viewed the primary responsibility of the radical lawyer, and indeed the radical leader, to use the attack of the enemy in the courtroom as an opportunity to launch a counteroffensive.

But this counteroffensive was never permitted to be detoured into the dead-end of an individual struggle against the court itself or the judges. This would have served no constructive political end whatsoever. It would have blocked an opportunity to center the attention of the people upon their main enemies: the dictator, the army, the ruling class. (It would have blunted, if not made impossible, the emphasis upon the illegality of the regime and the responsibility of the dictatorship for the destruction of the liberties of the people.) But most serious of all, it would have facilitated the development among the broadest circles of the people of a grotesque caricature of reality—the myth that the radical lawyer and the radical defendant are in fact the principal underminers of the system of "justice," of "democratic liberties," rather than the ruling class itself.

Today in the United States such a myth is facilitated by

the distorted image of a political trial as primarily a contest between political lawyers and defendants and a "hard pressed," if "irascible," judge. The development of such a caricature of the radical lawyer or defendant in the present period would be disastrous. It would undermine the effectiveness of radical lawyers and radicals in general in participating in the organizing of powerful movements to oppose the transition measures of repression and reaction. And most serious of all it would blunt the radicalization of the millions in struggle, since it would mask the reality of who is the real enemy of the elementary liberties of the people.

To understand the particularity of the contradictions which shape the present struggle and to mold one's role as a lawyer or teacher of law in such a fashion as to facilitate the resolution of the contradictions in a positive direction —which at this historic moment may mean participation in a gigantic step forward in the history of humanity: the taking over of the control of the political, economic, and cultural institutions of this country by the people—is, I confess, a most difficult and complicated task. It requires the utmost in skill, creative flexibility, patience, and courage. But it requires initially the willingness to study in depth the particular characteristics of the individual case or people's movement in which the radical lawyer is involved, so as to discover in *that precise situation* the most effective way to facilitate the interplay of *both* poles—the defense of the elementary forms of democratic liberties there under attack and, utilizing the arena the enemy has chosen, the development of a political counteroffensive which deepens the understanding of masses of people and accelerates their already swirling motion.

No one blueprint will provide the best course of conduct for every situation. In some cases the key may be found in an all-out fight against the steady and flagrant erosion of the right to bail, particularly for Black militant leaders—a struggle which has already begun to develop in trials involving the Panther Party. In other situations it may be found in the opening up of a massive and national struggle against current wholesale wiretapping in flagrant violation of the Constitution—an issue which may emerge out of any one trial of a political person on any charge. In still other situations the key may be found in the development of a full-scale struggle for the constitutionally guaranteed right to self-defense, in which the needs of a given political trial may call for political defendants, particularly when they are spokesmen of political parties or organizations, to represent themselves in the courtroom. Similarly, the other pole, the radicalization of millions now in motion, is assisted in many different ways. It may be furthered by skillfully placing the ruling military-political clique on trial as the real conspirators in trials charging conspiracy against antiwar activists, or by exposing as the real "law breakers" the racist remnants of the system of slavery, when Black men and women are placed on trial for alleged violations of "law and order."

But one thing is essential to any given solution of a particular problem. This is a political understanding that in *this period* in our history the effective development of a massive defense of the elementary forms of democratic liberties led by radicals is not antithetical to but, in fact, accelerates the radicalization of the millions who are daily being thrown into motion by the attacks and blunders of the governing circles. Such an understanding will permit the radical lawyer and the radical defendant to become the masters, rather than the victims, of the contradictions.

Notes

1. Those who may wince at the use of the term "the ruling class" as "alien jargon," should know that as a concept it has always been a part of the vocabulary of American politics, first appearing in James Madison's *Federalist Papers* and reappearing constantly throughout our history in the speeches and writings of such diverse figures as Wendell Phillips, William Lloyd Garrison, Clarence Darrow, and Eugene V. Debs, to mention only a few.

2. Mao Tse-tung, *On Contradiction.* New York: International Publishers, 1953, p. 16. A lecture delivered at the anti-Japanese Military and Political College in Yenan in August 1937.

3. Fredrick Engels, *Anti-Dühring.* New York: International Publishers, 1939, p. 133.

4. Mao Tse-tung, *On Contradiction,* p. 23.

5. V. I. Lenin, *Collected Works,* Vol. XXXI. New York: International Publishers, 1927, p. 143.

6. Ibid. In criticizing a contemporary, Lenin wrote: "He gives up the most essential thing in Marxism, the living soul of Marxism, the concrete analysis of concrete conditions."

7. *Proceedings of the Seventh Congress of the Communist International.* Moscow: 1939, Foreign Languages Publishing House, p. 127. I commend these proceedings to the careful study of all radicals, communist and noncommunist, Marxist and non-Marxist alike, not in the spirit of any dogmatic application of its entire analysis to the world of the 1970s, but for the insight it may give on occasion to the problems of the present. In this respect I find myself in agreement with Howard Zinn's recent comment that, in the study of history, "the crucial element is the present and the question of what we, the receivers of any assessment, will do in the present." Howard Zinn, *The Politics of History.* Boston, Mass.: Beacon Press, 1970, p. 28.

8. Greenville, Miss., *Delta Times,* May 17, 1970.

9. V. I. Lenin, "Left-Wing Communism, An Infantile Disorder," *Selected Works,* Vol. X. New York: International Publishers, 1935–1938, p. 136.

10. See Mr. Justice Black in *Offitt v United States,* Vol. 348, *U.S. Supreme Court Records* (1954), p. 11.

11. Fidel Castro, "History Will Absolve Me," in Leo Huberman and Paul Sweezy, "Cuba, Anatomy of a Revolution," Vol. 12, *Monthly Review* (July–August 1960), p. 30.

12. Ibid., pp. 30–31.

13. Ibid., p. 31.

14. Ibid., pp. 33–34.

15. Ibid., pp. 35–36.

16. Castro's argument that the right of insurrection against tyranny is a *legal, legitimate* right recognized by the finest minds of all humanity, "by men of all creeds, ideas, and doctrines" includes among its authorities "the philosophers of ancient India, the city states of Greece and republican Rome . . . John of Salisbury . . . Saint Thomas Aquinas . . . Martin Luther . . . Philipp Melancthon . . . Calvin . . . Juan Mariana, a leading Jesuit philosopher . . . the French jurist François Hotman . . . the German jurist John Althus . . . John Milton . . . John Locke . . . Jean-Jacques Rous-

seau . . . the Declaration of Independence of the Congress of
Philadelphia, on the 4th of July, 1776 [and] . . . the French
Declaration of the Rights of Man . . ."
17. "History Will Absolve Me," p. 47.

Soldiers
Say No

by Fred Cohn*

> *"Without a people's army, the people have nothing."*
> —Mao Tse-tung

It is a growing belief among a new generation of lawyers that the distinction between themselves and their clients is often arbitrary and elitist. Left political lawyers especially see their role as an arm of a political movement in which they serve alongside brothers and sisters struggling for a new and more viable society. As part of that struggle, a number of lawyers have chosen to apply their skills to the area of military law, either as individuals, as parts of legal teams, or as house counsels to GI "coffee houses" and groups of soldier and movement activists. Their involvement has one ultimate goal beyond the resolution of cases in the military courtroom—the development of a people's movement which includes a significant section of the working class.

Many New Left analysts have rejected the idea that the working class is a wellspring of people's revolution in this country. This assumption gained currency a few years ago, as a result of its espousal by Herbert Marcuse and other New Left theoreticians. New Left political theorists

---

* Copyright © 1971 by Fred Cohn.

generally consider the working class unsalvageable. The Old Left, however, regards the workers, in traditional Marxist terms, as the "vanguard of the revolution." In this continuing debate, many New Leftists justify their cynicism by pointing to the flag-waving activities of construction workers, the continuing overt racism of Southern segregationists, and the acceptance, if not encouragement, of government repression of youth protest by middle-aged middle America. These activities, in one sense, explain why the New Left has become identified, if not synonymous, with youth culture and youth protest. Yet the extent and direction of young people's hostility toward the traditional values will have its most profound effect when the sons and daughters of the working class also begin to express themselves in an organized way. It is becoming clear that increasing numbers of working class youth, by the time they reach an age when they are expected to become the economic and social replacements for their parents, are unwilling to accept their stratified roles in society. Youth is rebelling, including the children of conservative Right and Old Left parents. Their rebellion is catalyzing a general breakdown of the primary institutions in our society. As an aspect of this loss of faith in the system, youth has begun to demand from society the destruction of old forms and outdated institutions which do not serve its interests and needs. Young men in the military are no exception. In fact, it is through resistance within the armed forces that working class youth, whites and nonwhites alike, are emerging as a potentially dramatic force for social change.

Military service is, by its nature, a potentially radicalizing influence. Oppression in all its forms is magnified and institutionalized. Class structure is legislated. Initiative and skill often go unrewarded. The treatment of people as chattel is more overt and more visible than in any other institution. Each new recruit, unable to reconcile these obvious inconsistencies with the ideals of a true democracy, cannot completely accept, despite the enforced discipline, this terrible new reality. He realizes the impossibility of democratizing the structure of the military hierarchy and practices within the present system. It is no surprise, therefore, that the armed forces, especially during a period of domestic and foreign upheaval, have become a laboratory for the development of people's consciousness.

Of primary importance in the radicalizing process is the class basis of government methods for inducting men into the armed forces. All men in this country are faced with the possibility of military service. However, universal military training has built inequality into the induction process. For example, it is now an established fact that any middle class, white American can legitimately avoid conscription. Easy access to money and lawyers as well as a biased draft law insures that result. Not only is the role of the middle class assured in the capitalist economy, but military leaders assume that the exposure of the educated and privileged to military life will too soon convince them they should not be fighting. The military hopes that by excluding these potential malcontents and concentrating on working class and deprived youth a more malleable fighting force can be constructed. This also keeps lower classes, with fewer opportunities for work in the larger society, off unemployment rolls; in this way government maintains the illusion of "minimal" unemployment. The process feeds itself, for the values learned by those who go through the mill will be carried out into the body politic, forming, the system hopes, a forever silent majority. Veterans will then reaffirm their faith in the system to the next generation, who will take their designated places in the ranks.

The discriminatory nature of the induction process exposes current attempts to democratize the selective service system as a fraud. The aim of this deceptive plan is to convince those who are tired of being the cannon fodder in an immoral, illegal, and aggressive war that they are no longer the substitutes for a privileged class. It is even more a cause for cynicism because democratization of the recruitment process, through which all men are ostensibly chosen at random, is only the first step toward eliminating conscription altogether and creating an all-volunteer army. This political device supposedly will insure "freedom of choice" in determining how and when the citizen serves his country. It need not be stated, however, that the stampede to the enlistment centers for the volunteer army will not come from college campuses but from those who cannot subsist within the larger society. It will thus provide the general staff with its ideal soldier, a voluntary, paid, hopefully disciplined, trigger finger.

Even should this plan for an all-volunteer army succeed, thereby maintaining a majority of Blacks, Browns and working class whites in the enlisted ranks, it is too late to stop the tide of discontent and disenchantment within the military structure. The new awareness of Black and Brown youth particularly makes it evident that the inequalities inherent in the system will be challenged and that most cooptive strategies will be defeated. The white Left has also contributed to military headaches by organizing antiwar coffee houses where enlisted men gather off base to discuss local issues and to read "underground" newspapers. These organizing activities have provided welcome relief from the army's indoctrination process, exposing specific examples of stratification by rank, the privileges inherent in the selection of officers, stockade conditions, and the repression of voices of reform.

Because of the natural rigidity of army life, the undemocratic methods of recruitment, the class nature of army stratification, and the development of organized forces of antiwar and antimilitary sentiment, working class youth fully realize the lack of power they have over their own destinies and the fraud perpetrated on them by a supposedly democratic system. If this constituency can organize itself before it once again becomes absorbed into the system, and if more soldiers begin to respond actively to their deprivation of personal, economic, and social options, then in fact an alliance can be made between the white working class youth, their Black and Brown brothers, and middle class radical white youth. The possibilities for such an alliance have already been shown in GI demonstrations in Washington and around military bases, the latter in conjunction with military trials.

Much is made by radicals and their lawyers of the effects of political trials. They are treated in theory as educational and political forums for the community. While certain elements of a particular town or city are invariably educated and even radicalized by such trials as those involving popular antiwar leaders or Black revolutionaries, the extent of involvement by the majority of that community is diluted by the exigencies of mass communication, the class structure of the community, and its racial composition. This is not so in the case of the military trial. Military installations are like ghettos, no matter what their size and complexity. The general military population is bound together by the same ties that bind the ghetto—absolute denial of any freedom of self-determination. The soldiers understand that a violation of military law is in theory a crime but in many instances they simply do not care since they, in essence, do not think most violations should be crimes. Since all behavior is controlled by an alien and unsympathetic authority, the simplest violation, a disrespectful way of walking, for example, is subject to punishment. Indifference and contempt for law become a natural part of most soldiers' attitudes. The temporary soldier recognizes his own oppression and naturally focuses his attention upon persons who try to beat the system or run afoul of it in some way. News of the political trial sweeps the camp in the way least amenable to censorship and repression, word of mouth. As Professor Michael Tigar eloquently puts it, a "jurisprudence of insurgency" develops as the primary occupation of the people.

The nature of the radical lawyer's role as an opponent of the system is, first, to stand interposed between stringent military laws and his client. Second, and even more important, he acts as a mirror for his client's comrades to see those laws stripped of their pretensions and reduced to reflections of their real social purpose. In military courts the radical lawyer fulfills the second function better than in any other forum, for the democratic veneer over the laws applied to the dissident serviceman is thin. He has greater difficulty executing the first function, because it is the purpose of the military structure to instill fear and blind obedience by legislating every human function, systematizing the lack of due process, and preventing civilian judicial interference in the conduct of military affairs. Since military law is the orphan of the jurisprudential family, it has been neglected by legal scholars and governed by the militarists, including lawyers in the armed forces. The civilian lawyer on a military base has been the exception rather than the rule. The radical lawyer thus functions in the heartland of oppression as house counsel to those who have been alienated by the social crimes they see committed with impunity on every military base.

In recent years, radical lawyers have been asked to represent soldiers who have questioned the legitimacy of military service itself and many of its inherently undemocratic practices. AWOL (Absence Without Leave), for example, is no longer an unusual act of disobedience. Its increase over the last few years reflects growing contempt for law and the military obligation. The soldier knows that his participation in the armed forces flows out of a statutory duty to his country. But the treatment he receives and the military purposes for which he is used often make him view himself as above the law. Sometimes he cannot articulate the reasons for that feeling. Other times that articulation is in primitive terms of self-interest. Yet it is a feeling almost every GI understands; it is the crack in the foundation of the modern military.

The military lawyer who is politically motivated exploits this weakness in the military system at its roots. A classic example is the case of a sailor, Fred Patrick, who went Unauthorizedly Absent (the naval equivalent of AWOL) from his base. This sailor had thought out the political motivations for his actions. While in the service, he had joined the American Servicemen's Union, a group dedicated not only to extending the trade union movement to the military but to actively opposing the Vietnam War, racism, and oppression in and by the service. He demanded a political construct for his defense. It was clear to him that the Navy would have no difficulty proving the technical crime against him, but he wanted it made apparent to his brothers in uniform why he had gone UA, why he refused to cooperate with the military, and how, in continuing to acquiesce, his fellow servicemen were aiding not only his repression but their own.

Most political clients look upon their trials as a tool for organizing; the defense against a possible penalty is not a primary consideration. In fact, they may legitimately prevail upon their attorneys to emphasize the presentation of issues and to pay minimal obeisance to acquittal. This situation can only occur because of the unique relationship between the radical attorney and his clients, who themselves are responsible for most, if not all, decisions and do not rely on the professionalist's chant of "I know what is best for you." It is through the trust in this kind of relationship that the focus of a trial can be turned around and the burden of guilt be placed upon the accusers.

The young man in this case, who had been brought up in a working class environment, had originally enlisted in the Navy "to serve his country," a duty those before him had also accepted. When he recognized the purpose which his military commitment served, he left, after first trying to influence those who had power over him to change his role in the service. He did not want to be trained to kill; UA was his only alternative. When he returned to the Navy, he had in hand an application for discharge as a conscientious objector and sought to interpose that application between himself and the jurisdiction of the court. The application was denied.

The trial began with supporting demonstrations. Oppressive security precautions permeated the courtroom where there had never been any threat of violence or disruption. Counsel was forced first to fight the collateral issue of a public trial to get the nonservice friends and supporters of the defendant into the room. Finally, the commandant packed the courtroom with marines in order to deny seats to outside "agitators" and supporters.

The trial proceeded on the theory that the defendant had been defrauded. He had signed a contract, he argued, to defend liberty and had found himself assigned to pursue an aggressive war. This attack was the foundation for a frontal assault upon war crimes, the illegal and immoral activities in Southeast Asia, the role of the officer corps in that war, and the use of the citizen soldier as a tool of an imperialist foreign policy. Each marine and serviceman who was able to gain entry into that courtroom, including Vietnam veterans with apparent wounds, secretly or openly conveyed to counsel or to the defendant their belief that this courtroom had been transformed into a proscenium for exposing the truth, and that they were behind him.

The military had defeated itself, for with every new court ruling, the stock of this defendant grew, and increased credence was given to his arguments. The defendant had chosen a path which would probably lead to a maximum penalty (which in fact is what happened), but the political defense achieved its effect. The final sentence of six months in jail, loss of pay and allowances, and a bad conduct discharge were seen as an outrage, rather than a just result, by the entire base. A boy from middle America had helped to educate others to the nature of their own oppression.

In the case of the Fort Dix 38, a riot growing out of inhuman stockade conditions led to attempts to burn down the jail. Possible penalties for the rebellion were far more stringent than any AWOL violation, in some cases totaling fifty years in jail. Clearly these cases had to be tried on the facts showing guilt or innocence. This task was made more difficult when the Army singled out for general court martial, the most serious kind of trial, those persons who had the heaviest political commitment. These persons were kept for months in solitary confinement, euphemistically called "administrative segregation," until their trials were over. Confessions were extracted not only from the principal defendants, but also from others suspected of participating. "Suspects" were given promises of leniency and clemency if they would sign statements inculpating the politically involved defendants.

Throughout the trials the methods of the Criminal Investigations Division in extracting these confessions were challenged. One government witness took the stand for the defense and recanted his prior confession with the statement that it was a business deal: he had traded his incriminating statement for a reduction in the time he was already serving on another case. The reason that he was recanting and "telling the truth," he stated, was that the CID were "not gentlemen" and had not honored their word. Witness after witness recanted. One stated that he had read his statement before signing it, but it was shown that he was, for all purposes, illiterate. A seventeen-year-old defendant told how he had asked for a lawyer time and time again, but that at the end of three days of intermittent questioning and uncertainty, he had confessed.

In spite of all this evidence damning the government's case, all but one of the five soldiers referred for general court martial were convicted. The single acquittal was the result of a case so barren of facts that an unbiased civilian judge probably would not have sent it to the jury. Yet these cases, currently on appeal, brought to light the misery and squalor in which the inhabitants of the Fort Dix stockade lived. It was shown who went to the stockade: persons from poor and working class backgrounds. AWOLS made up the bulk of the inmates. No officer was sent to the stockade when accused of a crime. During the period of the trials, in fact, a lieutenant charged with stealing from military mail was merely restricted to post.

None of this escaped the attention of the population of the camp. People flocked to the Fort Dix Coffee House to work for the underground post newspaper, *Shakedown*, which was the only source of full reportage the GIs could get. The political attitude created among formerly apolitical people is best illustrated by the following anecdote:

Every evening at five o'clock on military posts the flag is lowered. Those persons outside a building must stand and salute during the ceremony. After one particularly unjust

conviction, a group of about fourteen soldiers were standing outside the courtroom. As the first notes of retreat
sounded, they rushed to go inside to avoid the salute. The
doors happened to be locked. Just then an officer passed
by and looked their way, so they stood at attention and
saluted. After it was over, a veteran of Vietnam who had
won a silver star plus other decorations and was expecting
yet another silver star said, "I feel as if my hand has committed a crime." Shortly thereafter he informed his com-
manding officer that he would refuse to accept the second
silver star.

It is not the realistic hope of the Movement that the
U.S. Army, as it now stands, will turn against its generals
and commence to serve the people today, tomorrow, or
next year. The hope and the goal of those involved in GI
organizing and those serving that Movement, such as lawyers, is that the politicization process will carry over, not
only out of the army and into the factories, but to the next
generation to be called upon to pick up the gun and defend this country from its so-called enemies, both foreign
and domestic. If this Movement is a success, that generation will know who the enemy really is, and act accordingly.

All armies are not evil. Given the proper function, the
form inevitably adjusts to fit it. A just purpose gives birth
to proper tools. An army that functions for a free people,
under a political system that will stand scrutiny, is a
people's army. Under that kind of system, rank, awarded
for merit and expertise, is not a dividing line between humanity and animalism. It is recognized in people's armies,
such as those in Cuba or China, that a military tactician
does not necessarily have the last word on political
thought, and it is the political implications of military actions which must have the highest priority. Criticism and
self-criticism among the troops and officer corps are es-
sentials. What should motivate an army is not unreason-
ing discipline and fear of reprisal, but a common cause,
openly arrived at.

When this is achieved, the army is truly the servant of
the people.

The First Law Commune

by Robert Lefcourt

Members of the Law Commune were surprised when an article in *The Village Voice* (March 1, 1969) called their office "one of the most innovative and extreme" law firms in the country. This comment appeared just a few weeks after the four attorneys and four "organizers" (all under thirty) began operation. The lawyers had not won any significant legal victories in the courts; their office was on Union Square, not Wall Street; they had not recently occupied any buildings; and the communards did not even live together in the usual sense of "commune." All they had done was to open a law office for the express purpose of supporting, in any way possible, the New Left.

But as the Law Commune enters its third year, this purpose in itself has been sufficient to fill some of the legal needs of many groups in political struggle, including various college student organizations, antiwar GIs, women's liberation groups, and the Black Panther Party. In addition, the firm offers a model for law students in search of alternative forms of law practice. Most important, the Law Commune distinguishes itself from most law firms by its challenge not only to the legal profession, but to the ideology of the judicial superstructure and the existing economic and political system.

The need for a law commune, its innovative internal structure, the conflicts of the lawyers as radicals, support of a broad range of political struggles—all these aspects of the Commune originate with the assumption that radical changes in society are necessary, and that lawyers can be more than neutral legal technicians if they pool their talents and resources in a collective format. The attorneys do not hesitate to affirm their New Left political identity as primary and their technical legal role as secondary. The reason they are together as a law firm is to earn enough money from paying, nonpolitical clients to support their predominantly free legal services for Movement individuals or groups. Just as the courts are the legal arm for the state, law communes and other radical law groups, it is hoped, will become the legal arm for a broad movement engaged in political struggles.

The birth of the first communal law firm was the result of many months of discussion (October '68 through February '69) among young lawyers, law students, writers, organizers, and Movement activists arrested during protests. In these discussions the necessity for a law firm whose primary purpose was defense of the radical movement was recognized and the outlines of such a firm were sketched.

The Commune emerged during a period of mass arrests of students, both in high schools and colleges, who were protesting conditions in schools and in society generally. A substantial part of the Black movement had shifted from the nonviolent tactics of the civil rights period of the 1950s to the armed defense of groups such as the Black Panther Party. Repression of Blacks by the police, the courts, and the government led to long imprisonments prior to trials. Politically sympathetic lawyers saw that those who participated in these and other sections of the Movement were not getting the legal support necessary to continue their struggles.

Government legal service agencies were not about to permit their attorneys to publicly support groups that opposed government policies. Notwithstanding the good faith of isolated individual members, public defender and legal aid lawyers were neither willing nor able to actively protect the rights of arrested protesters who appeared in criminal courts without lawyers, just as they have never been able to fight aggressively for the rights of the poor—their primary clients. Private attorneys willing to defend radicals were not only few in number, but none of their firms had as an express purpose the defense of Movement activists. A communal law firm was born out of necessity; the repression of so many parts of the Movement demanded it.

The young lawyers and nonlawyers wanted to create a new kind of law firm partly as an act of political honesty. It was not simply that the legal profession had avoided its responsibility to defend political activists. More seriously, the rebels recognized the inherently undemocratic nature of the legal profession, which they viewed as conservative, elite, and oriented to the upper middle class. The aim of the Commune, therefore, was to transform this lawyer-client relationship. In addition, as a political collective, the members would challenge the traditionally undemocratic practices of most law firms.

It was agreed, for example, that the mystique of the law and lawyers must be shattered. Abstruse rules and esoteric terminology prevent the masses of people from perceiving how the law relates to their lives. Traditional lawyers, who rarely communicate to clients what is being done in their behalf, presume a trust which actually breeds mistrust. Commune lawyers would close the gap between lawyer and client by turning legal jargon into everyday language and by encouraging mutual decision-making. They would work as closely as possible with political groups, not only in an advisory capacity, but in the actual planning of legal strategy as part of a political program. In these and other ways, it was thought that the traditional lawyer-client relationship could be altered.

The professional lawyer has always claimed that law, like surgery, is a specialized field requiring specific knowledge and training. But, in fact, a surgeon's tools are precise instruments; a lawyer's tools are people and their social relationships. The technicalities and complexities of

THE FIRST LAW COMMUNE

the law are designed only to obscure its class nature and its protection of the existing economic and political system.

As a result, even though Commune lawyers try to tear away the cloak of legal language and to discuss human and political possibilities, their clients, even the political activists, still expect them to make the decisions. A dramatic change in the lawyer-client communication and relationship has not been achieved. The trust which a political activist has for a Movement lawyer is based on the knowledge that the attorney is sympathetic. The trust which a nonpolitical client has for a Commune lawyer is based on the knowledge that at least this attorney is not as stuffy as the typical lawyer. (One potential client only wanted to speak with a longhaired lawyer.) But the result is that a certain amount of mistrust still exists between lawyer and client, with the client still suspecting that the attorney wants to make all the decisions because "he knows best." Sometimes, of course, the accusation is true.

On the other hand, the open identification of the Commune lawyers' politics with people's movements is a dramatic change in itself. As "people's lawyers," the Law Commune attempts to redefine the traditional lawyer-client relationship by choosing to defend those cases arising from struggles which attempt to give more power to more people. This is the primary criterion for accepting clients, usually members of an organization working for broad changes through specific issues.

A clear example of such a relationship is illustrated in a letter the New York Panther 21 defendants sent to their lawyers before their fifteen-month trial began and their unanimous acquittal in May of 1971:

Dec. 28th 1969

To the People's Lawyers:

. . . Would just like to say, what we have long felt: that not many can be called "People's lawyers," and for us, the Black Panther Party, the People and their struggle, you cats have been *beautiful* . . . It is true that very few People in the Mother Country can relate to why we as

Panthers will do, and continue to do what we must, in the way that we do. But it's because of People like you, that we know this sick Society *can* be transformed.

So, in the year coming, we can say truthfully that there is not a court in Racist Babylon that we would not be honored in confronting, where we will not unflinchingly be Proud and Confident in the Representation that you will give. And most of all, the sincerity in which it is given unifies us in our Purpose and respect for all the People's lawyers in our Particular way is the highest tribute we can pay you. We do not relate to holidays except in a revolutionary manner, but when the oppressed have triumphed, there will be a People's Lawyers Day, we and our children assure you.

Unity in struggle,
The "notorious" Panther 21

It is not surprising that five of the six Panther 21 trial lawyers were white (three of those belonged to the Law Commune), since ninety-seven percent of all lawyers are white. The fact that all the Commune lawyers are white (except for one staff worker and one ex-law student) is indicative of the political relationships between Blacks and whites in the current period. Political alliances have occurred nevertheless, out of necessity and shared goals, such as in factory workers' strikes, high school students' rebellions, and in political trials.

By not charging fees for representing particular causes, whether or not the client or group can afford to pay, the Commune commits itself to the political assumption that legal services should be free for everyone. Free, government-financed legal services for the poor do not meet the same need because they do not challenge the unequal economic relationships in society as a whole except for some programs such as the California Rural Legal Assistance. Until these relationships are changed, those clients of the Commune whose cases do not challenge social, economic, and political relationships will help to pay for those who do, and these paying clients are generally so informed. By not charging a fee and by closely identifying with the politics of the clients, the lawyers transform their traditional relationship with the people they serve, and in effect challenge the long-held assumption that a lawyer is an "officer of the court" first, and an advocate for the people second.

This approach made it necessary to redefine relationships and purposes within the Law Commune itself. The members attempted to change the structure from that of the typical law firm by instituting democratic practices. For example, the underlying principle of operation is that all workers, lawyers and nonlawyers, are equal. This concept has not been easy to apply. The easiest part, the lawyers found, was scrapping the traditional seniority system and distinctions based on age, experience, influence, and earning power.

The aim for equality had its major test in the determination of salary scales and in the use of surplus income. Pay scales are determined according to a deliberately vague definition of "need." All workers decide what they need to sustain themselves and their families "without having to worry." The unrevolutionary middle class life style became the basis of that definition. Ten thousand dollars was set as a maximum salary for a worker with a wife or husband and two children, or for a couple with high doctor bills. But by setting a maximum income, the members chose not to use surplus funds to create plush offices or suburban castles, even if the firm succeeds financially, thus opposing the traditional status-seeking "professional" whose wealth is the indication of "success," "influence," and how "good" a lawyer he or she is. Of the eight practicing lawyers, two require the maximum salary and two have outside incomes and do not draw any salary. Nonlawyers' salaries reflect similar extremes. Should one member require a higher income, the group as a whole makes the decision. A full discussion of what has come to mean "need" in the Commune would be very long, but it is sufficient to say that salary considerations have not caused any serious conflict. The elimination of titles, the practice of pay according to "need," and the establishment of moderate maximum personal incomes have demon-

strated the irrelevance of some traditions in the legal profession. Other law firms that have associated with the
Commune and new law practices that look to the Commune as a model are now also eliminating seniority titles
and democratizing financial and decision-making practices.

The group decided that "profits" would be spent in two
basic ways. The first would be expansion of the Commune, and the second would be the financial support of
law-related Movement projects. Both these conceptions
became realities. The Law Commune began with four
lawyers and four nonlawyers and expanded in its second
year to eight lawyers, between three and six rotating law
students, and between four and eight nonlawyers—typists, secretaries, and organizers. Lefcourt, Garfinkle,
Crain, Cohn, Sandler, Lefcourt, Kraft and Stolar is the law
firm's name. The legal workers include Carol Birnbaum,
Ruth Silber, Eunice Burnett and Carol Ramer; the current
law students, Bonnie Brower, Hersh Katz, Susan Tucker
and Mary Morgan; law graduate Gus Reichbach; law clerk
Susie Orbach; part-time participants Susanne Cohn, artist
and administrator, Bob Lefcourt, writer-in-residence, and
a half-dozen volunteers from colleges and various communities. In its first year, the firm earned enough money to
help support the publication of *The Bust Book,* a legal
handbook for political activists. In the second year, with
three of the lawyers working full-time as trial members on
the Panther 21 Conspiracy case, the surplus evaporated.
While there have been no records kept of precisely how
much time is given to clients, the attorneys estimate that
on the average well over fifty percent of each lawyer's
workday is devoted to nonpaying cases.

The lawyers' and nonlawyers' attempts to transform
lawyer-client relationships and their own relationships
and to develop a more rational and democratic internal
structure represent the beginning of a struggle against
their own class positions. For the lawyers this means a
rejection of professional status as elite members of the
middle class. For the legal workers, it means a refusal to

submit to an inequality enforced by traditions. In day-to-day practice this struggle has encouraged a family of interrelationships in which all are united in the desire to be involved in the political questions of the day, a comradeship surely unique in the conventional law office.

But this restructuring of relationships also reminded Commune members of how much further it was necessary to go. Like many thousands of young people, they had been radicalized by the wars in Southeast Asia and the continuing oppression of Black and poor people, but they were still unready for—the lawyers perhaps incapable of —a complete rejection of their bourgeois backgrounds. The conflict between the lawyer's role (middle or upper class) and the radical's role (the rejection of class position) is at the heart of two of the Commune's most difficult problems. The first is the question of life style, which includes the relationships between the lawyers and non-lawyers and men and women; the second can be called the "cult of individualism," which for lawyers refers to their "professional" status.

In the initial discussions about a law commune, it was suggested that the lawyers and nonlawyers in the collective should live together. By rejecting such middle class conveniences as separate households, and by pooling all resources and incomes, the trained lawyers would make a further advance in transforming the legal profession, and a deeper commitment to direct support of Movement clients. The savings on rents alone could have added to surpluses for use in political struggle.

However, the chance that lawyers would become full-time revolutionary legal technicians was remote at this period of political struggle. The number of arrests in colleges, high schools, and community groups in 1969 demanded of the lawyers a full-time effort in a cooperative defense. There was little opportunity for individual attorneys to develop political alliances with specific groups. The groups themselves were in a constant process of change. The lawyers did act in both a legal and political capacity, but they were lawyers primarily. They were

Movement attorneys whose politics were that they defended the Left. Members of the Commune were engaged in continual, time-consuming expansion during the first year. In addition, a fire in April 1970 burned down the building they occupied, and it took five months to relocate to their present Lower Broadway office, almost twice the size of the original location. However, friends of the Commune on the West Coast have organized a live-in collective law practice. Clearly this is a next step for some radical lawyers.

When the Law Commune began it had seemed possible that their relationships with nonlawyers in the firm would change. Three kinds of nonlawyers have become identified with the Commune—law students, secretaries, and, for lack of a better word, "organizers."

Law students traditionally have worked on a part-time basis for law firms, gaining experience which directly related to their school work, and the Commune took advantage of this tradition. One law school sent students to work in the Commune for school credit. A law students' association arranged for part-time paying jobs for other students. All the students became full participants in communal decisions. The students helped to organize law schools in New York's first demonstration of lawyers and law students protesting the treatment of prisoners, jail conditions, and injustices in the courts themselves in April 1969. One student wrote an article about his Commune experience for a school paper. A Black law student joined a white organizer in teaching a university course to community residents about the relationship between law and politics. These extracurricular office activities were not part of a planned program for law students associated with the Commune. The Commune as a whole has rarely discussed the responsibilities of law students who consider themselves radicals.

The role of secretaries is a more complicated problem. Initially, the lawyers hoped to find legal secretaries, who usually earn higher salaries than regular business secretaries, who were also politically committed workers. Although it was decided that technical competence was an indispensable requirement, the secretaries (or typists) have not functioned as isolated, hired employees. At least in the beginning all attended Commune meetings at which policy matters are determined. This participation in the decision-making procedure, along with economic equality, sharply distinguishes the Commune staff from the typical law firm worker. However, it has not completely resolved the basic fact that lawyer and secretary have different functions within the law firm. The tension between employer and employee persists, because the roles are still traditionally defined. The staff handles the paper work; the lawyers practice law. At Commune meetings, the staff does most of the listening; the lawyers do most of the planning, and until recently, the three staff workers attended these meetings less frequently.

Political equality is at the heart of the conflict. Of course the lawyer is a trained technician in a specialized area. But the secretary in a law office has the special advantage of being a lay person both familiar with legal problems and sensitive to contributing social forces. A nonlawyer in a law office can help to decide, for example, whether the firm should accept a particular case or enter a certain area of work rather than another. In fact, such a worker has a responsibility to influence the political posture and purposes of a law office. To some extent, this has happened in the Law Commune. The greater challenge for the Commune is to further narrow the distance between employer and employee, male lawyer and female secretary, and the class and sexist distinctions implicit in these relationships.

Unlike law students or secretaries, the role of the "organizers" had few precedents on which to base a relationship. The organizers were people who had an interest in working politically around questions of law. At first they intended to function as equal workers in the Commune, contributing income or drawing salaries as the situation required. The original four included a free-lance writer, an artist, a lawyer who gave up practice for political activity, and a college graduate turned community organizer.

It soon became apparent that a direct working relationship with lawyers was untenable. The organizers could function in special ways with the lawyers but not directly on cases. Three of the four wrote articles for underground papers on law-related subjects; the artist planned the office color scheme and layout, helped to set up a high school student defense group, and served as an administrator for a time; the ex-lawyer and the community organizer helped the lawyers in their contacts with Movement groups; and the writer encouraged other radical lawyers to write articles for the Movement. But after a few months, the formal relationship with the lawyers dissolved. Two of the nonlawyers joined full-time revolutionary groups, while the other two continued in their law-related projects, only indirectly connected with the firm. Yet the possibilities for a more dynamic relationship between radical lawyers and organizers cannot be dismissed by the experience of the Commune. As one of the organizers demonstrated with a high school student defense group, nonlawyers and lawyers together can plan training sessions on self-defense for lay people in both criminal and civil cases. Self-defense is the secularization of the law, the breaking of the lawyer's mystique as the all-knowing "professional," and the return of the law to the people. This relates directly to the political role of the radical lawyer in his relationship with nonlawyers.

The internal contradiction of the lawyer as radical manifests itself in the idea that the lawyer is a "professional." The most serious conflict, which actually threatened to split the Commune, was the cult of individualism. While a mechanism for allocation of salaries and profits had been worked out in the early stages, it was not discussed how cases would be distributed. It took almost a full year, after much conflict, for the Commune members to begin to face the problem of work allocation, or who gets which case. In the meantime, many traits from the business world that were anathema to Movement people crept into the daily world of the Commune. Competition among the male lawyers primarily centered, not on money, but on the "most important" cases, political and apolitical. It doesn't matter whether one calls this competition status-seeking, fame-hunger, egocentricity, or the personal eccentricities or neuroses of the men. The fact is that the "professionalism" of male lawyers carries with it the characteristic of many middle and upper class businessmen.

The women in the Commune were most affected by the individualism of the men. The secondary role of the two original women lawyers (one married, one single) and all the secretaries took some of the traditional forms in which women become second-class citizens, which contradict the purposes and hinder the effectiveness of the Commune as a whole.

True, the mere fact that the women are attorneys represents a breakthrough in the legal profession since women still comprise an insignificant percentage of those admitted to practice law. In addition, there is, of course, no economic discrimination. The women secretaries, like the women attorneys, earn salaries comparable to the men, but they have two additional battles to fight: their class position as employees working with "professionals," and the fact that "secretary" usually means "woman" in our society. The women lawyers, though free of these two battles, likewise found themselves in a secondary position to the men. The men they worked with had never fought against the traditionally oppressive roles designed for women in all job experiences. And despite the male lawyers' sympathy for women's liberation issues generally, their own professional and individualistic demands came between their understanding and their actions.

Since it would be unfair to the lawyers and their clients to cite actual examples, a hypothetical illustration will serve. Let us assume that 10,000 people "take over" the mass transit system and 500 are arrested, resulting in an important criminal case. The call for legal assistance comes into the office; a male or female lawyer responds, but the male aggressively seeks to assert his place as the head attorney. The woman does not compete because she is unaware that a battle is under way. She thinks that cases are shared, that work is divided. And this is true. Work is divided. In simple terms, the male writes the legal paper and the woman takes notes or the woman writes the paper and the man argues it in court. Division of labor is based on how successfully the male lawyers manipulate assignments so as to keep their primary role in a case secure.

One of the main rationalizations for male supremacy in most areas of work is not that women are inferior workers, but that it is necessary for men to be dominant in certain roles and women to be dominant in others. Each has a special role to play in society, so goes the rationalization, and both are important. In the above example, a criminal case which may lead to a trial is "heavy" work—men's work. In fact, law in general is men's work, created and perpetuated by men while women are "taken care of" by the law, by men. Therefore women lawyers should not get into men's work. "Male lawyers," says one woman attorney, "are conditioned to expect women to be nonlawyers in status, yet to be fully competent professionally, regardless of their lack of status." Despite professional competence, a woman attorney to this day is a "cute" aberration in a male-dominated profession. "As long as law office status and functions are sex-linked," the attorney continues, "promising women law school graduates are going to continue to be offered what amounts to glorified legal secretarial positions."

In the Commune's practice, the unstated assumption that women hold a special but secondary place led to a situation which duplicated many business establishments and reflected a larger problem—the isolation, not only of the men from the women, but the men from one another. Work was not a cooperative growth venture, as it might have been. Surely there were times when the lawyers discussed cases, pairing off in some instances. But this was still within the traditionally American system of competitive individualism. Each office was isolated from the others, the women were ignored, the secretaries were pressured to do the work of one lawyer before the other, law students served the male lawyer who had the best-known cases. The possibility for growth, for legal and political education, for helping their cause in a more constructive way, suffered.

The rebellion by the Commune women came many months after the firm began. The two women attorneys planned to split off and form a Women's Commune. They intended to give the men alternatives: (1) either cooperate with the split, telling the world that a second Commune was needed, consisting of women only at first, or (2) fight the split. (The women had not decided whether or not to demand reparations.) The women felt confident that they could successfully start a practice and receive political support from Movement groups and financial support from women seeking just such a law firm.

After discussions with sympathetic women activists and other women lawyers, it was decided to confront the men by remaining within the Commune. It became clear to the women that the basic problem of the group was not the women's secondary role (which had to be dealt with, of course) but the individualism/professionalism/competition syndrome among all the lawyers, including the women. The aim became to confront this more inclusive reality.

The first demand of the women was that all cases be allotted at a weekly Commune meeting, so that any case that came into the office would be brought before the group as a whole. The problem caused by differences in experience, varieties of specialization, age, sex, etc., would then be considered openly. The younger, less experienced attorney, who also has a special role, would be encouraged to share more work as an equal partner. Behind-the-scenes manipulation would have less chance of success.

The second demand was a transitional one, less fundamental than the first. The women refused to assist the men on any current case since they would invariably play a secondary role in that way. The men would have to assist one another if the work was to get done. In effect, the women put the men on notice that they must change their ways. The "or else" never openly threatened the Commune. The men knew that the survival of the group was at stake when the two women began to refuse assignments, assume new responsibilities, and propose practical alternatives to the cult of individualism.

The internal conflicts of the lawyer as radical are not the special problems of a small part of the legal profession; they are truly the problems of all lawyers in their relations with the people they employ, the clients they serve, and the profession they support. In a larger sense, they reflect some of the most important issues of our time, especially the need to restructure social, political, and personal relationships. As the experiences of the Law Commune illustrate, change cannot be accomplished in a vacuum; it must be linked to the larger struggles of those who are most oppressed.

The Commune opened its doors in March 1969. A year earlier, the individual lawyers had joined the defense of those arrested in the Columbia University student takeover of school buildings. When the Commune opened, the majority of the thousand cases resulting were still unresolved, while student protest had spread to other campuses. In most of these protests students did not turn to family lawyers for help. They chose lawyers who recognized their cases as "political," as a confrontation with institutional authority, not simply as disorderly conduct or trespass violations. In addition, the students remained a unified collective and planned their strategy with the radical lawyers. It was this relationship that created the first direct challenge to the courts in many years and which involved the Law Commune in many different struggles.

The Commune could not defend every student group that opposed oppressive school policies. Nor could it handle many of the legal assaults necessary in other areas of the people's movements. The choice of which areas claimed priority was left to all members of the firm, with occasional assistance from various New Left groups. Political cases included the defense of GIs opposed to the Vietnam War, draft resisters, community groups involved in fights against major institutions such as the public schools or the state legislature, women's liberation issues such as abortion reform, and the legal defense of revolutionary organizations such as the Pittsburgh Weatherwomen and the New York Black Panther 21. Fuller commitments to certain struggles, such as welfare rights or housing, did not materialize because of many factors, including the degree of broad public support and political impact and the analyses of the respective lawyers and potential clients. The fact is, however, that commitments were made to a variety of struggles.

The Law Commune has established the principle of self-control and self-support for political law firms. It offers legal and political support to individuals and groups engaged in people's movements. The particular organizational form which distinguishes the Law Commune from other law firms is not as important as the fact that a politically radical law firm can exist. Because of these facts, the firm has an important impact on legal training and the extent of alternative forms of law practice. Law students are not running to Wall Street law firms as they have in the past. To an increasing degree, especially in larger cities, radical law collectives are forming in response to the political needs of their own communities. The Commune originally had hoped to help set up more communes, and in many instances it has. It developed contacts with almost every one of the new radical law firms in Boston, Chicago, Detroit and Los Angeles.

The Commune's struggle to survive, however, is continual. Expansion was the Commune's first priority. But for two years, the work load of the lawyers, including political and apolitical cases, has been heavy. A fire, which the police labeled "suspicious," delayed expansion for several months. Furthermore, an Establishment lawyers' committee, which decides whether a prospective attorney is "morally fit" to practice law, has delayed issuing a license to one of the Commune's law students, who was active in the 1968 Columbia student rebellion, despite the fact that he has completed three years of law school and passed his examinations. Another law student, active in women's liberation causes, may have similar difficulties. And, of course, the Panther 21 trial occupied three of the eight lawyers full time for a year and a half. The expected contempt citations against the Panther lawyers were suddenly dropped when the jury acquitted all the defendants on all charges, but the courts have not said their final word about lawyers who defend radicals.

The Law Commune holds a special place in these times because it is the first law firm to declare openly its intention to defend those engaged in attempts to transform this corrupt capitalistic society. All young lawyers are taught, in what is called the Canons of Professional Ethics, that ". . . the stability of Courts and of all departments of government rests upon the approval of the people [and] . . . the public shall have absolute confidence in the integrity and impartiality of its administration." The people have now called for lawyers who will express their disapproval and loss of confidence. The primary responsibility of the radical lawyer is to serve the people when the laws and courts do not. A legal system that fails to respond to the needs of the people, especially the most oppressed, may soon learn that vital issues will be settled, not by laws and statutes, but in spite of them.

Socialist Law and Legal Institutions

by Michael E. Tigar*

The lawyer who has committed himself to work for radical or revolutionary change is like a sailor riding up the seaward side of a long wave. The great power which runs in every seaway is over, under, and around him. He has some ability to maneuver, but is restricted by the force of the wave. The most frightening aspect of the ride up the long seaward side is: One cannot see what is on the other side, whether rocks, shoal, or placid water. This fear leads the timid sailor to take his canvas down, turn, and point into the wind (so as to present the least resistance) and hope that the storm dies down. Or, despairing of hope that the storm will be over, he may seek shelter, perhaps in the shadow of a promontory.

Abandon the metaphor if it does not make the point. The "law," a system of positive legal rules and commands, looks to traditional values. The lawyer, a traditionalist *malgré lui*, finds it hard to imagine other ways of protecting human dignity and preventing arbitrary exertions of power than the ways he has been taught. The liberal bias of legal reform reinforces regard for tradition by emphasizing, in the United States today, the virtue of redeeming the promises of freedom and fairness of bourgeois consti-

---

tutional principle. Despite himself, the lawyer fears wholesale change because he cannot know what form state power will take in the wake of change. His task is difficult because he is likely to be a member of the middle class, driven to radical or revolutionary positions by the force of intellect and empathy rather than by his position of coercion and exploitation in the objective reality. Then, too, there are historical examples of revolutionary violence and terror which deter the thoughtful lawyer from advocating militant action for change.

Those who seriously advocate fundamental change cannot avoid the obligation to describe in outline the system they propose should replace the present one, and to apply their analysis of today's problems to those which are bound to follow in the wake of change. We must know not only where we are, but where we are headed.

It is the more important to take our bearings because lawyers share with law students a desperate sense of unease about their role, present or prospective. There are those lawyers who have idealized their own and others' role in defense of the movement for social change into a romantic picture of constant toil on behalf of embattled revolutionaries and constitutional principles under siege. The courage and dedication of such lawyers are examples to their less committed colleagues, but there is the unfortunate temptation in the course of such struggle to omit consideration of the basic questions of state power and law which undeniably influence the events with which one deals.

Some lawyers see their role as radical innovators in the service of constitutional principle. They well identify for us the tasks of this moment, but we must understand with them law's limits as well as its possibilities. We must know what are the motive forces behind the state's judicial and legislative branches when victories are bestowed upon the Left, such as in cases upholding rights of free speech and assembly, or when claims to equality are vindicated under the law.

There are lawyers who believe that if we conduct sufficiently vigorous defenses of the Movement, we will weaken the apparatus of repressive state power. And we must seek with them to understand their perception of the state that makes them so sanguine about our long-term prospects in its forums. On the other hand, there is arid theorizing about the institution of law and the state, which can, by stressing the immense force of the technology of repression, paralyze us.

This essay attempts, however briefly, to look beyond these modes of struggle within American capitalist institutions. One of its theses is that fundamental social change is necessary to fulfill claims to social justice. American society is built upon capitalist economic institutions. The right of property is a basic element of the constitutional legal order. Property is among the things which the state is committed to protect, just as it is theoretically committed to protect "civil liberties" and "civil rights." The protection of private property by the state is justified in the writings of eighteenth-century social theorists on the basis that the relationship between a man and "his" property is not a relationship of dominance and subordination, but one between a man and an object. John Locke even adopted a labor theory of property rights to underscore this point. Locke argued that when a man mixes his labor with the earth and produces, for example, some food, his right to ownership of that which he has produced is self-evident.

Locke's theory explodes, as does the theory that private property involves only a relationship between men and things, with the coming of industrial capitalism. In this society, some men own the means of production, and others sell their labor. The men who mix their labor with the raw material of production do not own the goods they make and are not considered as "selling" these goods to the capitalist. This division, it has been remarked in the writings of contemporary scholars, is the root of alienation in industrial society. This notion aside, however, the relationship between the owner of the means of production and his employee does involve dominance of one man

over another. If it is difficult to see this point in the context of a one-man shop, consider the great power of a large
corporation over the quality of life in its community. Job
opportunities, working conditions, living conditions—a
great deal depends upon the unilateral decision of the
plant owner.

A central theme in the new politics of change is a challenge to this unilateral decision-making power, and a willingness to question the legitimacy of capitalist relations of
production. This heightened insistence upon truly revolutionary change to redress social ills is responsible for the
escalation by public authorities and private power wielders
of their war against dissentient behavior. One cannot understand the "repression of dissent" without looking closely
at the forces in the interest of which it is employed. The
relationship between these forces and their tactics at this
period is but a special instance of the relationship between
the forms of state power and the system of social relations
which these forces protect. The state is not, despite emphasis in the legal forum on the adversary system, neutral.

Too often, however, this generation of Movement activists tends to regard the response of the state to protest as a
knee jerk, with the ruling class wielding the rubber ham-
mer. This simplistic view of the process of litigation and
adjudication is held because of an incomplete analysis of
the relationship between the state and the interests it protects. Since the state is a structure erected upon the basis
of social relationships at a given period, the set of formal
legal precepts about the way in which state power is to be
exercised is ideology with a kind of life of its own. That is,
though the principled application of formal rules—such
as the rule that freedom of speech shall not be abridged
—may under some circumstances cut against the will of
the holders of public and private power, these rules may
nonetheless be so applied. The ideology of law and legal
rules will not correspond at every moment with the wishes
and demands of the wielders of power. The judges, assigned the task of interpreting and applying legal rules,

are now more, now less, careful to follow out these rules to the limit of their logic regardless of whose interest they may serve in a particular case. Too, there are rules of law acquiesced in and indeed promoted by sections of the ruling class which advance and protect the interests of the poor, the dispossessed, and the discriminated. The genesis of such legislation is usually in social struggle, and its purpose is usually to buy off more fundamental demands for change.

To the extent that there is a conflict between ruling class self-interest and legal rules, there is an opportunity for creative and innovative litigation in present-day America. But those of us who are lawyers ought not fool ourselves that we are doing more than fighting a holding action against the power of the state and on behalf of the movement for social change. We must identify with and understand our Movement clients, for through them and not through us will the changes come that insure the realization of the ideal of justice. No system worthy of the name of justice can be built upon a foundation of social relations which put the means of production in the hands of private persons and the state's instruments of terror and coercion at their service.

Although most sections of the Movement recognize these facts, many still assume that a change in fundamental social relations—the coming of a socialist order of things—will of itself assure an end to injustice. Those who believe this forget that in neither capitalist nor socialist society is there a one-to-one mechanical correspondence between the interests served by the institution of state power and each particular decision made by each agency of the state. Continual struggle goes on in socialist countries to accommodate socialist legal norms and practice to fundamental socialist principle. A socialist society —the Soviet Union, China, Cuba—is one in which the means of production have already passed from private hands, or are being gathered up into public hands.

The long-range professed socialist goal is that the state "wither away," coercion and the apparatus of state power

becoming unnecessary. Adherence to rules of social conduct, the Marxist theory runs, will be secured through the
voluntary acquiescence of every man in shared goals, enforced by a kind of collective community sentiment. To
put it another way, the state is to be replaced by an apparatus for the administration of things.

Any thought that these changes would come automatically—and such thoughts have been expressed—is surely
visionary. Repression, bureaucratization, and even terror
have been used by almost every socialist regime. Too, socialist countries have determined—rightly or not—that
there is need for a more or less extensive system of state
organization run according to rules of order. By this
means is created a superstructure analogous to that existing in capitalist countries.

The question remains: what form should socialist legal
organization take? Although there is substantial room for
debate, some factors can generally be agreed upon. Such a
system must seek to accommodate and deal with attitudes
and behavior conditioned by life under capitalism; it must
command public acquiescence in the fairness of its rules
and procedures; and it must be amenable to change as the
experience of living in a new society changes the character of the people subject to its regime. It is an error to
assume that all problems of the achievement of justice become merely administrative under a new system of social
organization, just as it is wrong to assume that socialist
legal systems must be high-handed and arbitrary in the
single-minded pursuit of obseisance to the new order of
things.

Take the first of these problems, that of defining justice
in a socialist society. Under capitalism, Black and Brown
Americans are kept at an economic disadvantage. Given
menial jobs on the fringes of the labor force, they provide a source of cheap labor which is usable in times of
full employment at low wages. This subordination of
Blacks and Browns is the domestic analogue of American
capital's exploitation of labor in the Third World in the
production of primary products and semimanufactures

for shipment to this country. The existence, in this country and abroad, of a supply of cheap labor for the production of primary products and the performance of menial tasks has been a mainstay of capitalism.

The coming of a socialist society would abolish the economic necessity for superexploitation of nonwhites; it would not, however, do away automatically with racial attitudes which have been generated under capitalism. That is, the inferior position of Blacks and Browns in this country has come about because of the needs of a capitalist system. An elaborate system of ideological, superstructural justification for this fact has been generated by these concrete conditions. This justification, in the form of theories of racial superiority or their more sophisticated variants, has by now acquired a life of its own in the consciousness of millions of people. Social change alone will not eradicate that consciousness; experience and struggle may do so.

Consider too the question of sexism. In this society, the capitalist obtains from most workers the labor of two people for the price of one. The wife stays home to cook, clean, and tend the children, without pay. Suppose for a moment we did not have the institution of marriage and that each person either had to clean and cook his own meals or pay to have these jobs done. The cost to the worker of providing these services himself would be included in the definition of subsistence, or the wage that the owners of means of production will pay. The social determination of the basic wage would be different. As with the Blacks, an elaborate ideology about the natural role of women has developed to justify their subjection. While a system of socialist production relations would end the economic foundation for such a system, it would not end the attitudes conditioned over centuries which are part of almost every man's ideological baggage. Again, experience and struggle are the determinants of whether this question will be successfully resolved.

The governors of socialist societies recognize these and other problems, but in the Soviet Union, there is evidence that struggle to achieve a new concept of justice has not occurred. In the aftermath of the Khrushchev denunciation of Stalin there was much talk of the new socialist man and where he was coming from. The Soviet Communist Party Draft Program in 1961 spoke of achieving communism—the withering of the state—within twenty years. There has, however, been remarkably little discussion, in the Soviet Union or other socialist countries, of the precise meaning of "withering away of the state."

One goal of a new socialism, nevertheless, is the eventual transfer of power from the state to the people. Within the legal sphere, this means, in part, the development of an informal judicial system administered predominantly by lay people instead of a class of trained professionals. George Feifer's book, *Justice in Moscow*, describes the operation of people's courts, with jurisdiction over petty criminal offenses, domestic strife, and minor civil suits. These courts sit with one professional judge and two lay judges, in an atmosphere asserted to be informal. With some minor exceptions, these courts operate much like courts of first instance in Western countries.

At another level are "comrades' courts," a product of the post-Stalin era. These informal bodies, each with a territorial jurisdiction extending over a few city blocks, a particular factory, or some other living or working unit, are designed to dispense informal justice in minor social disputes, and to handle petty infractions of law best summarized as "disorderly conduct." Quite similar to the comrades' courts are the assemblies of the community, established in 1961 and possessing, among other features, the rather considerable power to deal with "parasitism" and incorrigible antisocial behavior by means of banishment from the community. The comrades' courts represent a genuine effort to place Soviet citizens in the midst of administering Soviet justice. In a future communist society, the Soviet Communist Party has written, "Comradely censure of antisocial actions will gradually become the principal means of eradication of bourgeois views, customs, and habits."

And yet, if the reports of observers can be credited, the participation of lay assessors in people's courts is generally desultory and pro forma, and the atmosphere little different from that of a municipal court in the United States. The comrades' courts, while they do cause excitement and interest in their proceedings, do not appear to have a significant impact on Soviet life. Moreover, there are indications that the existence and operation of these courts have met with some opposition from the Soviet legal establishment, in part upon the ground that, as René David reports, "their activity and their existence itself would be . . . rather difficult to justify in light of article 102 of the Soviet Constitution and the principle . . . in the . . . Penal Law in 1958 that a penalty may not be inflicted by the judgment of a tribunal except in conformity with a particular penal law." The comrades' courts operate informally both as to procedure and as to the rules they apply to judge and regulate conduct. Using such vague terms as "antisocial" and "disorderly," they appear to devise precise rules to settle individual cases in a rather freewheeling manner.

The story of the people's courts and comrades' courts points up a problem which, looking at the long-range prospects for the building of a society without a machinery of coercion, is perhaps even more serious than the departures from "legality" and the suppression of dissent which have been of relatively greater concern to Western observers. This problem is the rigidity of Soviet legal structures in the face of great underlying technological and social change, and the Soviet professional legal attitude towards the desirability of codified legal rules. Some background discussion on this problem is in order.

The civil law system, from the time of Justinian's codification of the Roman law, has placed great stock in writing down formal rules of positive law as a device for unifying and strengthening the power of the state. A notable expression of this use of codification is the Napoleonic code, which caps centuries of legal development. French law, in the thirteenth century, consisted of customary rules (each feudal fiefdom having its own set of customs), rules of "written law," principally obtaining in the south of France and deriving more or less directly from Roman texts, and the canon law, which had a rather extensive (by today's standards) secular jurisdiction. Beginning with Beaumanoir's reduction to writing in 1283 of the customary law of Beauvaisis and continuing through the officially sponsored compilations of the codes culminating in the eighteenth century, a move to consolidate French law under one sovereignty was evident. The Napoleonic code was but the highest expression of this aim, seeking not merely consolidation of the bourgeois nation-state, but the expression in legal rules of the will of the new ruling class. As Cambacérès said to the Conseil d'Etat in presenting an early Code draft: "It is indispensable to substitute for the old laws a code . . . which is at once the principle of social welfare and the safeguard of public morality."

The Soviet Union, even in 1917, had inherited a great deal of its law from the European civil law system. The nineteenth-century legal reforms in Russia had taken the form of a codification along the lines of the French model and in harmony with similar codification efforts in Germany and Austria. The same pattern was evident in the anticolonial revolutions of Latin America, which took the Code Napoléon as the basis of their positive law. In the Soviet move towards codification, codes, constitutions, and statutes have been regarded as the means of expressing socialist principle. This development leads to the creation and maintenance of a corps of legal technicians, concerned with writing, commenting upon, and administering these legal rules. This class of persons does not perform manual work or productive labor, but is concerned with the refinement and development of law as a system.

Alongside this development, Stalin contributed greatly to the development of a state apparatus which exacerbated the contradiction between the administration of positive legal rules and underlying social reality. Stalin vigorously opposed those who argued that the state could wither away by degrees as a socialist society built the technological basis and human consciousness appropriate to communism. Rather, he said, the socialist state would continue to be the strongest the world had yet seen, for contradictions between the dominant class, the proletariat, and its enemies would increase as socialism developed. This notion may be said to have some positive features. Stalin recognized that, in the words of one writer, "the ideological superstructure, though stemming from, and conditioned by, the economic base, also exerts a reflexive action upon the latter." He himself wrote of this as "the tremendous organizing, mobilizing and transforming value of new ideas, new political views and new political institutions." Vyshinsky wrote, in this vein, that "History demonstrates that under Socialism . . . law is raised to the highest level of development."

The assured consequence of projecting a statist view into Soviet legal thought was an increased separation of thought and action, of institutions and life reality. In the hands of the Soviet government under Stalin's direction, moreover, the Stalinist conception of law and legal institutions was the ideological foundation of the Stalin terror. Beginning no later than 1961, the Stalin theory of increasing contradiction was officially abandoned in favor of a theory that the Soviet state is a "state of all people." At the same time, there was a great reaction to the rigidity of Stalinist legal forms, particularly in the field of criminal law. In this atmosphere the comrades' courts were born.

But the comrades' courts cannot overcome a fundamental defect which remains in Soviet notions of law and its relationship to the level of social development. A dominant theme in Soviet thinking is that of "socialist legality," of harmony to written rules (including rules guaranteeing procedural rights) as the principal protection of "individual rights." This notion is no doubt comforting to Western observers, and even to radical lawyers in this country. So much of our time, as lawyers, is spent seeking to vindicate claims for justice founded upon written rules expressed as

limits upon the state's power to punish particular acts
(guarantees of free speech, for example) or to proceed in
particular ways (the guarantees of procedural rights). We
cherish these concessions and contradictions. But in a socialist society, there ought in theory to be a different approach. A socialist society is theoretically engaged in laying the technical basis for a new form of civilization, and
in that process human consciousness is to be transformed.
At bottom, Marxist theory emphasizes that there must be
a unity of theory and practice, of thought and work, of
rule and reality.

However, while the comrades' courts and assemblies of
the community in the Soviet Union pursue this unity
through the creation of forms of popular participation,
there remains a vast bureaucratic institution charged with
the development and elaboration of legal rules and structures. The Stalin terror is largely gone, but high valuation
is still placed on formal positive law. Soviet lawyers, and
some Western observers, would no doubt argue that the
maintenance of such a structure is necessary to insure
that state institutions follow certain basic norms of substantive and procedural law for the benefit of individuals.
But the experience of other socialist countries, engaged in
different experiments in developing legal institutions that
maximize popular involvement, suggests that the Soviet
thinkers are too firmly implanted in their European code
law tradition.

Contrast the Soviet view with that of the Chinese, for
example. The Chinese revolution was, it must be recalled,
fought over a long period of time and over an extensive
area. A far greater percentage of the people were engaged
in revolutionary struggle than in the Soviet Union. Institutions of governance were developed in the course of the
revolution and designed to return decision-making power
to the people. More important, perhaps, the Chinese legal
tradition has eschewed formal legal rules, which are regarded in Chinese philosophy dating to early Confucian
thought as inherently inferior to principles of behavior derived from common consent or custom, and enforced
through community pressure and community-based me-

diation agencies operating largely informally. Attempts made by Western imperialism beginning in the early twentieth century to impose "code law" in the tradition of the French and German experience were largely failures, serving only to regularize certain economic relations between the local bourgeois and comprador elements and the businessmen of the Occident.

René David has written, in *Les Grands systèmes de droit contemporains:*

> Marxist-Leninist philosophy contains elements which accord with this traditional philosophy: positive law has never appeared to the Chinese as being a necessary condition, or even a normal condition, of a well-ordered society; positive law is, on the contrary, a sign of an imperfect society, and a connection exists between the idea of positive law and that of coercion. Communism, presaged in Marxist thought, is nearly an ideal society as such a society is envisaged by the Chinese.

Others, including the American author Jerome Cohen, have also commented upon the connection between traditional Chinese views of law and the legal theory of the Chinese Communists.

Too, the Chinese revolution has been alert to the problem of separating mental from manual labor and to the important task of shaping institutional forms to reflect constantly changing material conditions of production and exchange. The restructuring of the universities in the Cultural Revolution is the most recent example of this process at work. The Chinese legal system reflects this systematic drive to prevent the formation of positive legal rules which acquire a life of their own, and a consistent attention to the application of principles derived from common experience and shared expectations about behavior in making legal rules. In defining criminal offenses, this process takes the following form: the single most important theoretical underpinning of the criminal law is Mao Tse-tung's work, "On the Correct Handling of Contradictions Among the People." There, Mao underscored the importance of the concept of contradiction in Marxist thought. Marxism, he reiterated, is based upon dialectical and historical materialism. Briefly, Marxist dialectics maintain that events in the real world, including historical events, move through the resolution of contradictions which inhere in all life situations. In society, the interests of social classes and groups are contradictory. The resolution of these contradictions takes the form of a synthesis on a new and higher level. Within that new synthesis there will develop a new contradiction in the form of an antithesis, leading to a still newer synthesis, and so on. Mao distinguished between contradictions which he termed "antagonistic," "between the enemy and us," and those which he termed "nonantagonistic," "among ourselves." An example of the former is the contradiction between the large bourgeoisie and comprador class and the majority of the Chinese people—workers, peasants, small farmers, small businessmen, and so on. The power base of the large bourgeoisie and the compradors had to be destroyed in order for the Chinese revolution to succeed; there could be no compromise with those whose means of livelihood depended upon the maintenance of a system of exploitation which was at the root of poverty and famine and kept in power by terror and coercion. Once the Chinese revolution was successful, however, there was no guarantee that the interests of workers, peasants, small farmers, and small businessmen would always be identical. Indeed, there was every reason to suspect that there would be contradictory demands upon social resources by these groups. Yet these demands were consistent with the maintenance of the basic system of social organization introduced by the revolution.

Chinese criminal law rests upon this basic formulation. Offenses committed in the name of bringing back the former system of social organization, or which objectively aid the reimposition of that system, are regarded as the occasion for severe measures. However, even in this field there is extensive concern with the rehabilitative potential of various social institutions, and careful attention to the problems of rehabilitation in individual cases.

More significant, however, for purposes of this essay, are the legal rules and institutions designed to deal with contradictions among the people. In general, there is a preference for dealing with disputes at the lowest and most informal level of adjudication. The farm community, the families living on a city block, and other informal groupings are enjoined to and do intercede freely to achieve an accommodation in both civil disputes and those which involve a minor infraction of criminal law rules. (Snow reports that there are only 250 lawyers in all China.)

As some observers have reported, a traffic law violator is likely to be pulled over to the side by a foot policeman and given a long lecture about the importance of abiding by rules so that the police and courts will not have to intervene. As the lecture continues, passersby are likely to join and turn the occasion into a discussion of the preferability of not having to have formal institutions of coercion. More serious disputes are thought to require more formal treatment, but the emphasis is not upon the vindication of abstract principle but upon the accommodation of conflicting interests to ensure protection of larger social goals.

Cohen recounts the case of a dispute, which turned to violence, between two farm work brigades over access to a source of fertilizer for the fields. Though there were injuries, the dispute was regarded as far less serious a matter than, for example, sabotage of an industrial plant which resulted in only property damage. The difference is attributable to the difference in the social concerns of the putative criminals in the two cases. The farm workers' dispute was handled without the imposition of criminal sanctions by meetings between the two communities involved and an agreement looking to an accommodation of their joint interest in maximizing output.

Chinese contract law, to take another example, is likely to be far less reliant upon formal rituals of contract law as conceived in Western business law contexts. In the Soviet Union, contracts between state organs and state-run enterprises have a decidedly managerial flavor, although there has been some effort to decentralize decision-making and put factory workers more directly into the process of management. In China, the making of economic contracts for production and supply involves thousands of people; these contracts are the basis of output predictions and relations between the various sectors of the economy. It is not unusual for an entire farm community, an agricultural or factory commune or similar economic unit, to have a mass meeting to decide upon the terms of a contract of production and supply. The thought, no doubt, is to integrate the managerial and production functions, and take from the "contract law" the aura of a legal rule or principle divorced from the participation of those whose labor power makes up the goods which will fulfill the contract.

In sum, the Chinese legal system is built upon a sense of community, and seeks to prevent the creation of an ideology of law and state which would be a barrier to social development and contradict the goal of eliminating the coercive aspect of state power. There are, of course, risks and disadvantages in such a system. Most obvious to Western critics is the absence of an orderly and organized system of insuring procedural fairness and respect for substantive rights. American constitutional scholars, proceeding in most cases from premises narrowly defined by the dominant assumptions of constitutional doctrine in this country, regard the absence of such a system as an incurable defect. How can one secure respect for rights unless those rights are written down in a code and unless some branch of government is given the duty to see that they are not denied? The answers are difficult to find, since our knowledge of the Chinese legal system is gained largely from the distorted perspective of refugees in Hong Kong interviewed by American scholars on Ford Foundation grants. However, it seems likely that in terms of Chinese tradition, a system of social organization which relies upon constant and active debate about social goals and priorities has a great chance of developing a broad consensus about minimal human rights and securing respect for them.

Consider, too, the development of legal institutions in

Cuba. The available evidence suggests that the entire tone and tenor of Cuban life have been changed by the Revolution. There has been, since the Revolution left its liberal reformist phase and embarked upon a program of socialist construction, detailed and consistent attention to non-material incentives to production, involving the entire population in setting social priorities, and developing informal systems of dispute resolution.

Interestingly, part of the pre-Revolutionary system of courts and judges, still staffed to a large extent with lawyers whose experience and education antedate the Revolution, continues to function. The judges in their robes still sit in large courtrooms and hear major cases, basing their decisions (at least in criminal matters) on the 1938 Cuban Code. Why this system has been permitted to continue is difficult to know. Perhaps its existence is tolerated because it is being undermined from two directions by newly developed institutions of justice.

The first of these is the revolutionary tribunals which try alleged counterrevolutionary activity. These tribunals are manned by the armed forces. It would be worthwhile to conduct an independent evaluation of their procedures, including the sort of evidence relied upon and the standards of proof required for conviction. In the absence of such a study, one can only report that the existence and functioning of the tribunals do not appear to have caused great concern, distrust, or dismay on the part of the Cuban people. Cuba is, after all, still under siege and subject to armed attack, overt and clandestine, by groups operating from the United States and elsewhere in Latin America.

The second set of institutions, undercutting the jurisdiction of traditional courts, is the popular tribunals. These bodies, run by nonlawyer judges elected by a majority of the citizens in a particular area, have extensive powers to deal with a wide range of criminal and civil matters. Their emphasis, we know from reports of those who have spent a great deal of time observing them, is upon nonpenal solutions to problems brought before them. Their powers include incarceration (in jail or under house arrest), compulsory psychiatric treatment, compulsory work in agriculture for a stated period, attendance at a school to complete one's education through the sixth grade, and a host of other corrective or compensatory sanctions. The most common minor sanction is the public admonition. The jurisdiction of these courts is defined by category of offense rather than by a code of laws. These categories include delicts, a category sharing some notions of the common law tort and crime categories, and contraventions, a category of conduct less serious than delicts and including "disorderly conduct" sorts of behavior. Delicts include conduct analogous to defamation, threats and coercion, violation of rationing regulations, cheating one's business customers, and other kinds of conduct regarded as affecting fundamental social interests. These categories are familiar to the civil law tradition.

The basis for determining whether an individual has by his conduct committed a delict or contravention is uncertain, except that the lay judges feel a sense of obligation to reflect revolutionary consciousness in their judgments, and to find a basis of decision that reflects the community will. There is no code as such, only a very general manual for the lay judges. Since the sessions of the tribunals are held in the evenings and extremely well-attended, the educational value of the proceedings is considerable. Since the judges are not only elected, but hold regular jobs in the daytime, they are unlikely to regard themselves as separate from the communities they serve.

The crucial distinction between the Soviet and Cuban popular tribunals is in the revolutionary character and commitment of the societies of which they are a part. There appears to be an effort in Cuba to rely very little upon rigid structures and forms, a constant effort to renew institutional norms with revolutionary experience. There is a marked fear of creating a class of persons— whether they be students, lawyers, professors, or governors—who do not work but merely live from the labor of others. Evidence of this same effort appears in China, where the historical suspicion of rigid forms makes the task easier at least in the realm of law. This is not to doubt, in either the Cuban or Chinese experience, the role of a central authority in making social and economic decisions. The presence and influence of the state are felt everywhere in these societies. Clear, however, is a commitment to move away from reliance upon state power as the instrument of social cohesion and control.

What can be the lesson of this historical sketch for the Movement in this country? We have, all of us, been schooled to believe that protection of basic rights requires a quasi-independent class of lawgivers expounding a detailed set of rules which contain, as monuments to social struggle, some concessions to fairness and justice ranging from formal guarantees of political freedom to wage-and-hour legislation.

In the courts and in political forums we have sought to create progressive legal rules to protect and extend the rights of people's movements. But we have not sought to hear the people's authentic voice on the courts and halls of justice, only to keep that voice from being stilled by the application of legal rules which are at bottom designed to protect privilege. It has been the principle that we have sought to defend, not the institution which administers it.

In considering a new system of social relations for this country, we must ask what forms are likely to protect revolutionary gains and at the same moment ensure respect for persons against the arbitrary exercise of power. The Soviet experience shows, I think, that reliance upon formal legal rules to embody fundamental social decisions about goals is an error. The creation of a class of persons whose task is thought and speculation is not merely futile but dangerous: Such a class does not work but lives off the labor of others, and has no practice with which to integrate its theory.

Thus, the model of the Movement lawyer must be seen as a temporary expedient. The law-trained technician applying his set of knowledge, seeking to mate one legal concept with another to produce an innovation which will secure judicial recognition, is a valuable defender of the

Movement. The exposure of the extent to which formal legal rules are not honored, and to which the reality of the administration of justice falls short of its ideal, is important as well. But these efforts are understandable and reasonable for two purposes only: first, they expose contradictions in present society and contribute to the growth of a movement for change which seeks to resolve contradictions in a new synthesis; second, they win concessions from legal institutions. These concessions are won from a legal order which, as the thesis of this collection of essays asserts, is "against the people." A legal order befitting a socialist country must attempt to embody popular aspirations and goals.

If this is so, then the most important questions about the structure of a legal order in a new society are answered not by lawyers as technicians of the existing order, but by Movement activists in seeking to live and work together to bring about change. How does the Movement deal with sexism and racism in its midst? How are disputes settled? What respect is given the views of others? What steps are taken to prevent elitism and the separation of theory and theorists from practice and struggle? The dominant form of Movement organization today is the collective group organized in a particular area or around a particular issue or set of issues. The truly remarkable fact about Movement groups is the recognition that life together in struggle is not possible unless these interpersonal issues, which are microcosms of social conflicts in a larger arena, are raised, discussed, and dealt with.

Indeed, if the goal of a new society is the demystification of law, one must consider demystifying the Movement lawyer here and now. Certainly lawyers have skills, experience and knowledge to share. But the increased moves toward self-defense by Movement people on trial, toward breaking down barriers to real communication with juries in criminal trials, and toward making lawyers responsible to the Movement they seek to serve, are concrete steps toward understanding and building a legal system in a new order of things. This attack on "professionalism" and "elitism" by lawyers is part of a broader concern which the Movement must have with solving its own internal problems while struggling with problems outside itself, rather than deferring consideration of internal problems.

The Movement must abandon the notion that questions of racism, sexism, regard for the rights of others, and fairness may be postponed in intra-Movement relations and taken care of "when the revolution is won" by dint of an invocation of substantial state power or *dirigisme*. The kind of society we get, as the experience of socialist countries has shown, is the kind we build for. This has been and is true of every revolutionary struggle in the past twenty years. The building of legal institutions, in the sense that procedures and rules crystallize out of struggle, is an ongoing process which involves everyone in the movement for change. There is no reason, in this process, to forget the lessons of our own history as a people and the regard traditionally paid in bourgeois rhetoric to such matters as freedom of discourse and procedural regularity. Indeed, failure to recognize a fundamental American commitment to these principles would be wrong. It would be equally mistaken, though, to regard these rights as the creatures of a state apparatus and necessarily bound up with the creation and maintenance of such an apparatus. Today, these rights, to the extent their protection contradicts the interests of the commanders of power, are concessions wrested from reluctant institutions. These concessions are just that, and their extent is tested by the strength of a movement for change which demands respect for them.

How does the movement for change propose that America be governed? Just in the way that it creates and maintains means to govern itself.*

---

* The books and articles to which the author refers are included in the Selected Annotated Bibliography under Section III C., *Socialist Legal Institutions*.

Selected Annotated
Bibliography

The purpose of this selected annotated bibliography is to provide the reader with a number of books and articles that could be useful in a nontechnical study of the law. It therefore seemed important not only to include those works to which articles in the anthology refer but to offer a sampling of material which indicates the relationship between the law, the legal system, other primary institutions and some of the predominant values and ideas in American society.

I. THEORIES OF LAW, STATE AND SOCIETY

Adamic, Louis. *Dynamite: The Story of Class Violence in America.* New York and London: Chelsea House, 1931. A poorly written but informative account of government repression of Left-wing movements historically.

Arendt, Hannah. *On Revolution.* New York: Viking Press, 1963. A must for all political thinkers—a study of the history and meaning of revolution.

Bernstein, Barton J. *Towards a New Past: Dissenting Essays in American History.* New York: Vintage Books, 1967. An important collection by radical historians; moves away from "consensus" interpretations of history.

Cahn, Edmund. *The Sense of Injustice.* Bloomington, Indiana: University of Indiana Press, 1964 (1949). An anthropocentric view of law, concentrating on justice and power, freedom and order, security and change.

Domhoff, William. *Who Rules America?.* Englewood Cliffs, New Jersey: Prentice-Hall, 1967. The American upper class exposed! Corporation lawyers discussed, pp. 58–62.

Emerson, Thomas I., David Haber and Norman Dorsen. *Political and Civil Rights in the United States.* New York: Little, Brown & Co., 1967. One of the most comprehensive collections of legal documents in political and civil rights, accompanied by an analysis of the legal problems involved.

Engels, Fredrick. *Anti-Dühring.* New York: International Publishers, 1966 (1935). Gives the best and most comprehensive explanation of the dialectic, a good introduction to Marx's *Capital,* and lays the theoretical foundation of socialism.

———. *The Origins of Family, Private Property, and the State.* New York: International Publishers, 1942. A Marxist analysis of the oppressive nature of the family and its necessary dissolution.

Hart, H. L. A. *The Concept of Law.* London: Oxford University Press, 1961. One of the recent attempts to revive legal theory by providing an "analysis of the distinctive structure of a legal system" and the relation between law and other values.

Hegel, Georg W. F. *Philosophy of Right.* Oxford: Clarendon Press, 1967 (1952). Freedom is the fruit of necessity. The old absolutes are revealed in human affairs, not in philosophical thought.

Kolko, Gabriel. *Wealth and Power in America.* New York: Frederick A. Praeger, 1962. "An analysis of social class and income distribution"—an excellent reference for the Left. Useful bibliography.

Lenin, V. I. *Left-Wing Communism. An Infantile Disorder.* New York: International Publishers, 1940. "A popular essay in Marxian strategy and tactics." Attacks Left opportunism and doctrinairism.

———. *What Is To Be Done?.* New York: International Publishers, 1929. Discusses some of the major questions involved in the development of a revolutionary situation.

Mao Tse-tung. *On Contradiction.* New York: International Publishers, 1953. "A lecture delivered at the anti-Japanese

Military and Political College in Yenan in August 1937." A study of the law of unity of opposites, the basic law of thought.

Marcuse, Herbert. *Eros and Civilization*. Boston: Beacon Press, 1955. A philosophical and political analysis of Freud.

————. *One Dimensional Man*. Boston: Beacon Press, 1964. "Studies in the ideology of advanced industrial society." Some of the New Left's theoretical foundations.

Marx, Karl, and Fredrick Engels. *German Ideology*. New York: International Publishers, 1947 (1932). One of the first statements on historical materialism; it shows the relationship between the economic, political, and intellectual activities of man.

Mills, C. Wright. *The Power Elite*. New York: Oxford University Press, 1957. One of the first studies to document the military-industrial-government complex.

Proudhon, P. J. *What Is Property?*. New York: H. Fertig, 1966 (1890). "An inquiry into the principle of right and of government."

Sweezy, Paul M. *The Theory of Capitalist Development*. New York: Monthly Review Press, 1956. "Principles of Marxian political economy."

Williams, William Appleman. *The Great Evasion*. Chicago: Quadrangle Press, 1964. A theoretical treatment of America's failure to meet its economic and social crises during this century.

Zinn, Howard. *Disobedience and Democracy*. New York: Random House, 1968. "Nine fallacies of law and order."

II. HOW THE LAW OPPRESSES

A. *Racism and the Law*

Berger, Monroe. *Equality by Statute: the Revolution in Civil Rights*. Garden City, N.Y.: Anchor Books, 1968. Revised edition of Berger's analysis of the role of law in the civil rights struggle.

Billingsley, Andrew. *Black Families in White America*. New York: Prentice-Hall, 1968. Positive analysis of the history, structure, aspirations, and problems of Black families in a white-controlled society.

Blaustein, Albert P., and Robert L. Zangrando, eds. *Civil Rights and the American Negro*. New York: Trident Press, 1968. Useful compilation of documents, cases, etc.

Burns, Haywood. "Can a Black Man Get a Fair Trial in This Country?", *New York Times Magazine* (July 1970). An analysis of racism in the functioning of the criminal justice process in the United States.

————. "Racism and American Law, a New Course in Legal History," No. 2, 3, *University of Toledo Law Review* (October 1970). A new course offered at N.Y.U. Law School in 1969–1970, and why such a course is needed by law students, Black and white.

Catterall, Mrs. Helen Honor (Tunnicliff), ed. *Judicial Cases Concerning American Slavery and the Negro*. 5 vols. Washington, D.C.: Carnegie Institute of Washington, 1926–1937. Definitive work for overview of slave cases.

The Challenge of Crime in a Free Society, A Report by the President's Commission on Law Enforcement and the Administration of Justice. New York: Avon Books, 1968. Examines the extent and methods of preventing and combating crime, and calls for fundamental reform in the judicial system. See Section 5, "The Courts."

Cossett, Thomas F. *Race: The History of An Idea in America*. Dallas, Texas: Southern Methodist University Press, 1963. Traces development of ideas on race from the seventeenth century to the present.

Curry, J. E., and Celen D. King. *Race Tensions and the Police*. Springfield, Illinois: Thomas, 1962. Discussion of law enforcement and how it is affected by racial attitudes.

Donner, Frank. "The Epton Case: Southern Justice in New York," *Guild Practitioner* (Winter 1965). The case marked the government's attempt "to tie the civil rights movement to subversion; to find a scapegoat for rioting in the North."

Fanon, Frantz. *The Wretched of the Earth*. New York: Grove Press, 1963. Both the book and Sartre's preface are essential background to understanding Third World thought and its relation to the white international Establishment.

Foote, Caleb. "A Study of the Administration of Bail in New York City," Vol. 106, *University of Pennsylvania Law Review* (1958). A blistering, statistically documented attack against the use of bail to detain the poor—a classic.

Franklin, John Hope. *From Slavery to Freedom: A History of Negro Americans.* New York: Vintage, 1969 (1947). One of the best histories of Blacks in America.

Friedman, Leon, ed. *Southern Justice.* Cleveland and New York: Meridian Books, 1963. An anthology of writings by a number of the lawyers involved in the struggle for justice in the South.

Ginger, Ann Fagan, ed. *Minimizing Racism in Jury Trials.* Berkeley, Cal.: National Lawyers Guild, 1968. Charles Garry's *voir dire* of the jury in the Huey P. Newton murder trial in 1968, revealing prejudice among white jurors.

Greenberg, Jack. *Race Relations and American Law.* New York: Columbia University Press, 1959. Deals with capacity of the law to affect race relations and discusses basic law in wide range of civil rights areas.

Grimshaw, Allen D. "Lawlessness and Violence in America and Their Special Manifestations in Changing Negro-White Relations." Vol. XLIV, no. 1, *Journal of Negro History* (January 1959), pp. 52–72. Argues that the most intense Black-white conflict has taken place when the minority group has threatened the status quo.

―――. "Police Agencies and the Prevention of Racial Violence," Vol. 54, *Journal of Criminal Law, Criminology and Police Science* (March 1963), p. 110. Suggests that good policing alone *can* make a major contribution to interracial peace.

Hopkins, Vincent C., S.J. *Dred Scott's Case.* New York: Atheneum, 1967. A scholarly account of the Dred Scott case in legal and historical context.

Jordan, Winthrop D. *White Over Black, American Attitudes Toward The Negro, 1550–1812.* Chapel Hill: University of North Carolina Press, 1968. Scholarly examination of early

American racial attitudes, with invaluable sections on the role of law.

King, Donald, and C. Quick, eds., *Legal Aspects of the Civil Rights Movement*. Detroit: Wayne State University Press, 1965. Collection of materials on civil rights law, strong on Civil Rights Law of 1964.

Knowles, Louis L., and Kenneth Prewitt, eds. *Institutional Racism in America*. Englewood, N.J.: Prentice-Hall, 1969. Description and analysis of institutional racism aimed at providing tools to help in struggle against it.

Leadership Conference on Civil Rights, New York. *Federally Supported Discrimination*, 1961. Surveys its extent, and proposes executive action to eliminate it.

Litwack, Leon F. *North of Slavery*. Chicago: University of Chicago Press, 1961. Shows face of historic racism above Mason-Dixon line, 1790–1860.

Lynd, Staughton. "Slavery and the Founding Fathers," in Drimmer, Melvin, ed., *Black History*. Garden City, New York: Doubleday, 1968. Good job in exposing the founding fathers and their interests.

Mack, Raymond W., ed. *Race, Class and Power*. New York: American Book Company, 1963. Useful selection of papers on a theoretically structural view of dominant-minority relations.

Mangum, Charles. *The Legal Status of the Negro*. Chapel Hill: University of North Carolina Press, 1940. Documents race discrimination against Blacks in areas of civil rights, education, property rights, family, juries, right to counsel, etc., ahead of its time.

Miller, Loren. *The Petitioners, The Story of the Supreme Court of the U.S. and the Negro*. Cleveland, Ohio: Meridian Books, 1967. A chronicle of Supreme Court decisions in respect to Blacks, slave and free, between 1789 and 1965.

Myrdal, Gunnar. *An American Dilemma*. New York: Harper & Row, 1963 (1944). Classic study of the Black American, on theme that inequality affects every phase of Black life and personality.

———. *To Establish Justice, Insure Domestic Tranquility*. New York: Bantam Books, 1970. Final Eisenhower Report, calls among other things for an end to racial discrimination and reform of the judicial and police systems as major factors in social disruption.

Report of the National Advisory Commission on Civil Disorders. New York: E. P. Dutton & Co., Inc., 1968. The Kerner Commission not only identifies the cause of ghetto insurrection as "white racism" but argues that if Blacks are not allowed to enter the mainstream of American life civil strife will prevail.

Robinson, A. L., Craig C. Foster and D. H. Ogilvie. *Black Studies in the University.* New York: Bantam Books, 1969. Symposium arising out of a conference at Yale on need for curriculum change.

Rostow, Eugene V. "The Japanese-American Cases—A Disaster," Vol. 54, *Yale Law Journal* (1945), p. 489. An attack on the imprisonment of Japanese-Americans as unconstitutional and a political expediency.

Schwartz, Barry N., and Robert Disch. *White Racism, Its History, Pathology and Practice.* New York: Dell, 1970. An anthology of historical and contemporary writings on white American bigotry.

Skolnick, Jerome H., ed. *The Politics of Protest.* Report of the Task Force on Violent Aspects of Protest and Confrontation of the National Commission on the Causes and Prevention of Violence. New York: Ballantine Books, 1969. See Ch. VIII, "Judicial Response in Crisis" for an account of the inherent racism in judicial procedures.

"Special Issue on Racism in the Law," *Guild Practitioner* (Fall 1968). Six attorneys (including Judge George W. Crockett, Jr.) indict the law itself as criminal and racist.

Steel, Lewis M. "Nine Men in Black Who Think White: A Critic's View of the Warren Court," *New York Times Magazine* (October 13, 1968), p. 56. Argues that the Supreme Court has struck down only the symbols of racism, leaving intact practices that ensure the survival of white supremacy.

Steiner, Stanley. *The New Indians.* New York: Harper & Row, 1968. A popular account of recent developments.

Tenbrock, Jacobus. *Equal Under Law*. New York: Collier Books, 1965. A documentary account of the men and forces that shaped the legal cornerstone for civil rights.

Tussman, Joseph, ed. *The Supreme Court on Racial Discrimination*. New York: Oxford University Press, 1963. Useful compilation of Supreme Court decisions on various areas of racial discrimination.

U.S. Commission on Civil Rights. *Justice*. Washington, D.C.: Government Printing Office, 1961. A comprehensive survey of race and justice at the trial. Book V, Part VIII, "The American Indian," invaluable on relations with the government, legal status and status as a minority.

————. *Mexican Americans and the Administration of Justice*. Washington, D.C.: Government Printing Office, April 1970. Another minority group suffers at hands of white-oriented legal system; a strong condemnation of police abuse of Mexican-Americans.

————. *Racism in America and How to Combat It*. Washington, D.C.: Government Printing Office, 1970. Comprehensive study by Anthony Downs.

————. *Law Enforcement: A Report on Equal Protection in the South*. Washington, D.C.: Government Printing Office, 1965. Considers denials of constitutional rights, and remedies, and recommendations for criminal and civil remedies and executive action.

Wolfgang, Marvin E., and Bernard Cohen. *Crime and Race: Conceptions and Misconceptions*. New York: Institute of Human Relations Press, 1970. Significant study for the American Jewish Committee, examines relations between criminal statistics and race, and explodes many myths.

Woodward, C. Vann. *The Strange Career of Jim Crow*. New York: Oxford University Press, 1966. Revised edition of this classic analysis of the birth of Jim Crow and the growth of Black disfranchisement.

Wright, Judge J. Skelly. "The Courts Have Failed the Poor," *New York Times Magazine* (March 9, 1969). A judge describes the injustices in the administration of the courts; assumes, however, that hope lies in the higher courts.

B. Women and the Law

American Women. The Report of the President's Commission on the Status of Women, Margaret Mead and Frances B. Kaplan, eds. New York: Scribner, 1965. Typical government report about the inequities in various fields toward women. See especially the chapters on "Women Under Law" and "Civil and Political Rights."

Beauvoir, Simone de. *The Second Sex*. New York: Knopf, 1953. Explores women's secondary role in society.

Boyles, George James. *Woman and the Law*. New York: Century, 1901. A perfect example of traditional male paternalism before the time when women could vote or practice law. A male gives advice to women on the laws regarding domestic and property relations.

Fenberg, Matilda. "Blame Coke and Blackstone," *Women Lawyers Journal* (Spring 1948). A history of the legal status of women in America.

Flexner, Eleanor. *A Century of Struggle*. Cambridge, Mass.: Harvard University Press, 1959. Good history of the development of women's struggles in the United States.

Glasgow, Maude. *The Subjection of Woman and Traditions of Men*. M. I. Glasgow, 1940. Not a history but a depiction of the adverse environment in which woman was confined culturally, physically, and emotionally.

Grimes, Alan P. *The Puritan Ethic and Woman Suffrage*. New York: Oxford University Press, 1967. "Struggling for power and status behind the relatively innocuous phrase of equal rights for women were the social forces whose ultimate goal was the establishment of a system of values (the so-called 'puritan ethic') embedded in the law."

Kanowitz, Leo. *Women and the Law: The Unfinished Revolution*. Albuquerque: University of New Mexico Press, 1969. Indicates that even a thorough, intelligent study of how the law continues to oppress women does not necessarily help a male to see through his own male chauvinism.

Komarovsky, Mirra. *Blue-Collar Marriage*. New York: Random House, 1964. More scholarly than Rainwater's study on working class families, but almost unique in its attempt to analyze workers' values and norms.

Kraditor, Aileen S. *Up From the Pedestal.* New York: Quadrangle Books, 1968. A collection of many original documents, including such law-related excerpted material as Margaret Failler's "The Great Lawsuit" (1843) and Ernestine Rose on "Legal Discrimination" (1851).

Millett, Kate. *Sexual Politics.* New York: Doubleday, 1970. One of the most important studies of women's oppression in the last fifty years.

Morgan, Robin, ed. *Sisterhood is Powerful: An Anthology of Writings from the Women's Liberation Movement.* New York: Random House, 1970. Today's struggles by radical American women. Some law-related material; a good bibliography.

Murray, Pauli, and Mary Eastwood. "Jane Crow and the Law: Sex Discrimination and Title VII," Vol. 2, *George Washington Law Review* (1965). A review of women's legal status, especially in employment.

Pilpel, Harriet, and Theodora Zavin. *Your Marriage and the Law,* rev. ed. New York: Collier, 1965. Nonradical view of marital duties, responsibilities, and rights as seen in American law.

Rainwater, Lee, Richard P. Coleman and Gerald Handel. *Workingman's Wife: Her Personality, World, and Life Style.* New York: Oceana Pub., 1959. One of the only studies of working class families. Incomplete but useful.

Reverby, Susan, Ellen Bellet and Joan Jordan. "The Equal Rights Controversy: Past and Present," *Up From Under* (August-September 1970). Argues that equal rights legislation will hurt lower class women. Protective laws should be extended to apply to all working men and women.

Schulder, Diane B. "Does the Law Oppress Women?" in *Sisterhood is Powerful,* Robin Morgan, ed. New York: Random House, 1970. A survey of sexist U.S. Supreme Court decisions which are used today to justify unfair laws against women.

The Woman Question: Selections from the Writings of Karl Marx, Fredrick Engels, V. I. Lenin and Joseph Stalin. New York: International Publishers, 1951. Although they were all men, their contribution to the possibility of a worldwide women's liberation movement cannot be underestimated. A must for men especially who wish to understand the male role as oppressive.

White, James J. "Women in the Law," *Michigan Law Review* (April 1967). Examines the status of women in the legal profession, what they do, compared with men, and the forces that might narrow the gap between male and female status.

Women and the Law. The Cornell Law Forum. New York: Cornell University, 1969. A whole issue devoted to such topics as NOW (National Organization of Women), women as lawyers, and male opinions of women in the law.

C. *Poverty Law*

Brownell, Emery A. *Legal Aid in the United States.* Rochester, New York: Lawyers Co-operative Publishing Co., 1951. "A study of the availability of lawyers' services for persons unable to pay fees." Paternalism personified.

Cleary, John J. "National Defender Project: A Progress Report," Vol. 26, no. 3, *The Legal Aid Briefcase* (February 1968), p. 99. Survey of the major defender programs throughout the country.

Hagwood, Leon Carl. "Indigent Defendants: The Need for Effective Aid in Addition to Counsel," Vol. 34, *Mississippi Law Journal*, p. 145. "The question is whether assistance of counsel means the effective assistance of counsel." Unfortunately, the definition of effective can be interpreted from a liberal or radical perspective; conservatives control the definition now.

Hunter, Robert S. "Slave Labor in the Courts: A Suggested Solution," *Case and Comment* (July-August 1969). Argues that attorneys will do a better job for the poor if they are paid better; also shows a state-by-state breakdown of attorney compensation.

Karpel, Craig. "Defending the Poor: Lawyer as Hangman," *The Village Voice* (June 12, 1969). Fine exposé of the Legal Aid Society in New York City.

Silver, Carol Ruth, "The Imminent Failure of Legal Services for the Poor: Why and How to Limit Caseload," Vol. 42,

Journal of Urban Law (1968). A thorough discussion of why lawyers cannot handle all the problems of the poor; suggests a short-run strategy out of the current failure of direction.

Silverstein, Lee. *Defense of the Poor: The National Report.* 3 Vols. Chicago: American Bar Association, 1965. The most complete report on who gets defended and how, where, and why.

Smith, Reginald H. *Justice and the Poor.* New York: Scribner's, 1919. One of the first important studies attacking the denial of justice to the poor.

D. Law, Lawyers and Legal Institutions

Beil, Marshal. "The Contempt Weapon Against Lawyers in Court," *Harvard Civil Rights—Civil Liberties Law Review* (April 1970). The reasons for contempt, the constitutional protections and why contempt is an abuse of the court's power at any time.

Bert, R. "Lawyers May Challenge Court System," *Guardian* (July 20, 1968). The "political" nature of the firing of Gerald Lefcourt from the Legal Aid Society in New York.

Black, Jonathan. "Lawyers of the Left: A Crisis of Identity," *The Village Voice* (May 1, 1969). This article surveys radical law firms in New York (where most of them are), the cases they handle, the life styles they lead, and their differences in approach.

Boudin, Kathy, Brian Glick, Eleanor Raskin and Gustin Reichbach. *The Bust Book: What to Do Till the Lawyer Comes.* New York: Grove Press, 1969. Informs young people, especially, on how to prepare for "the law" in demonstrations, while using drugs, when arrested, at arraignment, etc.

Burnstein, Malcolm. "Trying a Political Case," *Guild Practitioner* (Spring 1969). A useful discussion of all aspects of a political trial, aimed at encouraging lawyers to take on such legal activity.

Cahn, Jean and Edgar Cahn. "The New Sovereign Immunity," Vol. 81, *Harvard Law Review* (1968). A theory for the use of legal attacks on government agencies and programs.

————. "What Price Justice: The Civilian Perspective Revisited," Vol. 41, *Notre Dame Lawyer* (1966). Decentralize the courts—the courts belong to the people.

Carlin, Jerome, and Jan Howard. "Legal Representation and Class Justice," *UCLA Law Review* (January 1965). Discusses class difference among attorneys. The significance of these detailed distinctions seems rather limited.

Chevigny, Paul. *Police Power: Police Abuses in New York City.* New York: Vintage Books, 1969. Various accounts of the daily routine of institutionalized police brutality.

Cloke, Ken. "Conspiracy: Ruling Class Weapon," *Guardian* (February 28 and March 7, 1970). A radical analysis of the government's use of conspiracy laws to crush movements for social change.

Cohen, Morris R. "Constitutional and Natural Rights in 1789 and Since," *National Lawyers Guild Quarterly* (March 1938). Argues that because law is not absolute, the courts must be held responsible for their decisions.

"The Credibility of American Justice," Special Issue of *Transaction* (July/August 1967). Deals mostly with lawyers and the indigent, but raises questions concerning the failures of the whole legal process.

Delany, Judge Hubert T. "The Lawyer's Right to Exercise the Privileges of Citizenship," Vol. 13, *Lawyers Guild Review* (Winter 1953). Discusses the nature of the attacks against lawyers during the McCarthy period.

Dershowitz, Alan M. "On 'Preventive Detention'," *The New York Review of Books* (March 11, 1969). Analyzes the historical background, and argues for the unconstitutionality of detaining a suspected criminal in prison on the theory that the person may commit another crime.

Disruption of the Judicial Process. American College of Trial Lawyers (July 1970). A reactionary lawyers' group attempts to lay the groundwork for punishing lawyers who defend Movement clients.

Edises, Bertram. "Contempt of Court and the Lawyer: The Unequal Combat," Vol. 18, *Lawyers Guild Review* (Summer

1958). An argument against the use of overwhelming judicial power to jail defendants and lawyers.

Harris, Paul. "You Don't Have to Love the Law to be a Lawyer," *Guild Practitioner* (Fall 1969). Discusses the useful role of the radical lawyer during prerevolutionary times despite the fact that legal institutions constitute a reactionary force.

Harris, Richard. *Justice: The Crisis of Law, Order and Freedom in America.* New York: Avon Books, 1969. An incisive attack on the political use of the U.S. Justice Department under John Mitchell as compared with the previous administration.

Hayden, Tom. *Rebellion and Repression.* New York and Cleveland: Meridian Books, 1969. Illustrates the gap between the Establishment and the New Left. Tom's testimony before the House Un-American Activities Committee (HUAC) and the National Commission on the Causes and Prevention of Violence.

Horowitz, Harold W., and Kenneth L. Karot. *Law, Lawyers and Social Change.* New York: Bobbs-Merrill, 1969. An introduction to the American legal system, through cases and materials that show the legal process involved in the movement for social change.

Kinoy, Arthur. "The Present Crisis in American Legal Education," Vol. 24, *Rutgers Law Review* (Fall 1970). In a passionate call for fundamental change in legal education, the writer has opened a dialogue, along with the article in this collection, that has already had its effect in challenging the status quo in legal education.

Kirchheimer, Otto. *Political Justice: The Use of Legal Procedure for Political Ends.* Princeton, New Jersey: Princeton University Press, 1961. An important attempt to show the influence of contemporary politics on the legal principles and procedures underlying the law; the myth of the law's impartiality is analyzed.

Marion, George. *The Communist Trial: An American Crossroads.* New York: Fairplay Publishers, 1950. Written during the McCarthy period, the book documents all the horrors of the political persecution of Communist Party members; however, it fails to place the conspiracy trial in any historical or political focus.

"The National Lawyers Guild: Legal Bulwark of Democracy," Vol. 10, *Lawyers Guild Review* (Fall 1950). Since most of the Left lawyers belong to the National Lawyers Guild, it would be important for all concerned to read the Guild reply to charges of subversion by the Committee on Un-American Activities during the McCarthy witchhunt.

Nizer, Louis. "What To Do When the Judge Is Put Up Against the Wall," *New York Times Magazine* (April 5, 1970). The Witchhunts begin again as an Establishment lawyer outlines various punishments for today's radical lawyers on the pretext that they "intend" to disrupt the judicial process.

Pecora, Ferdinand. "Democracy and the Legal Profession," Vol. 2, *National Lawyers Guild Quarterly* (April 1939). The importance of the National Lawyers Guild (three years old in 1939)—its goals are not too dissimilar from those of today's young lawyers, although its methods may be.

Rainwater, Lee, and William L. Yancey. *The Moynihan Report and the Politics of Controversy.* Cambridge, Mass.: The M.I.T. Press, 1967. As one of the most sophisticated forms of racism, the report at least stirred a political controversy. Read the full text.

Riesman, David. "Law and Social Science: A Review of Michael and Wechsler's Casebook on Criminal Law and Administration," Vol. 50, *Yale Law Journal* (1941). A classic argument on the relation between law and other disciplines, and the need for integration.

Rockwell, David N. "Bar Associations and Radical Lawyers: The Politics of Ethics," *Harvard Civil Rights—Civil Liberties Law Review* (April 1970). Analyzes the history of elite and conservative bar associations and the means of punishing attorneys who deviate from the accepted political philosophy.

"Special Issue on the Movement and the Lawyer." *Guild Practitioner* (Winter 1969). Two dozen Movement lawyers comment on their participation in various struggles.

Task Force Report: The Courts. The President's Commission on Law Enforcement and the Administration of Justice. Washington, D.C.: U. S. Government Printing Office, 1967. An important study about how the courts work and how they should work. Racism, of course, doesn't exist as an element in the court functionings.

III. TOWARD ALTERNATIVE INSTITUTIONS

A. Trade Unionism

Barkin, Solomon. *The Decline of the Labor Movement, and What Can Be Done About It.* Santa Barbara, California: Center for the Study of Democratic Institutions, 1961. A trade union intellectual writing from a liberal point of view gives a detailed analysis of labor's failure in terms of its own limited goals.

Jacobs, Paul. *The State of the Unions.* New York: Atheneum, 1963. A former trade union organizer chronicles the decline of unions in America and their developing conservatism.

Lens, Sidney. *The Crisis of American Labor.* New York: A. S. Barnes, 1961 (1959). Despite its failure to go beyond unions in understanding working class needs, it provides good overview of where labor is at and is still the best analysis of the labor movement generally.

————. *Left, Right and Center: Conflicting Forces in American Labor.* Hinsdale, Illinois: H. Regency Co., 1949. One of the better analyses of the ideological conflicts within trade unions at the end of World War II.

Preis, Art. *Labor's Giant Step: Twenty Years of the CIO.* New York: Pioneer Publishers, 1964. Written from a Marxist viewpoint—an essential for those wanting to understand the decline of trade unionism in America.

Wellington, Harry H. *Labor and the Legal Process.* New Haven and London: Yale University Press, 1968. "Examines the national policy toward labor and explores the role of law and legal institutions" or how the labor movement has submitted to the legal superstructure.

B. *Signs of Fascism*

Bullock, Alan Louis Charles. *Hitler: A Study in Tyranny*. New York: Harper and Row, 1964. Despite its theoretical short-comings, this is the best biography of Hitler available in English.

Dimitroff, Georgi. *The United Front*. New York: International Publishers, 1938. The classic statement by the general secretary of the Communist International in the 1930s concerning the strategy and tactics for combating fascism—still used by the Communist Party and other revolutionary groups as contemporary political strategy.

Dutt, Rajani Palme. *Fascism and Social Revolution*. New York: International Publishers, 1935. "A study of the economics and politics of the extreme stages of capitalism in decay." Written from a Communist point of view, it is a powerful and scholarly study of the relation between the rise of fascism and the economic and social crisis of the 1930s.

Guerin, Daniel. *Fascism and Big Business*. New York: Pioneer Publishers, 1939 (1936). A convincing analysis of the relationship between the large corporations and fascist governments in several European countries—shows that fascism was not a movement of small shopkeepers and disillusioned workers, but was also a product of the requirements of capitalism.

Hitler, Adolf. *Mein Kampf*. New York: Stackpole Sons, 1939. Hitler laid it all out, but nobody believed him.

Ibarruri, Dolores. *They Shall Not Pass: The Autobiography of La Pasionaria*. New York: International Publishers, 1966. A head of the Spanish Communist Party during the civil war writes her autobiography justifying and glorifying the sorry record of international Communism in Spain.

Neumann, Franz L. *Behemoth: The Structure and Practice of National Socialism, 1933–1944*. New York: Harper and Row, 1966 (1942). The best of all books about fascism.

Orwell, George. *Homage to Catalonia*. New York: Harcourt, Brace, and Co., 1952 (1938). Personal account of the Spanish Loyalist coalition formed to defeat the dictator Franco.

Reich, Wilhelm. *The Mass Psychology of Fascism.* New York: Orgone Institute Press, 1946. Probably one of the most important books about fascism because it attempts to understand its rise as part of the daily life and mentality of the German people; also shows the authoritarian personality and structure as factors in determining the failure of the Left to stem Hitler's seizure of power.

Salvemini, Gaetano. *The Fascist Dictatorship in Italy.* New York: H. Fertig, 1967 (1927). The most eminent of Italian intellectuals concisely and brilliantly presents the anatomy of Italian fascism.

Shirer, William L. *The Rise and Fall of the Third Reich: A History of Nazi Germany.* New York: Simon and Schuster, 1960. Monumental in bulk and superficial in content, but essential for understanding the relation between people and events.

C. Socialist Legal Institutions

Babb, Hugh W., trans. *Soviet Legal Philosophy.* Cambridge, Mass.: Harvard University Press, 1951. Discusses the revolutionary role of law and state in context of Soviet legal theory.

Berman, Jesse. "The Cuban Popular Tribunals," Vol. 69, *Columbia Law Review* (1969), p. 1317. These courts not only represent a "considerable step forward in popular involvement in the administration of justice, [but they] . . . are close to being institutions which truly administer popular justice."

Blaustein, Albert P., ed. *Fundamental Legal Documents of Communist China.* South Hackensack, New Jersey: F. B. Rothman, 1962. One of the few valuable collections in English of Chinese legal materials.

Cohen, Jerome A. "Chinese Mediation on the Eve of Modernization," Vol. 54, *California Law Review* (1966), p. 1201. An historical perspective on informal grievance in Communist China.

————. *The Criminal Process in the People's Republic of China, 1949–1963.* Cambridge, Mass.: Harvard University Press, 1968. Although the book contains useful insights into the criminal process, its chief value lies in the extensive collection of theoretical works on law and the state which is included in the appendix.

Conquest, Robert, ed. *Justice and the Legal System in the U.S.S.R.* London, Sydney, etc.: Booley Head, 1968. Some valuable factual material written from the perspective of a Western English opponent of the Soviet legal process.

Cuba and the Rule of Law. Geneva: International Commission of Jurists, 1962. A contentious and superficial critique of Cuban legal institutions.

David, René. *Les Grands systèmes de droit contemporains.* Paris: Dalloz, 1966. An excellent compendium of the main outlines of the world's principal legal systems—contains sensitive discussions of Soviet and Chinese law.

Feifer, George. *Justice in Moscow.* New York: Dell Publishing Co., 1965. A chatty, non-Marxist report on Soviet courts, from the lowest workers' tribunal to the Supreme Court of the land.

Hazard, John N., and Isaac Shapiro. *The Soviet Legal System.* Dobbs Ferry, New York: Oceana, rev. ed., 1969. Post-Stalin documentation and historical commentary by two eminent Western scholars.

Hsiao, Gene T. "The Role of Economic Contracts in Communist China," Vol. 53, *California Law Review* (1965), p. 1029. The role of law (despite the rejection of the rule of law for the revolution) as it applies to China's (1) economic bureaucracy, (2) meaning of property and (3) the national plan.

Mouskhely, Michel, ed. *L'U.R.S.S.—Droit, Economie, Sociologie, Politique.* Paris, 1964. A valuable collection of studies on Soviet law and institutions.

Nee, Victor, with Don Laymen. *The Cultural Revolution at Peking University.* New York, Monthly Review Press, 1969. The only complete and accurate report in English about the Cultural Revolution in China.

Romashkin, Peter, ed. *Fundamentals of Soviet Law.* Moscow: Foreign Languages Publishers, n.d. An introduction to Soviet law—a good beginning for new students.

Schlesinger, Rudolf. *Soviet Legal Theory: Its Social Background and Development.* London: K. Paul, Trench, Trubner & Co., 1946. One of the outstanding analyses of Soviet legal thought to be produced in the West, written from an independent, although sympathetic point of view.

Vyshinsky, Andrei I. *The Law and the Soviet State.* New York: Macmillan Co., 1948. The writer was the principal legal theoretician during the Stalin period and this book was his major work.

D. Ideas of Resistance

Althusser, Louis. *Pour Marx.* Paris: F. Maspero, 1966. Theoretical attempt to bring Marxist theory up to date with behavioral theory development.

Berrigan, Daniel. *The Trial of the Catonsville Nine.* Boston: Beacon Press, 1970. The poetic account of an exemplary act (destroying Selective Service files) against the war in Southeast Asia and the trial that followed.

Castro, Fidel. *History Will Absolve Me: The Moncada Trial Defense Speech, Santiago de Cuba, October 16, 1953.* London: Jonathan Cape, 1968. This is perhaps Castro's most famous speech prior to the Revolution. He appears before the Court of Justice as a defendant and outlines his program for a new society.

Cohn-Bendit, Daniel. *Obsolete Communism: the Left-Wing Alternative.* New York: McGraw-Hill, 1968. An excoriating critique of the role of the old Marxist Left in relation to the 1968 rebellions in France in which the traditional Left parties became instruments of the capitalist state.

"The Constitutional Right to Advocate Political, Social and Economic Change—An Essential of American Democracy," National Committee on Constitutional Liberties, Vol. 7, *Lawyers Guild Review* (March-April, 1947). One of the important responses by Left lawyers at the beginning of the McCarthy period to those who believed in the "Communist menace" cry.

Dennison, George. *The Lives of Children: The Story of the First Street School.* New York: Random House, 1969. A personal account by a dedicated humanist teacher with no politically radical perspective—his attempt to change the system and how all efforts fail.

Douglas, William O. *Points of Rebellion*. New York: Vintage, 1969. A U. S. Supreme Court justice attacks the inadequacies of the legal system and the failure of the Establishment to respond to the needs of the people.

Foner, Philip, ed. *The Black Panthers Speak*. Philadelphia and New York: J. B. Lippincott Co., 1970. "The Manifesto of the Party: the first complete documentary record of the Panthers' program," including statements of Huey P. Newton and other leaders.

Gardner, Fred. *The Unlawful Concert: An Account of the Presidio Mutiny Case*. New York: Viking Press, 1970. The crime of the twenty-seven soldiers is analyzed. As the longest court martial in military history, the case represents one of the important challenges to military authority.

Gramsci, Antonio. *The Modern Prince and Other Writings*. New York: International Publishers, 1967 (1957). A founder of the Italian Communist Party develops a theoretical study of political and legal theory under conditions of revolutionary crisis following World War I.

Hayden, Tom. *Trial*. New York: Holt, Rinehart & Winston, 1970. The Chicago Eight Conspiracy trial, its prelude, aftermath, and a program for action as told by one of the defendants.

Henry, Jules. *Culture Against Man*. New York: Random House, 1963. Invaluable to those who wish to study the relationship between the mass media and the configuration of political and social consciousness.

Huberman, Leo, and Paul M. Sweezy. *Cuba: Anatomy of a Revolution*. New York: Monthly Review Press, 1960. One of the best Marxist histories of the Cuban revolution.

Jackson, George. *Soledad Brother: The Prison Letters of George Jackson*. New York: Bantam Books, 1970. Some of the best writing to come out of the Black revolutionary movement. Jean Genet's introduction is a perfect complement of a white man's relationship to the necessity for Black freedom.

Jacobs, Paul, and Saul Landau. *The New Radicals*. New York: Vintage Books, 1966. "An analytical portrait of the young radical activists who have repudiated traditional liberalism and who seek a new vision of America through civil rights, university reform, and anti-war and anti-poverty activities."

Kohl, Herbert R. *36 Children*. New York: New American Library, 1967. Letters, stories, etc. by the author's students in an East Harlem elementary school. Suggests the anger and failure of children because of a bankrupt school system.

Kozol, Jonathan. *Death at an Early Age: The Destruction of the Hearts and Minds of Negro Children in the Boston Schools*. Boston: Houghton, Mifflin, 1967. See the George Dennison and Herbert Kohl annotations.

Lefebvre, Henri. *The Explosion: Marxism and the French Revolution*. New York: Monthly Review Press, 1969. An important attempt to relate the 1968 French student and worker rebellion to the institutional crisis in French society.

———. *The Sociology of Marx*. New York: Pantheon Books, 1968. One of the best attempts to extract from Marx's writings his concepts of class, the state, and social change.

"Lenin Today," Vol. 21, no. 11, *Monthly Review*. Collection of articles that analyze socialist political institutions, focusing of the possibility of achieving socialism in Western capitalist countries.

Lenin, V. I. *State and Revolution*. New York: International Publishers, 1932. Marxist teaching on the state and the tasks of the proletariat in the revolution, especially on the relationship between revolutionary consciousness and socialist governmental institutions.

Levine, Mark L., George C. McNamee and Daniel Greenberg, eds. *The Tales of Hoffman*. New York: Bantam Books, 1969. An edited account, especially aimed at fulfilling the irony in the title, of the "Chicago 8/7" Conspiracy trial.

Long Live Leninism. Peking: Foreign Languages Press, 1960. These articles, published in commemoration of the ninetieth anniversary of Lenin's birth, serve the historical function of opening the Soviet and Chinese theoretical dispute on revisionism.

Mitford, Jessica. *The Trial of Dr. Spock*. New York: Alfred A. Knopf, 1969. The first important trial by the government in its attempt to suppress dissent against the Vietnam War. Convictions obtained.

Rogers, David. *110 Livingston Street*. New York: Random House, 1968. "Politics and bureaucracy in the New York City schools." A call for reform where reform is no longer possible.

Rubinstein, Annette, ed. *Schools Against Children: The Case for Community Control*. New York: Monthly Review Press, 1970. A movement of parents, teachers and community activists analyze and attack the New York City bureaucracy.

Sherrill, Robert. *Military Justice is to Justice as Military Music is to Music*. New York: Harper & Row, 1970. One of the first books in recent years to document the abuses of military authority—some key political cases discussed.

Silberman, Charles E. *Crisis in the Classroom*. New York: Random House, 1970. A liberal's interpretation of what the Left has been arguing for years, that schools are "jails" and the kids want to be liberated. Breaking the formality of the school structure does not lead, however, to a new education.

Snow, Edgar. *The Other Side of the River: Red China Today*. New York: Random House, 1962. One of the most accurate accounts of life in China, including a study of the legal apparatus, since the writer is one of the few American journalists permitted to visit and study the country and its institutions.

Student Power: Problems, Diagnosis, Action. Baltimore, Maryland: Penguin Books, 1969. The student movement analyzed from a world perspective by New Left, predominantly student, writers.

Stenographic Report of the Proceedings of the Seventh Congress of the Communist International, 1935. Moscow: Foreign Languages Press, 1939. Recommended to radicals, communist and noncommunist alike, for the insight these proceedings may give to the problems of the present.

Training Manual on Public School Law. Schools Defense Network, 640 Broadway, New York, New York, 1969. One of the first efforts to guide parents and students (in New York City) to an understanding of legal rights in the public schools.

Trials of Resistance. New York: A New York Review Book, 1970. A collection of essays by New Left writers on some of the major trials for civil disobedience and resistance in the late 1960s.

Those interested in a further study of progressive and radical legal thinking in the past thirty years may find it useful to obtain a one-volume reference work called the *Index to National Lawyers Guild Periodicals*, which includes:

The National Lawyers Guild Quarterly, Vol. 1, 2.
The Guild Review, Vols. 1–20.
Law in Transition, Vols. 21–23.
The Guild Practitioner, Vols. 24–28.

For information, write:
Meiklejohn Civil Liberties Library Publications
Box 673-a,
Berkeley,
California 94701

Notes on Contributors

Stanley Aronowitz, former steelworker and trade union organizer, was a columnist for the *Guardian* and the *Liberated Guardian*. Born in New York City in 1933, he was a former editor of *Studies on the Left*. He has written an article on the new working class for *The Revival of American Socialism* (Oxford University Press, 1971), and on council communism in *The Unknown Dimension* (Basic Books, 1971). He is currently an educational planner in New York City, active in community control struggles in East Harlem and Yorkville.

Haywood Burns, National Director of the National Conference of Black Lawyers, is the author of *The Voices of Negro Protest in America* (Oxford University Press, 1963), "Federal Government and Civil Rights" in *Southern Justice* (Pantheon, 1965), and "Can a Black Man Get a Fair Trial in This Country?" *The New York Times Magazine* (July 12, 1970). Born in Peekskill, New York in 1940, he worked with New Haven CORE and the Council of Federated Organizations in Mississippi while attending law school. After clerking for U.S. District Judge Constance B. Motley, he served as a staff attorney for the Poor People's Campaign (1968) and is presently an adjunct member of the New York University Law School faculty.

Kenneth Cloke, Reginald Heber Smith fellow with the Venice Neighborhood Legal Services. He is the author of a *Guide to Draft Resistance* (1969), *Military Counseling Manual* (1970) and an earlier essay, "Law Is Illegal." Born in San Francisco, California in 1941, he attended Boalt Law School. The California Bar Character Committee held a special hearing to determine whether his political views would hinder his role as a future lawyer, but he was finally admitted to the practice of law. Upon graduation, he became the Executive Secretary of the National Lawyers Guild (1967–1968). He is currently working in the military movement, associated with such groups as Support Our Soldiers (sos) and Movement for a Democratic Military (mdm).

Fred Cohn, born in New York City in 1939, is a member of the firm of Lefcourt, Garfinkle, Crain, Sandler, Lefcourt, Kraft and Stolar, known in the Movement as the Law Commune. A partner with Julius Cohn (1968–1969), he became active in Movement law work during the student rebellion at Columbia University. He represented defendants in such cases as the Fort Dix 38 and the Fort Hood Three (1969–1970) and remains active in the antimilitary movement.

Ann M. Garfinkle is one of the original members of the Law Commune. Born in New York City in 1942, she was a partner with Carol Lefcourt and associated with Florynce Kennedy (1968–1969). She was co-counsel in *People v Berkowitz,* in which the off-Broadway play *Che* was closed because the actors appeared nude (1970) and *Abramowitz v Lefkowitz,* a suit which attacked the constitutionality of New York State's abortion laws (1970). She has tried numerous women's liberation cases.

Lennox S. Hinds, Chairman, Association of Black Law Students at Rutgers Law School, was born in Trinidad, West Indies, attended the City University of New York, did graduate work at the University of Minnesota and Brooklyn Polytechnic Institute, and was a research chemist for ten years before he decided to devote his full energies to social change. He is presently a candidate for J.D. at Rutgers Law School, and as Executive Director of the Heritage Foundation, Inc., does work for community groups developing programs for reordering social priorities and with colleges for the development of Black studies programs.

George Jackson, sentenced to from one year to life for stealing seventy dollars from a gas station, has been in jail more than ten years, over seven of which were spent in solitary confinement. Just twenty-eight years old, he is a legend in the California prison system. His letters to friends and family, written during incarceration, have been collected in a book, *Soledad Brother,* with an introduction by Jean Genet.

Florynce Kennedy, an infrequent attorney and frequent lecturer was born in Kansas City, Missouri in 1916. Counsel for the estates of Billie Holiday (1959–1965) and Charlie Parker (1960–1965), she is presently active in the Black liberation movement and the women's liberation movement. She was a delegate to the National Conference on Black Power (1967–1970) and associate counsel in the New York abortion repeal suit (*Abramowitz v Lefkowitz*, 1969–1970). Miss Kennedy has recently co-edited, with Diane Schulder, *Abortion Rap* (McGraw-Hill, 1971).

Michael John Kennedy, born in Spokane, Washington in 1937, is a partner in the firm of Kennedy and Rhine. In addition to handling numerous military cases, he has represented Students for a Democratic Society in an Iowa conspiracy case (1967), Rennie Davis and David Dellinger at House Un-American Activities Committee hearings (1968), and contributed to the pretrial work for the Chicago Eight conspiracy trial (1969), at which time he was arrested illegally by the presiding judge. His clients have included the Gay Liberation Front, Los Siete, and Dr. Timothy Leary in San Francisco.

Arthur Kinoy, Professor of Law at Rutgers University and a member of the firm of Kunstler, Kunstler and Hyman, is presently appellate counsel in the Chicago Eight conspiracy trial. Born in New York City in 1920, he was former staff counsel to the United Electrical Workers (1947–1950) and Morton Sobell (1951–1968). He has argued *Dombrowski v Pfister, Cameron v Johnson, Dombrowski v Eastland* and *Powell v McCormack* before the United States Supreme Court. His published essays include "The Constitutional Right of Negro Freedom," Vol. 21, *Rutgers Law Review* (1966–1967), "The Constitutional Right of Negro Freedom Revisited," Vol. 22, *Rutgers Law Review* (1967–1968) and "The Present Crisis in American Legal Education," Vol. 24, *Rutgers Law Review* (Fall 1970), among others. Political attacks against him include appearances before the House Un-American Activities Committee (*District of Columbia v Kinoy*, reversed 1968) and others. He is presently associated with the Law Center for Constitutional Rights.

William M. Kunstler, born in New York City in 1919, is an attorney with the Law Center for Constitutional Rights. His numerous publications include *Beyond a Reasonable Doubt?*

(1961), *Deep In My Heart* (1966) and the bestseller, *The Minister and the Choir Singer* (1964). In addition to representing Dr. Martin Luther King, H. Rap Brown, and members of the Black Panther Party, he was co-trial counsel in the Chicago Eight Conspiracy case (1969). While his four-year contempt of court sentence in the latter case is in the appeal courts, he is seeking to prevent the disbarment of other Movement attorneys, including Daniel T. Taylor in Kentucky and Frank Oliver in Illinois.

Carol Lefcourt, co-counsel in the New York Panther 21 Conspiracy case, is a partner in the firm of Lefcourt, Garfinkle, et al. Born in New York City in 1943, she was a partner with Florynce Kennedy (1968–1969). One of the original organizers of the Law Commune in New York, she was active in the defense of parents' groups, students, and teachers around the fight for community control (1968–1969). In addition to representing various women's liberation groups, such as the Feminists, she joined in bringing a suit which challenged the constitutionality of New York State's abortion laws (1970).

Gerald B. Lefcourt was born in New York City in 1942. While a staff attorney for the Legal Aid Society in New York, he helped to organize the Association of Legal Aid Attorneys (1968). He was later the Legislative Director of the National Emergency Civil Liberties Union (1969) and joined the Law Commune in the first expansion. His other clients have included Abbie Hoffman, Mark Rudd, the New York Panther 21, as well as other activists.

The New York Panther 21 include Jamal Baltimore, Lee Berry, Joan Bird, Robert Collier, Analye Dharuba, Lonnie Epps, Ali Bey Hassan, William King (Kinshasa), Alex McKiever (Catarra), Baba Odinga, Curtis Powell, Lee Roper, Afeni Shakur, Lumumba Abdul Shakur, Clark Squire and Michael Tabor (Cetewayo). At the time of their arrest on April 2, 1969, for allegedly plotting to bomb police precincts and other public buildings, the defendants had actively supported the school community control struggle, organized breakfast programs, initiated a drive against narcotic dealers, and sought to encourage community control of the police department. They were acquitted on all charges on May 13, 1971.

Howard Moore, Jr., the Legal Director and founder of Southern Legal Assistance Project (SLAP), is the author of "Black Barrister at the Southern Bar," National Lawyers Guild, *Guild Practitioner* (Winter 1967). Born in Atlanta, Georgia in 1932, he was general counsel to the Students Nonviolent Coordinating Committee (SNCC) and has tried *Bond v Floyd*, the Julian Bond ouster case (1966) and *Carmichael v Allen*, the Stokely Carmichael riot case (1966). Cited for contempt in 1963 by Judge Turwood T. Pye, Fulton County Superior Court, Atlanta, Georgia, for moving that the judge disqualify himself because of racism. Attorney Moore plans to expand SLAP into an effective instrument against racism and repression. He is presently co-counsel in the *People v Angela Davis*.

Eve Pell is a free-lance journalist and co-author, with Paul Jacobs and Saul Landau, of *To Serve the Devil* (Random House 1971), a history of minority races in America. Born in New York City in 1937, she has taught school in San Francisco and has worked for Joseph S. Clark, United States Senator.

David N. Rockwell, a third-year law student at Harvard Law School at the time of this writing, was born in Minneapolis, Minnesota in 1947. A graduate from Shimer College, Illinois (1968), he worked for the New York Law Commune (Summer 1969), and the Shelter Half Coffeehouse (Summer 1970). His publications include "Bar Associations and Radical Lawyers: The Politics of Ethics," *Harvard Civil Rights—Civil Liberties Law Review* (Spring 1970). He plans to join the Boston Law Commune upon graduation.

Diane B. Schulder, a graduate of Columbia Law School, originated and taught the first course on "Women and the Law" in a United States law school at the University of Pennsylvania. Her seven years in law practice include a year with a federal district court judge, working with Leonard Boudin on the Dr. Benjamin Spock trial, and serving as a Legal Aid Society attorney in New York. She has written "Does the Law Oppress Women?" in *Sisterhood Is Powerful* (Random House, 1970), and, with Florynce Kennedy, was the editor of *Abortion Rap* (McGraw-Hill 1971). She has worked in support of antiwar GIs and is currently doing research on political conspiracy trials while writing a novel.

Michael E. Tigar, formerly Acting Professor of Law at the University of California, Los Angeles, is the author of numerous articles and essays in law reviews, in addition to "The Jurisprudence of Insurgency," soon to be published. Born in California in 1941, he entered private practice with Edward Bennett Williams (1966–1969). He was Editor-in-Chief of the *Selective Service Law Reporter* (1968–1969). Some of his cases include the *United States v Dellinger* (the Chicago Eight), which led to his arrest by Judge Julius Hoffman (later dismissed); the *United States v Marshall* (the Seattle Eight) and the *People v Angela Davis.*

Robert Lefcourt, born in New York City in 1939, is a former English instructor at the Pleasantville High School and at Suffolk County Community College. He has written articles on the law for underground media publications, helped form the New York Law Commune, and coordinated experimental law courses for community residents at Columbia University and for students at Park East High School in New York. He is presently studying alternative education experiments in New York City.

Index

A

C

D

E

F

G

H

I

J

K

S

T

DATE DUE